AF608249

ROCKING THE BOAT

Migration and Race in Contemporary Spanish Music

Rocking the Boat

Migration and Race in Contemporary Spanish Music

SILVIA BERMÚDEZ

UNIVERSITY OF TORONTO PRESS
Toronto Buffalo London

Toronto Buffalo London
www.utorontopress.com

ISBN 978-1-4426-4852-4

Toronto Iberic

Library and Archives Canada Cataloguing in Publication

Bermúdez, Silvia, author
Rocking the boat : migration and race in contemporary Spanish music / Silvia Bermudez.

(Toronto Iberic series ; 29)
Includes bibliographical references and index.
ISBN 978-1-4426-4852-4 (bound)

1. Spain – Emigration and immigration – Songs and music. 2. Music and race. 3. Songs, Spanish – Spain – History and criticism. 4. Popular music – Spain – History and criticism. I. Title. II. Series: Toronto Iberic ; 29

ML3498.B516 2018 782.421640946 C2017-905445-7

This book has been published with the assistance of the University of California, Santa Barbara.

University of Toronto Press acknowledges the financial assistance to its publishing program of the Canada Council for the Arts and the Ontario Arts Council, an agency of the Government of Ontario.

Canada Council for the Arts
Conseil des Arts du Canada

Funded by the Government of Canada
Financé par le gouvernement du Canada

For Salvador Bermúdez Escalante, Sandra Bermúdez Rosell,
and Sergio Bermúdez Rosell, in memoriam

Contents

Illustrations

Acknowledgments

My deepest and sincerest gratitude goes to the following friends and colleagues for helping me rethink and polish sections of the research, but above all for their many and varied acts of kindness over the years, in particular, during the writing of this book: Jorge Pérez, Roberta Johnson, Mary Coffey, Robert Pavich, Juan Pablo Lupi, Jorge Olivares, Parissa Tadrissi, Eyda Merediz, Bill Nichols, Roberto Strongman, and Tony Geist. I especially appreciate that in the final stages of producing *Rocking the Boat*, Roberta Johnson brought her scholarly acumen and generosity to see me through the last hurdles. And that Tony Geist's munificence worked its magic in the securing of permits when nothing else did. I am also most grateful to José Colmeiro, musicologist Eduardo Viñuela, and Jonathan Mayhew for insightful comments and suggestions. Special thanks to Hakim Abderrezak for his intellectual largesse and commitment to locating sources. My gratitude to Lorena Barret, interpreter *extraordinaire,* for suggesting more nuanced translations of some of the songs. For their help with chords and musical analysis I am indebted to Eduardo Viñuela and David Thurmaier. For their steadfast assistance with the manuscript and around the manuscript I thank Amber Workman and Ana Requena, who also has become a dear friend. At the University of Toronto Press I thank Mark Thompson and Frances Mundy for their guidance. Siobhan McMenemy was instrumental in my signing with the University of Toronto Press, and Toronto Iberic – thank you.

During the writing of this book, the following universities invited me to discuss my research on Spanish pop music, race, migration, and borders. For their feedback and proving questions I thank students, colleagues, and participants at the "Burning the Sea: Clandestine Migrations in the Age of Globalization," the symposium at the University of Minnesota-Minneapolis; at the Department of Spanish and Latin American Studies at the University of Sydney; at the Department of Spanish and Portuguese at UCLA; at the Department of Modern Languages and Classics at the University of Alabama, Tuscaloosa; and the Department of Modern Languages and Literatures at Sonoma State University. My own institution, the University of California-Santa Barbara, generously provided funding, first in the form of two Academic Senate Grants (2008 and 2016) to finalize research and complete publication. At the final stage I very much appreciated the assistance of Mary Gay (Director) and Teresa Salinas (Manager of Financial and Academic Services) at the Phelps Administrative Support Center. For his good offices I am thankful to Leo Cabranes-Grant, the chair of my department, and to John Majewski, the Michael Douglas dean of Humanities and Fine Arts for the financial support to complete the publication of this book.

For their companionship, constant support, and encouragement I am thankful to Griselda Pérez, Alexis Rodríguez, Igone Etxebarria, Fernando Lafora, Alma Alfaro, Brinda Metha, Eloi Grasset Morell, Jackie Peláez, Gustavo Montes and Araceli Trujillo. Though he is no longer with us, may he rest in peace, I thank Javier Lafora's kindly granting permission to use his photographs of Madrid and migrant newcomers, including musicians performing on city streets. Thank you to the talented Catalan photographer Manel Armengol for sharing his beautiful photographs with me, in particular the 1976 one of Joan Manuel Serrat. Several of the artists approached were most gracious with granting copyrights to quote their work: my gratitude goes to Santiago Auserón, Concha Buika, José María Cano, Chambao's Lamari, Joaquín Sabina, and Joan Manuel Serrat. I also thank Editorial Pre-Textos and Manuel Ramírez's help.

And last but not least, for their unending support and sense of humour I am grateful to my beloved family, Marta Rosell Navalles, Sonia, Alejandro, and Lorena Bermúdez, Enoc and Clea Armengol Bermúdez, and Alejandra Bermúdez Llanos. And for providing a home away from home I am forever thankful to my other family, Gonzalo Gurmendi, Raquel Mazer, Gabriel, Natalia, and Marina Mazer Gurmendi.

Permissions

"A ba 'ele" ("Los Extranjeros")
Lyrics and Music: J. Loribo Apo / C. Apo Botupa
Copyright by Warner/Chappell Music Spain, S.A.
"Coplas añadidas a Semilla Negra" (pages 42–3) from *Canciones de Radio Futura* (1999) by Santiago Auserón
Poem by Santiago Auserón
Copyright by Santiago Auserón
Copyright by Editorial Pre-Textos of the 1999 edition of *Canciones de Radio Futura*
"Disculpe el señor"
By Joan Manuel Serrat
Copyright by Joan Manuel Serrat at www.jmserrat.com
"El blues del esclavo"
By José María Cano
Copyright by José María Cano at www.grupomecano.com/EL_BLUES_DEL_ESCLAVO.php
"La Casa por la Ventana"
Lyrics: J.R. Martinez Sabina
Music: F. J. Lopez Varona / A. Perez Garcia de Diego
Copyright by El Pan de Mis Niñas, S.L.
(All rights administered by Warner/Chappell Music Spain, S.A.)
"Mi Primo el Nano"
Lyrics and Music: J.R. Martinez Sabina
Copyright by El Pan de Mis Niñas, S.L.
(All rights administered by Warner/Chappell Music Spain, S.A.)
"New Afro Spanish Generation"
Lyrics and Music: M.C. Balboa Buika

Copyright by Warner/Chappell Music Spain, S.A. / Intuition Media, S.L.

"No es serio este cementerio"
by José María Cano
Copyright by José María Cano at www.grupomecano.com/NO_ES_SERIO_ESTE_CEMENTERIO.php

"Paseo con la negra Flor" (pages 44, 45) from *Canciones de Radio Futura* (1999) by Santiago Auserón
Poem by Santiago Auserón
Copyright by Santiago Auserón
Copyright by Editorial Pre-Textos of the 1999 edition of *Canciones de Radio Futura*

"Salam Rashid"
Poem by Joan Manuel Serrat
Copyright by Joan Manuel Serrat at www.jmserrat.com

"Semilla negra" (page 40) from *Canciones de Radio Futura* (1999) by Santiago Auserón
Poem by Santiago Auserón
Copyright by Santiago Auserón
Copyright by Editorial Pre-Textos of the 1999 edition of *Canciones de Radio Futura*

"Tirso de Molina"
Lyrics and Music: J. Loribo Apo/C. Apo Botupa/J. P. Guerrero
Copyright by Warner/Chappell Music Spain, S.A./Grupo Gestor de Ediciones Propias, S.L.U.

"Un africano por la Gran Vía" (pages 33, 34) from *Canciones de Radio Futura* (1999) by Santiago Auserón
Lyrics by Santiago Auserón
Copyright by Santiago Auserón
Copyright by Editorial Pre-Textos of the 1999 edition of *Canciones de Radio Futura*

ROCKING THE BOAT

Migration and Race in Contemporary Spanish Music

Introduction

In 1900, at the annual meeting of the American Negro Academy, when delivering his lecture "The Present Outlook for the Dark Races of Mankind," W.E.B. Du Bois introduced his well-known and much quoted premise that "the problem of the twentieth century is the problem of the color-line" – central to the *Souls of Black Folk* (1903). In the 1900 lecture, Du Bois explains that he wants to broaden his horizons and assess "the problem of the color line, not simply as a national and personal question but rather in its larger world aspect in time and space" (1900, 47). I mention Du Bois's words because they go to the heart of my discussion of the role of race and racism – "the problem of the color line" – in the musical narratives produced in Spain beginning in the early 1980s and up to 2011 by a diverse array of musicians in which, for the most part, undocumented migrants became subjects of popular songs.[1] The "larger world aspect in time and space" refers in this case to the securing and militarization of borders in the European Union in relation to mass migration. But "mass migration" is actually about the individual migrants and refugees from the Global South and East, escaping persecution, poverty, warfare, ethnic and religious conflicts, or environmental instability seeking to reach the Global North, in this case Europe.

These are among the reasons that led Thomas Nail to begin his landmark study, *The Figure of the Migrant* (2015) asserting that "[t]he twenty-first century will be the century of the migrant" (1). As per the data from the *World Migration Report 2010* and the 2015 "Migrant Health" report by the World Health Organization there are, in many diverse manifestations, more migrants at the turn of the twenty-first century "than ever before in recorded history" (Nail 2015, 1; see note 1). Thus, if race and racism are the problem of the twentieth century, that problem is compounded in the twenty-first century by the subjectivities of undocumented migrants and refugees who are socially expelled and cast out through processes of racialization, which I detail later in this introduction – one of the many strategies used to prevent their moving freely, forcing the migrant to attempt to cross fences and/or borderlines. It is within these social and historical premises that the situation in Europe is described by the global media as the worst migration/refugee crisis since the Second World War (Nordland 2015; Safdar 2016).

I also maintain that the dramatic circumstances we witness since 2015 in regard to Europe's migrant and refugees crisis is but a further development of what has been taking place for the past five decades: the movements of the destitute, stateless, and desperate from the poor Global South and East – *les damnés de la terre* as per Frantz Fanon's (1925–61) seminal 1961 essay – to the real and imagined riches and freedom of the Global North here centred on the European Union (EU), minus the United Kingdom since June 2016 because of the so-called Brexit, the British exit from the EU.[2] I further argue that the musical narratives produced in Spain beginning in the early 1980s in regard to the migratory processes taking place as Spain becomes "the southern outpost of 'Fortress Europe'" (Tilmatine 2011, 579), need to be understood as an earlier cultural manifestation attesting to the migratory movements towards Europe within the Mediterranean routes described by Frontex, the European Agency for the Management of Operational Cooperation at the External Borders of the Member States of the European Union (see http://frontex.europa.eu/about-frontex/origin/). Frontex also places Spain within the Eurosur category (see http://frontex.europa.eu/intelligence/eurosur/). Spain is a front-line state, a Mediterranean nation on Europe's southernmost border; Italy and Greece are two other so-called Eurosur nations that are either destinations or gateway nations.

The agency is the materialization of the notion of "Fortress Europe," a concept favoured by Hitler during the Second World War (Seaton 1981) but used at different times in history; today it is primarily employed to describe the fortification of Europe to prevent entry from the outside (Geddes 2008). In regard to the aims of the present study, the term comes "into pointed focus when looking at the hazardous crossings taken by would-be migrants trying to reach the EU's Southern frontiers" (Bermúdez and Strongman 2015, 138). Frontex, as a symbolic and material emblem of Fortress Europe, currently delineates eight different access routes from other geopolitical locations to the European Union in its "Migratory routes map" (see http://frontex.europa.eu/

trends-and-routes/migratory-routes-map/). *Rocking the Boat* focuses on the movements through the routes by land and sea that pertain to Spain's becoming the primary point of entry to the European Union in the last decades of the twentieth century – while also serving as a major transit country for those seeking to reach other destination countries. Beginning in early 2015 the impacted points of entry to Fortress Europe moved further east, to the so-called Eastern Mediterranean route when Greece overtook Italy as the first European Union country of arrival. The privileging of the Eastern Mediterranean route, "has placed Turkey at the center of how Fortress Europe seeks to deal with migrants, refugees, and asylum seekers" (Bermúdez and Strongman 2015, 138).

That music is the first field of cultural production to engage with migration and the changing Spanish social landscape at the turn of the twenty-first century (as early as the 1980s; literature and film begin in the 1990s) is not surprising.[3] In his *Crónica sentimental de España* (1971), Manuel Vázquez Montalbán asserts that one of the social functions of music is to provide emotional catharsis (Bermúdez and Pérez 2009, 127–8). And that is what the popular songs of the 1940s, mostly *cuplés,* did by making bearable the brutality of the so-called "years of hunger" (Colmeiro 2003, Sieburth 2014).[4] Although the Franco regime used the songs and other forms of commercial popular culture to numb the Spanish people, the reception of these songs can also be read "as a form of cultural resistance which helped people in the enormous task of 'getting by'" (Graham 1995, 241). In *Crónica sentimental de España,* Vázquez Montalbán reminds us that music, both artistically and culturally, allows us to assess the current state of events, processes, and social situations. This is a point argued by musicologist Richard Middleton (2006), who contends that popular music encapsulates forms of identity because of its intrinsic collectivizing quality: its ability to form adherences. Vázquez Montalbán's and Middleton's assessments of the social function of music – as a way of expressing that which has been repressed and as a mode of forming adherences – are central to my analysis of the developing body of songs on migrant subjects, racial hierarchies, and racism.

I view the songs as cultural texts that are to be understood as "texts," both "in the sense that we are able to *read* [them] – to *interpret* [them] – just like a book" and "in the sense that, like everything else in culture, [they have] been constructed, 'stitched together' using material that has been used before" (Bowman 2008, 35). It is as cultural texts that *Rocking the Boat* foregrounds the importance that lyrics play in popular music's communicative power, for they are a valuable tool for reading ideological intentions and the changing political and economic tendencies of the 1980s, 1990s, and first decade of the 2000s in Spain (see Shuker 2001 and 2005 for the understanding of popular music and key concepts, respectively). As such, lyrics are the focal point of my analysis and, following Simon Frith in *Performing Rites: On the Value of Popular Music*, they are simultaneously considered as "words, rhetoric, and voices" (1981, 159). Focused on difference and the change they bring to what, after the adoption of the Spanish Constitution of 1978, is articulated as a multilingual but supposedly homogenous nation state, the songs thematize racialization processes: the strategies, methods, and procedures by which race has become salient when discussing migration to the European Union (EU). Racialization is an act "done" to others as part of a power relationship such as apartheid, Jim Crow, or the Final Solution (Omi and Winant 1994). But it is also "a consequence of institutional operations, an intrinsic feature of the modern state's functions of classification, biopolitics and governance" (Garber 2007: 62–3). In both instances, race is a significant factor in the way social resources are allocated.

I concur with the assessment that the European Union has "*racialized immigration* ... by rendering the conditions of entry and settlement more difficult for those people not racialized as 'white'" (Garber 2007, 62; emphasis mine). In the case of Spain, I argue that the songs document the symbolic and institutional operations that have taken place to classify and categorize migrant newcomers and so-called second and third generation Spaniards as "non-white." When considering the notion of race we are dealing with ideological constructions of difference that use the phenotype as the marker to articulate said difference (Radano and Bohlman 2000; Gates Jr 2008). More importantly, as an unfixed and constantly evolving and negotiated category, the category "race" needs to be contextualized within the specific social, political, economic, and cultural contexts in which it is articulated. *Rocking the Boat* focuses on a particular body of songs produced in Spain at the turn of the twenty-first century that narrate the presence of migrant newcomers and migratory movements within racial hierarchies. In so doing, *Rocking the Boat* also attends to how the songs document the legacy of racism – traced back to empire building and colonial relations – while appealing, directly or indirectly, for solidarity.

The processes and practices of imagining race are not new to Spain. Indeed, considering that the rise and expansion of European modernity rest heavily on the emergence of the colonial enterprises of the fifteenth and sixteenth centuries and on the articulation of racial differences "to manage work, reproduction, and the social organization of the colonized" (Lowe 2006, 204), Baltasar Fra-Molinero (2000) reminds us that early modern Spain and colonial Spanish America are initial contributors to the practices of racial hierarchization (see also Fra-Molinero 1995; Berta Ares Queija and Allessandro Stella 2000). More to the point, Jerome C. Branche in *Colonialism and Race in Luso-Hispanic Literature* insists on considering "the broader Occidental imaginary on race" (2006, 3) when assessing a written tradition that over five hundred years has reified the negative connotations assigned to the Spanish words *negro/negra*. It is within and against the backdrop of this literary canon that I evaluate the body of songs focused on the terms *negro/negra* and *negrito/negrita* as used in the racialization processes taking place in democratic Spain as a result of migration and disparic movements.

The Historical Context

It is telling that the band Radio Futura, the pop group Mecano, and later the hard rock group Barricada, as well as *cantautores* (singer-songwriters) Carlos Cano and Joaquín Sabina came to prominence between 1982 and 1992, the decade of Spain's postmodern and global transformation and the period in which the nation established itself as a model democracy, a postmodern cultural haven, and a rising economic presence in Latin America. The triumph of Felipe González's Spanish Socialist Workers' Party (PSOE) in the 1982 general election – the same year Mecano and Barricada released their first records and Radio Futura toured all over Spain – cemented Spain's democratization process and meant the implementation of widespread changes thoroughly reshaping the nation. But Felipe González's consolidation of power and the survival of the democratic process were not without serious opposition, since many in the Spanish armed forces considered the processes taking place during Adolfo Suárez's administration (1977–82) a threat to "the unbreakable unity of the Fatherland" (Aguilar 2002, 314). The growing frustration within the police and the armed forces were embodied in the person of Lieutenant-Colonel Antonio Tejero of the *guardia civil* (civil guards) who led the assault on Parliament on 23 February 1981 (23F) while a vote was in progress to elect Leopoldo Calvo Sotelo as prime minister. Already in 1978 Tejero was plotting to overthrow the government in what came to be known as *Operación Galaxia* (Operation

Galaxia) (Clemente 1994). By appearing on television, King Juan Carlos I was able to stop the coup. On 28 October 1982, the PSOE's leader Felipe González helped his party win the general election with an absolute majority. By 1992, the PSOE had lost its allure due to corruption and fraud that reached the highest level of the government.

Corruption and fraud notwithstanding, the series of celebrations in 1992 – the Olympic Games in Barcelona, the Seville World's Fair, the commemoration of the quincentenary of Columbus's arrival in the Americas, and the naming of Madrid as the "European City of Culture" – allowed Spain to project a global image by which Spanish cities became emblems of cosmopolitan appeals and European wealth. These events were compared with a carnival that provided an "effective distraction from the negative consequences of the PSOE's economic policies and from the gathering gloom of the oncoming recession" (Graham and Sánchez 1995, 413). The celebrations of 1992 marked Spain's return to centre stage in the geopolitical landscape, to a position of significance and power worthy of a nation that once had been a mighty empire. But 1992 also heralded the bleak times to come for the remainder of the decade with a Socialist government involved in political deception, marred by criminal investigations, and undergoing a severe economic recession with unemployment at 24 per cent (Juliá 2000). All the while the social fabric of the nation was torn apart by the alarming rise of racist and xenophobic events and attacks.

The seriousness of the problem became painfully clear in November 1992, when Spaniards woke up from the celebratory hangover to the news of the murder of Lucrecia Pérez, a black Dominican woman who had recently arrived in Madrid to toil as a domestic worker in a private home. Killed in Aravaca, Lucrecia Pérez became an emblem of what was left after the party was over, a literal leftover that embodied the violence of racism, which could not be silenced by the rowdy revelry. Migration, already discursively presented as "an invasion," was becoming a serious issue, which needed to be urgently addressed to avert the decomposition of the body of the nation. The tragic event revealed not only racist behaviour but also, more disturbingly, the workings of racist doctrines that established false connections between physical type and character. Lucrecia Pérez's murderers, invoking such a causal relation, victimized her for belonging to what was perceived as a threatening race. And since "the segmentation of the world along racial lines has as its corollary an equally definitive segmentation of the world along cultural lines," black and Moroccan migrants in Spain became the target of racial attacks throughout the 1990s (Todorov 2006, 214). The attacks culminated in the episode that took place in February 2000, in El Ejido, Almería province, when locals targeted the Moroccan migrant population for three days, harassing them and destroying or burning their shops, houses, and mosques (Checa 2001).

None of this was yet obscuring the promising political horizon that opened up for the PSOE and the Spaniards in general in late 1982 and early 1983, after they had survived the hovering phantom of another military dictatorship after the failed military coup of 23 February 1981. Nor did it put an end to the endless carousing in clubs, concerts, and art exhibits in the wake of the cultural phenomenon known as *la movida* (the happening) (Pérez-Sánchez 2007; Fouce and del Val 2013; Nicholas and Song 2014). There was, after all, much *pasotismo* (disengagement) and *desencanto* (disenchantment) from the deluge of transcendental historical events that led to 23F – the assassination of Luis Carrero Blanco by Basque nationalist group ETA (Euskadi Ta Askatasuna, Basque Homeland and Liberty) in 1973, Franco's death in 1975, the king's declaration of democracy in 1976, the democratic elections of June 1977, the ratification of a democratic constitution in 1978, the centrist government of Adolfo Suárez (1977–82), and the declaration of autonomy by Catalonia (1977), the Basque Country (1979), and Galicia (1981). Thus, as a way of coping with the dizzying speed of the *transición* and a difficult economic situation, much of the younger generations decided to commit themselves to fashion, the visual and graphic arts, and to new wave pop and hard rock. It is at this social, political, and economic juncture that Radio Futura, Mecano, and Barricada burst onto the Spanish musical scene. All three bands enjoyed extraordinarily successful musical careers that ended, respectively, in 1992, 1998, and 2013.

Let me rewind to July 1985, during Felipe González's first term, and the enactment of the "Ley Orgánica sobre derechos y libertades de los extranjeros en España" (Organic Law of Rights and Liberties of Foreigners in Spain), shortly after Spain had signed the treaty to join the European Union (EU) in June of that year. To convince Spaniards and other countries in the European Union that a Socialist party could be tough on migration, the PSOE-led Congress passed what has become known as *La Ley de Extranjería* (The Immigration Law), one of the harshest immigration laws in all of Europe at that time, criticized for its restrictiveness and for advocating tough police practices, with a subsequent reform in 1991 (Sánchez Jiménez 2005, 95). A more severe stance on immigration follows during the José María Aznar's administrations (1996–2004), reflecting the underlying right-wing agenda of the People's Party made evident by transferring all responsibility for immigration from the Spanish Ministry of Labour to that of the Interior (Balfour 2005). The Popular Party also waged culture wars with an ambitious program implementing reforms in the teaching of the humanities to highlight Spanishness, *patriotismo constitucional* (constitutional patriotism), and issues of national pride including "the struggle of the Christian kingdoms against the Muslims in the Middle Ages" (Núñez Seixas 2005, 127; see Epps 2010 on *patriotismo constitucional*).

The PSOE won the general election of 14 March 2004 by a narrow margin and José Luis Rodríguez Zapatero became Spain's prime minister as a result, many consider, of the political manipulation of the Atocha terrorists attacks of 11 March 2004 by José María Aznar's ruling government (Porras Nodales 2004; Béroud 2006). Despite strong evidence that Al Qaeda-inspired militants were behind the attacks, then Prime Minister Aznar and his Popular Party ministers insisted in blaming ETA for the bombings of the four commuter trains making their way to the Atocha station in the early morning hours. Aznar and the Partido Popular (Popular Party) lost the March 2004 elections, and Rodríguez Zapatero went on to secure a second term on 9 March 2008, with a political program that emphasized social issues, including fighting gender violence and discrimination, expediting divorce, and legalizing same-sex marriage. But even Rodríguez Zapatero's progressive agenda failed to address racism, a major social issue affecting Spain during his tenure as attested by, among other events, the anti-migrants attacks that took place on 16 September 2004 in the industrial park of Carrús in Elche (coastal province of Alicante). In this instance, around five hundred people set fire to several Chinese shoe warehouses. At the anti-migrant protest held six days later, placards and chants of "No Chinese!" and "Stop immigration!" did nothing to calm the situation.

And while the achievements of the LGBTQ community under Rodríguez Zapatero's watch cannot be trivialized, neither can be ignored the brutal immigration policies that Rodríguez Zapatero's government began enforcing more assiduously from 2004 onwards but more repressively at the onset of the economic recession in 2008. The draconian measures included police profiling in Madrid and Barcelona to meet weekly quotas of arrests of immigrants, especially Moroccans, who could be returned to their country expeditiously and inexpensively (Kern 2009). In committing to a policy that concentrated the government's efforts in border patrolling, detention, deportation, and repatriation, Rodríguez

Zapatero abandoned previous processes of regularization, like the one promoted in 2005 allowing 580,000 undocumented migrant workers to achieve legal status.

Rodríguez Zapatero's austerity measures eroded support for his party, prompting him to call for an early general election in July 2011. The impact of the protests by *Movimiento 15-M*, the *Indignados* (Outraged), and other grass-roots movements on this decision cannot be overstated. The 15-M was one of the faces of the anti-austerity movements that were born in response to the financial crisis, inequality, corruption, and the high rate of unemployment among Spain's youth (Romanos 2013; Sampedro and Lobera 2014; Snyder 2015, among others). Prompted by social networks, the demonstrations began on 15 May 2011. The general election of 2011 took place in November; Mariano Rajoy, the leader of the People's Party since 2004, won with the strongest majority in three decades and was appointed as prime minister. Rajoy's cabinet immediately approved what is known as the "first austerity plan," a series of drastic measures that froze public workers' salaries, reduced the workweek, and froze the minimum wage, among other actions. Immigration continued to be a sensitive issue as Spain grappled with a double-dip recession and a 26 per cent unemployment rate in the final quarter of 2012 and as Prime Minister Rajoy marked his first year in office.

In 2013, Spaniards continued to take to the streets across the country to protest against not only these measures but also against a long list of corruption scandals implicating bankers, politicians, unions, and even members of the royal family. The scandals are behind the abdication of Juan Carlos I in favour of his son who ascended to the throne as Felipe VI on 19 June 2014. This political shake-up was preceded by the foundation by Pablo Iglesias of the left-wing party Podemos (We Can) in January 2014 – a byproduct of the Indignados/15-M social movement. In the December 2015 general election Podemos secured 69 seats out of 350 in the Spanish Parliament, forever redrawing the political landscape known to the nation since 1978. The securing of 40 seats by the party *Ciudadanos* (Citizens), which emerged in Catalonia in 2006 as anti-separatist and centre-right, also contributed to the so-called paradigm shift in Spanish politics. Since no party secured a majority, rounds of negotiations were held attempting to establish a governing coalition. The failure of these negotiations sent Spain into a second general election in the span of six months. The political deadlock prompting the 26 June 2016 election was not resolved. To the surprise of many, the results had the People's Party winning by securing 137 seats, the PSOE further losing political clout with 85 seats. Podemos, which went into these elections as *Unidos Podemos* (United We Can) in coalition with *Izquierda Unida* (United Left), suffered a blow by only securing 71 seats to the 32 secured by Ciudadanos. After a ten-month political impasse, Prime Minister Rajoy formed a minority government in October 2016 with limited ability to enact legislation. The political turmoil attested to the fact that Spain continued to tussle with finding common ground in the articulation of the Spanish State.

Democratic Spain as Europe's External Border

Spain's accelerated transformation from dictatorship to democracy and, in particular, that of its rapid socio-economic development, which in 2008 turned into a severe economic and social crisis with no end in sight in 2016, cannot be told without also considering the demographic forces that continue to shape its present-day identity. For the purpose of this study, I specifically consider the migratory movements from Latin America, sub-Saharan Africa, and the Maghreb region, particularly Morocco, that has had such a significant influence on Spanish society that the infamous *pateras* and *cayucos* transporting would-be migrants and refugees to Spanish shores are but ironic images of the ships that were once powerful instruments of economic development and colonization for the Spanish empire.[5] These tattered boats have come to signify the undocumented migrants as threatening hordes (Flesler 2008), reversing Spain's status as a sending nation in the 1970s – between 1962 and 1976 almost two million Spaniards mainly from Andalusia and Galicia migrated to northern European nations – to a receiving nation.[6] Spain's transformation from a country of emigration to one of immigration, with a rapid increase in the number of migrants from non-EU countries is an issue in the debate about national identity. However, as I point out in the conclusion, at the onset of the 2008 economic crisis, Spain once again experienced being a country of emigration because of high unemployment rates among young Spaniards (Nogueira 2012).

But the reversal experienced between the 1980s and the first decade of the twenty-first century literally and metaphorically rocked the nation to the core, since the (mis)representation of migrant newcomers, among other issues pertaining to assumptions about Spain's national identity, continue to play a crucial role in the discursive construction of Spain since the adoption of the 1978 Constitution. The document establishes Spain as a nation composed of seventeen autonomous communities and two autonomous cities, Ceuta and Melilla, with Catalonia, Galicia, and Euskadi (the Basque Country) recognized as *Comunidades históricas* (Historical nations) (see Bermúdez 2010). Ceuta and Melilla are to play a central role in the militarization and protection of the European Union, signalling the fluid nature of borders by which Europe now legally begins in northern Africa.

In calling attention to how migration has been mostly symbolized as "an invasion," *Rocking the Boat* explores how the presence of migrant newcomers as well as that of naturalized citizens and so-called second- and third-generation nationals, challenges notions of Spanishness. This is not an inconsequential matter since decades after the transition to democracy, the idea of a unified Spanish nation proclaimed in the Spanish Constitution of 1978 was shaken by, among other factors, Catalonia's push for independence as per the nonbinding vote of the 2014 Catalan self-determination referendum, the November 2015 Declaration of the Initiation of the Process of Independence of Catalonia, and the October 2017 independence referendum. Another factor "influencing the debate about national identity in Spain is migration" (Kleiner-Liebau 2009, 18).

In relation to the discursive construction of national identity, I argue that these new migrant subjects are "rocking," as in the shaking called upon by rock 'n' roll and the urban dances derived from it, Spain's notions of homogeneity, boundaries, accommodation, and incorporation. By metonymically referring to this musical genre, *Rocking the Boat* also underscores the role urban popular music plays both in the negotiation of cultural difference and in the narration of these dangerous crossings. The telling of these crossings, along with the complex processes by which the Spanish nation simultaneously rejects and welcomes the newcomers, is a central theme in contemporary Spanish film, literature, and photography (see note 3).

As I elaborate in "Rocking the Boat: The Black Atlantic in Spanish Pop Music from the 1980s and the '90s" (Bermúdez 2001), popular music is the first cultural and artistic sphere in Spain that turns its attention to the materiality of migration and to the racialization of transnational migrant subjects. In particular, I pay attention to the processes of racial containment by which prevailing cultural and social values shape the figuration of migrants and so-called second- and third-generation Spaniards as racialized subjects primarily described by their ethnicity. Written and performed by an array of bands, singers, duets, *cantautores*, and a rapper, the songs I analyse here bear witness to the racialization of not only migrant newcomers but also of the successive generations "of locally born descendants ... trapped in the *vulnerable role of perpetual outsider*" (Gilroy 1993, 123; emphasis mine). This book seeks to illuminate how popular music has imagined race in connection with the migrant subject by considering twenty-five songs produced between 1984 and 2011 by the groups Radio Futura (rock-pop), Mecano (pop), Barricada (hard rock), Ska-P (ska, alternative rock), Chambao (flamenco fusion), Chab Samir (Spanish/Moroccan raï), and Che Sudaka (*música mestiza*) (hybrid music); the duets Amistades Peligrosas, Ella Baila Sola (both pop), and Las Hijas del Sol – aunt and niece duet originally from Equatorial Guinea (marketed under the world music banner); *cantautores* Joan Manuel Serrat, Carlos Cano, Pedro Guerra, and Joaquín Sabina; artist Concha Buika (Latin jazz, *copla*, and other musical styles), and rapper El Chojin. This is not by any means an exhaustive index of all the groups and performers that have paid attention to migrant subjectivities and racialization processes in the musical arena.[7]

The main criterion for this selection – unavoidably arbitrary as all selections are – has been the popularity of the songs and their interpreters. The artists were – in the case of those no longer performing – and are widely popular transnationally, and their compositions are broadly distributed and consumed. This is not the case of Chab Samir (born Samir El Quichiri, in Oujda, Morocco, 1969–, and now a Spanish citizen, also identifying as Catalan). As I discuss later in chapter 2, he is the author of the first raï music album in Arabic produced in Spain in 1999 by Afro-Blue Records self-titled *Chab Samir* (Játiva 2004; Nair 2006, 69). Though Samir was already a musician in his native Morocco, and somewhat familiar to Spanish audiences because of his role in the migration film *Saïd* (1999, directed by Llorenç Sole), he did not achieve the kind of commercial popularity enjoyed by the other artists studied here. For one, by singing in Arabic he deliberately chose to address the Maghrebi communities in Spain opting to not enter non-Arabic-speaking markets. Second, by focusing solely in Spain, Chab Samir did not participate in the ever-popular world of Arabic music mega stars such as raï global phenomenon Khaled (formerly known as Cheb Khaled, born Khaled Hadj Ibrahim in Algeria in 1960). It is also pertinent to disclose that I know the majority of the 1980s and 1990s songs by heart, since they were part of what Vázquez Montalbán has termed "educación sentimental" (sentimental education) for songs' contribution to shaping individual and collective imaginations (1971). Thus, the selection reflects personal preferences that join millions of other listeners and fans pledging their allegiances in varying degrees to the individual performers, bands, and duos seeking to denounce racism and call attention to the predicaments of migrants and refugees. Except for a few earlier manifestations of the 1980s, all the songs, despite and against having some of them participate in racialization processes do, in one way or another, actively seek to denounce the situation and raise the public's awareness about how "the illegal immigrant [is presented] as a bogeyman, a perennial outsider who in waves and floods invades Western countries" (Andersson 2014, 2).

Three caveats are in order. First, the songs and musicians I focus on, for the most part, have migrants as subjects of popular songs but only Las Hijas del Sol, Chab Samir, and Che Sudaka are either exiled or migrants themselves, as I discuss in the corresponding chapters. Second, their music has been produced and disseminated through the transnational recording industry, alternative record labels, new technologies, and new social media beginning in the 1980s. Since music is such an integral part of our daily existence, we must also keep in mind that migrant musicians negotiate cultural difference, literally and metaphorically, in the normalcy of the quotidian by performing the music of their countries of origin in public spaces throughout the Spanish territory – squares, subway entrances, street corners – as they seek to make a living. Every day, as a cross section of Spaniards go about their business, they are exposed to an array of musical traditions, instruments, and sounds that go from Andean bands playing their *quenas* (Andean flutes) to accordion-playing Romanians (see figure 1) and everything in between, including classically-trained immigrant musicians playing violins.

These migrant musicians transform places such as Barcelona's Catalonia Square, *Parc de la Ciutadella* (Ciutadella Park), and Madrid's Puerta del Sol, as well as many other emblematic Spanish public spaces, into veritable technospaces (Appadurai 1996) where hybridization, diasporic communities, and postcoloniality reshape and refashion urban landscapes imbued with essentialist attributes that speak to national roots, be it Catalan or Spanish. Precisely in chapter 4, by focusing on the band Che Sudaka – the name a play on the popular Argentine expression "ché" and the pejorative Spanish expression "sucada" to mean someone from South America – I call attention to these aspects in the *música mestiza* (hybrid music) sound that emerged in Barcelona when the professionalization of some of these migrant street musicians and the intervention of the music industry catapulted "the *mestizo* sound from the confines of social centers, public parks and 'alternative' music venues to the stages of 'world music' festivals and the playlists of mainstream radio formulas" (Sánchez Fuarros 2013, 146). The third caveat is

1. Eastern European migrant musicians in Madrid.
Copyright Javier Lafora, 2014.

that the majority of the songs I study narrate accounts of migration from Latin America – mostly from the Caribbean – and from sub-Saharan Africa; only three songs attend to the plights of migrants from the Maghreb.

In regard to the negotiation of cultural difference and new identity markers for the Spanish nation, the songs by Las Hijas del Sol, Chab Samir, Che Sudaka, Concha Buika, and El Chojin are the best examples. Las Hijas del Sol voice the experiences of exiled newcomers in the 1990s, while Chab Samir and Che Sudaka that of illegal migrants from Morocco and South America, respectively, arriving in the early 1990s in the first case and the early 2000s in the second.[8] Concha Buika and El Chojin represent so-called second-generation Spaniards. Significantly, while Spanish film and literature have been more in tune with the diasporic narrations of the Moroccan community and Muslim Spaniards, a lesser number of songs have focused on the Moroccan community per se, despite their being, historically, one of the oldest and one of the largest migratory groups in the last three-and-a-half decades.[9] This lack of representation is illustrated in *Rocking the Boat* since only three of the twenty-five songs I study openly depict the trials and tribulations of Muslim migrant workers from the Maghreb region as they seek employment either in the Catalan Maresme region, as in "Salam Rashid" (Hello Rashid) by singer songwriter Joan Manuel Serrat, or throughout Europe, as in "Alí, el magrebí" (Ali, the Maghrebi) by Ska-P, or when embarking on perilous migratory journeys, as in the song "Patera" by Chab Samir. A fourth song, Chambao's "Papeles Mojados" (Wet Papers), implicitly refers to migrant subjects from the Maghreb by the opening statements in Berber at the beginning of the song and by the desert-like landscape presented in the song's video. Ultimately, the particular migration social history narrated in the songs studied here does not fully address the complex and diverse migratory patterns that have defined Spain in the late twentieth century.

Relevant to my discussion of musicianas and their works are the postcolonial responses of Moroccan born Catalan writer Najat El Hachmi (1979–) and Equatoguinean writers Francisco Zamora Loboch (1948–) and Donato Ndongo Bidyogo (1950–). Exiles from Equatorial Guinea have taken up permanent residence in Spain as a result of Francisco Macías Nguema's brutal dictatorship (1969–79) and that of his successor, Teodoro Obiang Nguema.[10] In Madrid, Ndongo Bidyogo, seeking to establish his nation's literary history, published in 1984 the first *Antología de la literatura guineana* (Anthology of Guinean literature), which includes, in addition to Zamora Loboch and Bidyogo himself, writers such as Juan Balboa Boneke (1938–2014), María Nsué Angüe (1945–2017), Ciríaco Bokessa (1947–), Raquel Ilonbé (1939–92), Justo Bolekia Boleká (1954–), and Joaquín Mbomio Bacheng (1956–) (see Ngom 1993, 2004; Lewis 2007; Ugarte 2010). Three years later, in 1987, eight-year-old Najat El Hachmi, a native of Nador in northern Morocco, arrived in Vic, a city in Barcelona province, where she attended school and learned the language with which, in 2004, she announced to the world her new-found identity in the poignant essay *Jo també soc Catalana* (I Too Am Catalan). In 2008, she was awarded the Ramon Llull Prize, the most prestigious award in Catalan letters, for her *L'Ultim patriarca* (The Last Patriarch). In contrast, Ndongo Bidyogo's anthology did not receive much critical attention from the Spanish intellectual milieu when it first came out in

1984, two years after Felipe González's Spanish Socialist Party landslide win in the 1982 elections. *Antología de la literatura guineana* is now considered a foundational text in the Equatoguinean literary corpus (Ngom 1993; Lewis 2007; Ugarte 2010).

In the musical arena, I first take into account the 1999 postcolonial responses by Chab Samir in the song "Patera," as an expression of migrant consciousness and denunciation of the criminalization of migration. I then pay attention to "Sin papeles" (2003) from the band Che Sudaka, formed in 2002 in Barcelona by four South American musicians – two Argentinian and two Colombians – all undocumented migrants that met in Barcelona's George Orwell Square, located in *Ciutat Vella* (Old town), and popularly known as Tripi Square. There are two reasons for such a moniker; it is a reference to the drug scene that once dominated the place as well as an homage to the unique sculpture by avant-garde Catalan artist Leandre Cristofol (1908–98), both fomenting "trips." The Square became a meeting point for buskers from all over the world and source of inspiration for a fusion of various styles. The four undocumented migrant musicians began jointly busking on street corners and metro stations to earn a living, transitioning to the recording industry in 2003 with the release of their first album *Trippie Town* (label K Industria) in homage to where they first met (see http://www.chesudaka.com/index.php/es/.

Music and Transnational Capitalism

Theodor W. Adorno's (1990) emphasis on the economic base of music production, although useful, is not enough to fully explain the terrifying experience of racially- and ethnically-marked migrants/musicians. (I am fully aware that economic issues loom large in the transnational movements of people.) For one, Adorno neglects to consider fully the symbolic dimension of the practice of music. Although his analysis is quite subtle and useful even today, it fails to take into account more complex processes of social identity formation: identification, attachment, and what Lacan would term enjoyment. Indeed, if enjoyment is relevant to processes of social identity formation, it is also central to the consumption of music, and to the many pleasures we derive from it individually and collectively.

In regard to the many different musical styles and genres that need to be considered when evaluating songs contributing to the imagination of race in Spain in connection with migration at the turn of the twenty-first century – pop, rock and hard rock, flamenco fusion, ska, *música mestiza* (hybrid music), raï, rap, and the patently Hispanic tradition of *cantautores* – we must pause when considering the "world music" category in which artists such as Las Hijas del Sol and Concha Buika have been placed. The musical trajectory of the aunt (Piruchi Apo) and niece (Paloma Loribó) duo, whose five albums were produced in Spain, is inseparable from the postcolonial history of West Africa and from the musical productions of the African diaspora. Their global impact can be assessed in terms of "the popularity of world music ... and the connections with other displaced groups throughout the world" (García-Alvite 2004, 155). But we cannot overlook that Las Hijas del Sol accepted the marketing of their songs under the world music banner because their survival as musicians and performers was linked to their being promoted as world music artists. As García-Alvite rightly points out, lack of freedom and of an infrastructure to produce and distribute records in Equatorial Guinea, as well as the prospect of becoming associated with the entourage of the dictator, led them to leave their country. In return, Apo and Loribó use the means provided by the world music machinery to their advantage negotiating cultural difference in the metropolis while establishing themselves as postcolonial citizens and performers at the top of World Music Charts Europe (García Alvite 2004, 157).

Success – transatlantic success – which is intimately tied to transnational capitalism, also defines the musical trajectories of, among others, Mecano, Joan Manuel Serrat, and Joaquín Sabina. It is also transnational capitalism that brings to the Spanish shores the vessels – *pateras* and *cayucos* – with human cargo from Africa, and the planes from all over Latin America, the Caribbean, and other parts of the world to serve as maids, cleaners, and hand labourers in the fields of Almeria, Catalonia, Andalusia, and the Canary Islands. Within the new modes of flexible production and financial deregulation of transnational capitalism, African, Moroccan, Caribbean, and Latin American migrant workers came to Spain in the last decades of the twentieth century to form an easily exploited labour force.[11] The presence of all these migrant newcomers is portrayed as a sociopolitical problem that needs to be controlled to avoid the disintegration of the nation and the danger migrants supposedly represent to the "sovereignty, identity, and well-being" of Europe (de Wenden 2007, 29). Étienne Balibar forcefully argues that racism and neo-racism are ills that define nation states and the European Union as a whole (1991, 15–23).

Indeed, depicting migration and transnational movements as invasions is the norm when discussing these processes in the age of globalization. The "familiar language of borders and threats" is used to describe how those "inside" fear the migrating hordes coming from "outside" – Mathew Coleman explains how similar imageries are used to describe the arrival of migrant Chinese nationals by boat to Canadian shores (2005, 294). One cannot overstate how migration is construed within a discourse of fear, since anxiety and dread appear to be the driving forces behind the bloc-wide immigration policy adopted by the European Parliament on 18 June 2008 in Strasbourg (France), which, among other measures, authorizes the jailing of undocumented workers for as long as eighteen months pending deportation. Although the policy is decried by the United Nations and human rights organizations as excessive and inhuman, Spain is one of the main beneficiaries of the funds established by the EU to help deter migration to the European Union, since over 131 million euros were destined for Spain's use until 2010.[12] In the 1980s, Spanish musicians turned their attention to this particular narrative of migration – a racially construed discourse of "borders and threats" – that can be traced back to 1 July 1985 when Felipe González's Socialist administration passed and enacted the Ley Orgánica 7/1985 de 1 julio, sobre derechos y libertades de los extranjeros en España (Organic Law of Rights and Liberties of Foreigners in Spain).

The exploding musical scene of the late 1970s and early 1980s signalled Spain's assimilation to the neoliberal capitalist model within a globalized economy. Spain was rapidly transformed into a consumer society in which music became a highly commodified product that helped advance the modernization process (Tango 2006). If Spain's new urban modernity generated an ebullient musical landscape with an inordinate number of successful bands during the 1980s, it also brought about a new social landscape because of the arrival of migrant workers mostly from North and sub-Saharan Africa, Latin America, and the Caribbean.[13] The impact on the Spanish social imaginary of migration and the rejection to the presence of workers from the Global South and East were made apparent in 1985 with the enactment of the Ley Orgánica sobre derechos y libertades de los extranjeros en España aimed at controlling both legal and illegal migration. The Organic Law 4/2000 of 11 January, as amended by Organic Law 8/2000, Organic Law 14/2003, and Organic Law 2/2009 of 11 December is the one in effect in 2017.

In what follows I assess how migration was first used by Felipe González and the PSOE as a political tool to win the presidential electionof 1986 and how it was later articulated as a sociopolitical problem during Popular Party's José María Aznar's two terms as prime minister (1996–2004, winning the 2000 general election by absolute majority). I also consider the embracing and rejection of migrant subjects during the two-term Socialist administration of José Luis Rodríguez Zapatero (2004–11) and the protectionist stance of the Partido Popular's Mariano Rajoy during his tenure as prime minister (2011–16) after the People's Party landslide victory in the 2011 general election. And while my study ends with a song, "Rap vs. Racismo" produced in 2011, in chapter 4 and the conclusion I do briefly take into account how the success of Podemos and the rise of Ciudadanos marks a radical change in Spanish politics since 1978 from a two-party to a multiparty system. I also explore how the general elections of December 2015 and June 2016 show that Spaniards continued to be troubled by corruption, unemployment, and recession but, tellingly, and in contrast with other nations in presidential elections such as the United States or Britain's vote to exit from the European Union, there is no mass anti-immigration party contesting Spain's elections – a radical change from preceding ones, as previously stated.

Mapping the Trajectory of the Music

Within this political and social context I study how the racialization of migration is sometimes reified and often questioned in the following twenty-five works listed by group, artists, or duos and in order of publication: Radio Futura's two 1984 poems "Un africano por la Gran Vía" (An African on the Gran Via) and "Semilla negra," the 1987 "Paseo con la negra Flor" (Walk with the black Flower), and the 1992 "Coplas añadidas a Semilla Negra"; Mecano's 1986 "No es serio este cementerio" (This is not a proper cemetery) and 1988 "El blues del esclavo" (The slave's blues); Joan Manuel Serrat's 1989 "Salam Rashid" (Hello Rashid) and 1992 "Disculpe el Señor" (Pardon Sir); the 1991 "Africanos en Madrid" (Africans in Madrid) by the duo Amistades Peligrosas; the 1992 "Oveja negra" (Black sheep) by the Basque hard rock group Barricada; three songs published in 1994 – Carlos Cano's "Canción para Lucrecia" (Song for Lucrecia), Joaquín Sabina's "La casa por la ventana" (Going for broke), and Ska-P's "Alí, el magrebí" (Ali, the Maghrebi); three songs published in 1995 – Pedro Guerra's "Contamíname" (Contaminate me) and Las Hijas del Sol's "A ba'ele" (The foreigners), in their native Bubi, and "Tirso de Molina" in Spanish; by the duo Ella Baila Sola the 1996 "Que se te escapa el negro" (The black guy is getting away from you); two 1999 songs "Mami, el negro está rabioso" (Mama the black man is mad) by rapper and hip hop artist El Chojin and "Patera" by the band Chab Samir, led by Chab Samir; Ska-P's 2000 "Lucrecia" – a revisitation of Lucrecia Pérez's murder and criticism of the *Ley de Extranjería*; Che Sudaka's 2003 "Sin Papeles" (Without papers); Concha Buika's 2005 "New Afro-Spanish generation"; the 2008 hit "Papeles mojados" (Wet papers) by Chambao, the flamenco-electronic group from Andalusia; and two raps by El Chojin conclude the musical trajectory delineated by *Rocking the Boat*, his 2009 "N.E.G.R.O." and the 2011 "Rap vs. Racismo," a joint venture by El Chojin and a team of Spanish rappers that served as the anti-racist campaign promoted by the NGO Movimiento contra la Intolerancia (Movement against Intolerance) to principally reach the younger student population (see "Campaña Rap contra el Racismo" (www.movimientocontralaintolerancia.com).

In analysing these songs I subscribe to Frith's (1981) notion that when listening to the lyrics of pop songs one hears three things simultaneously: words, rhetoric, and voices. As to words and their ability to endow songs with meaning, Frith notes that "in everyday terms a *song* – its basic melodic and rhythmic structure – is grasped by people through its words" (1981, 159; emphasis in the original). Despite all the controversies surrounding the value of content analysis in musicology, Frith reminds us that lyrics – "words" – need to be taken into account when analysing pop songs. And since words are central to the musical narratives on migration and race in Spanish pop music, I concentrate on a close reading of the lyrics of songs focused, mainly, on undocumented migrant subjects in Spain at the turn of the twenty-first century.

Words in pop songs are words "in performance," resting on specific rhetorical strategies and, as such, we are to treat them "in terms of the persuasive relationship set up between singer and listener" (Frith 1996, 166). Meaning is thus produced through the performance, which, in turn, draws attention to the words and to the singer. Voice, for obvious reasons, also plays a crucial role in my analysis of the songs. We are to understand voice "as a musical instrument; as a body; as a person; and as a character" (Frith 1996, 187). Aware that the meaning of popular music is dependent also on melody and sounds, I am including the musical analysis of four songs to further expose how racialization processes are also inscribed in the harmonic and melodic features of the songs. In all instances, the musical analysis adds to the understanding of the lyrics, and I rely on the expertise of musicologist Eduardo Viñuela for the musical analysis of three songs: Radio Futura's "Un africano por la Gran Vía" in chapter 1, and Amistades Peligrosas's "Africanos en Madrid" and Ska-P's "Alí, el magrebí" in chapter 3. Thanks to the help of musicologist David Thurmaier, I include the musical analysis of Joan Manuel Serrat's "Disculpe el Señor" in chapter 2. All translations to English are mine, and the help of Lorena Barrett and Eyda Merediz is noted when pertinent. Due to the need to abide by stricter Canadian copyright regulations because of the book being published by University of Toronto Press, and despite many and incessant attempts, for diverse reasons I was not able to secure permits for the following songs, "Africanos en Madrid," "Contamíname," "Alí, el magrebí," "Lucrecia," "Mami, el negro está rabioso," "N.E.G.R.O," "Oveja negra," "Papeles mojados," "Patera," "Que se te escapa el negro," and "Sin papeles." I do address the narrative of the songs and point everyone to the many digital music venues and YouTube videos where the songs can be directly experienced.

In assessing Spanish racism in the historical context of the turn of the twenty-first century I am particularly indebted to Jerome C. Branche's (2006) *Colonialism and Race in Luso-Hispanic Literature* and to the work of Margarita Cervantes-Rodríguez, Ramón Grosfoguel, and Eric Mielants in the volume *Caribbean Migration to Western Europe and the United States: Essays on Incorporation, Identity, and Citizenship* (2009). The first premise guiding the discussion of the twenty-five songs with which I am concerned in *Rocking the Boat* is that migrant workers arrive in territories that are "always already informed and constituted by coloniality" (Grosfoguel, Cervantes-Rodríguez, and Mielants 2009, 8). The second is how important "race as *narrative* has been and continues to be" in the close to five-hundred-year canon of Luso-Hispanic culture (Branche 4; emphasis in the original, see also Branche 2008).

In chapter 1, "The Roaring 1980s: From La Movida to Racial Naming, Slavery, and Muslims in the Catalan Maresme," I analyse four songs by Radio Futura ("Un africano por la Gran Vía," "Semilla negra," "Paseo con la negra Flor," and "Coplas añadidas a Semilla Negra") and two by Mecano ("No es serio este cementerio" y "El blues del esclavo") within the articulation of "blackness" and the enactment of the Organic Immigration Law of 1985. I also consider the poem "El prisionero de la Gran Vía" (The Prisoner of the Gran Via), a postcolonial response to these racialization processes, by Equatoguinean Francisco Zamora Loboch, a long-time *madrileño*. The chapter concludes with an analysis of Joan

Manuel Serrat's "Salam Rashid," a song in Catalan that deals with the trials and tribulations of a Maghrebi migrant worker.

In chapter 2, "The 1990s, Take One: Fortress Europe, Racism, Apologies, and Contestation," I address the social and cultural value assigned to *cantautores* in the Hispanic cultural imaginary to explore how this value allows them to sing from an authorial and privileged position. I then evaluate Spain's new geopolitical status in light of the celebrations of 1992, the paradigms of transnational capitalism during the period that now is described as the first mass migration movement to Fortress Europe (Andersson 2014, xviii). Transnational capitalism and racism are the central focus of the songs I analyse in this chapter: Serrat's "Disculpe el señor," Cano's "Canción para Lucrecia," Sabina's "La casa por la ventana," and Guerra's "Contamíname." I conclude the chapter with Chad Samir's "Patera" and El Chojin's "Mami el negro está rabioso," with particular attention to El Chojin's scathing denunciation of Spanish racism. Relating it to the crime that inspired Cano's song, I also discuss Zamora Loboch's *Como ser negro y no morir en Aravaca*, an essay whose writing was prompted by Lucrecia Pérez's murder.

In chapter 3, "The 1990s, Take Two: The Racial Profiling of Black and Maghrebi Migrant Subjects," I first attend to the articulation of blackness in "Africanos en Madrid" by the duo Amistades Peligrosas. I then study the colonial underpinnings of the violence exerted on black men by the Spanish police in "Oveja negra" by Barricada and "Que se te escapa el negro" by the duo Ella Baila Sola. I also consider two songs, "A ba'ele" (The foreigners) in Bubi and "Tirso de Molina," a Spanish rendition of "A ba'ele" in the Equatoguinean responses to racial profiling articulated by the aunt and nice duo Las Hijas del Sol, that advance a gendered understanding of the social process of migration. How religious difference is racialized through the conflation of migration and Islam is evaluated in "Alí, el magrebí" by Ska-P, a song seeking solidarity for the Maghrebi subject, which I read in conjunction with Chab Samir's Spanish/Moroccan raï "Patera" and Najat El Hachmi's *Jo també soc catalana* (2004) and within the epistemology of *pensament de frontera* (frontier thought; see also Gloria Anzaldúa's borderlands). In connection with the articulation of blackness, I further discuss Zamora Loboch's *Como ser negro y no morir en Aravaca* (1994) along with Donato Ndongo's (2007) novel *El metro* (The subway).

In chapter 4, "Twenty-First Century Spanish Musical Landscapes: From Ska and *Música mestiza* to Flamenco Fusion Singing and Chilling, to Rapping Against Racism," I consider Ska-P's "Lucrecia" within discussions of multiculturalism and against the 2000 xenophobic attacks against Moroccan migrant workers in El Ejido in Almería province, and the Partido Popular's *Ley de Extranjería* 4/2000 and 8/2000. I then look closely at the significance of the song "Sin Papeles" by the band Che Sudaka within the *música mestiza* scene in twenty-first century Barcelona and as a manifestation of *mestizaje* hybridity – as lived experience by encounter due to migratory movements (Wade 2005). In relation to the September 2004 anti-migrant attacks against Chinese owners and workers in the industrial area of Carrus in Elche, I discuss how racism and xenophobia continue to look for new targets. I then continue the musical analysis with Concha Buika's enactment of hybridization and creolization in "New Afro Spanish Generation," a song formulating a new social landscape for the nation and that, in its use of English and Spanish, appears to question the imposition of racial categorizations from the United States. I also analyse the rhythms of flamenco fusion in Chambao's powerful "Papeles mojados," which focuses on the continuous symbolic relevance of *pateras* and *cayucos* in the Spanish imaginary. I conclude the evaluation of racialization processes in contemporary Spanish popular music by turning my attention to El Chojin's 2009 "N.E.G.R.O." – where the rapper as activist uses identity politics to argue for the empowerment of black Spaniards – and to his 2011 joint-venture and self-explanatory "Rap vs. Racismo." But first, let's rewind and explore the musical landscape of the early 1980s in Spain in chapter 1.

1

The Roaring 1980s: From La Movida to Racial Naming, Slavery, and Muslims in the Catalan Maresme

As Spain negotiated a European – "white" – identity, by being granted entrance in 1986 to what was then the European Economic Community (EEC), musicians from two very distinct musical genres imagined racialized identities in the 1980s. The earlier productions were by Radio Futura and Mecano, two groups emerging from the exuberant musical scene of the *Movida madrileña* during the late 1970s and early 1980s (Ordovás 1984 and 1989; Gallero 1991; Cervera 2002; Fouce 2006; Fouce and de Val 2013). The later manifestation, the 1988 song "Salam Rashid" from the album *Material sensible* (Sensitive material), by Joan Manuel Serrat (1943–), a towering figure among Iberian and Latin American *cantautores*, is about a clandestine Maghrebi migrant in the Catalan Maresme. Already an established transatlantic start for albums such as, among others, *Dedicado a Antonio Machado, poeta* (Dedicated to Antonio Machado, poet) (1969, Zafiro/Novola) and *Mediterráneo* (Mediterranean) (1971, Zafiro/Novola) by the time Radio Futura and Mecano became fundamental musical references in the 1980s, Serrat's prolific recording career in Catalan and Spanish begins in 1965 (Vázquez Montalbán 1972). Since then, the singer-songwriter has penned and published over three hundred songs and has produced an extensive recording career, in Spanish and Catalan, the two languages that have allowed him to communicate with millions of listeners and concert-goers throughout the world (Martínez and Sales Casanova 2013; see also http://jmserrat.com/). And choice of language is at the heart of "Salam Rashid" (Hello, Rashid) a song in Catalan narrating the trials and tribulations of the Muslim migrant worker identified by first name in the title.

A paradigmatic musical text in more ways than one, Serrat's song is, chronologically speaking, the first of only two songs among those examined in this book where religious difference is racialized through the conflation of migration and Islam. The other, which I address in chapter 3, is "Alí, el magrebí" (Ali, the Maghrebi) by the ska hard rock band Ska-P. In terms of melody, "Salam Rashid" relies heavily on musical hybridization, since in the published CD album Serrat brought the virtuoso guitar playing of flamenco star Paco de Lucía (1947–2014) to bare relevance on the telling of this migrant's story. Born Francisco Sánchez Gómez in Algeciras, in the province of Cádiz in Andalusia, the famed guitarist and composer, redefined flamenco by expanding its musical horizons and was also recognized as an outstanding jazz player (see www.pacodelucia.org). Thus, from very early on flamenco melodies play an important role in delineanting the musical landscape that attests to the racialization processes taking place in constitutional Spain.

Before turning our attention to "Salam Rashid," we must first focus, as per the songs' publication dates, on the ebullient Spanish musical scene of the late 1970s and early 1980s that gave birth to a parade of bands during the years of the Movida. Radio Futura emerged in Madrid in 1979, first as the creation of Herminio Molero in 1978 when he first fashioned Orquesta Futurama, a macro-band that later changed its name to the one that would become famous under the leadership of Santiago Auserón. Following a different musical path, the trio Mecano erupted into the musical scene in 1982 with their self-titled album *Mecano* (CBS), the same year the PSOE won the general election by a landslide, which led to sweeping reforms and modernization programs. Despite their opposing musical conceptualizations and radically different styles and aims, both Radio Futura and Mecano have become embedded in the cultural imaginary and sentimental vocabulary of generations of Spaniards. Mecano gave voice to a range of emotional situations, reactions, and relationships not musically addressed before so openly in Spanish music – lesbian love in "Mujer contra mujer" (Woman against Woman) or street violence in "Cruz de navajas" (Cross of Knives). Radio Futura produced songs such as "Escuela de calor" (School of Heat), "and "La estatua del Jardín Botánico" (The statue in the Botanic Garden) conveying meanings beyond their invitation to dance. Four productions by Radio Futura – "Un africano por la Gran Vía," "Semilla negra," "Paseo con la negra Flor," and the 1992 "Coplas añadidas a Semilla Negra," which, as the title indicates, needs to be read alongside "Semilla negra," and two by Mecano – "No es serio este cementerio" and "El blues del esclavo" – document the racialization processes taking place in the

Spain borne after the 1978 Constitution. In particular, I pay attention to how these six songs, in their specific uses of the terms *africano* (African man), *negra* (black woman), *negro* (black man), and *negrito* (little black man), delineate a classificatory system that becomes operative when discussing Spanishness and Europeaness in the wake of Spain's transformation from a sending to a receiving society (Triandafyllidou, Modood, and Zapata-Barrero 2006). I conclude the chapter by analysing how Joan Manuel Serrat's "Salam Rashid" works within and against this classificatory system.

Radio Futura: New Musical Frontiers, Old Racial Anxieties

At the time of their first live performance in October 1979, Radio Futura consists of four members – Santiago Auserón, Luis Auserón, Enrique Sierra, and Hermino Molero. A few months later, they are chosen, among all the other emerging bands, to open for Elvis Costello's first-ever concert in Spain, held on 20 March 1980.[1] The performance signals Radio Futura's impact in the development of what has now been labelled by media and cultural critics as the golden era of Spanish pop, what Héctor Fouce calls the Spanish *Nueva ola* (New wave) (Fouce 2006, 51).[2] The event forever linked Radio Futura to a foundational musical moment in Spanish pop music since the Elvis Costello concert marked the beginning of the internationalization process by which Spain became known, both economically and musically, to the field of popular music. Two days after their momentous opening act, Radio Futura went into the recording studio to produce their first album with the hit single "Enamorado de la moda juvenil" (In Love with Youth's Fashion), released in May 1980. The song became an anthem for young Spaniards, a popish homage to the relevance youth and a youth culture was to have in the emerging democratic Spain; foreshadowing, if you will, that in 1982, Felipe González was to be, at that time, the youngest European prime minister at the age of forty. After the departure of Herminio Molero in 1981, Santiago Auserón fronted the group as lead singer until its dissolution in the spring of 1992.

Santiago Auserón brings to Radio Futura's musical projects his charisma but, more importantly, his intellectual acumen. Co-author with his brother Luis Auserón of some of their most successful songs, he produced *Semilla del son* (The roots of son) (BMG-RCA) in 1992 – a two-CD compilation of Cuban music – and is the author of *La imagen sonora: notas para una lectura filosófica de la nueva música popular* (1998) (The sound image: notes for a philosophical reading of the new popular music), the volume of his creations titled *Canciones de Radio Futura* (1999) (Songs by Radio Futura), and of *El ritmo perdido: Sobre el influjo negro en la canción española* (2012, re-edited in 2015) (Lost rhythm: On the black influence on the Spanish song), another publication from the artist confirming his dedication to documenting the impact of Arab and African rhythms in Spanish music.[3] Known for his expertise in the Cuban *son*, Santiago Auserón's production of the *Semilla del son* CD was a pioneering enterprise, undertaken well before Cuban music and Cuban musicians such as Compay Segundo became fashionable and profitable – like in the case of the Grammy winner The Buena Vista Social Club's self-titled 1997 album and the award-winning 1999 documentary (of the same name) by Wim Wenders and Ry Cooder.

In committing to the dissemination, revalorization, and celebration of Afro-Cuban music in late twentieth-century Spain, Auserón contributes to the hybridization of Spanish music (Tango 2006). When discussing Afro-Cuban's influences in twentieth-century Spain, we ought to remember that before Radio Futura embarked on the hybridization of Spanish pop/rock music in the early 1980s, Spaniards had been enamoured of Afro-Cuban rhythms and, in particular, from the 1930s onward, of a particular Afro-Cuban performer Antonio Machín (born Antonio Abad Lugo Machín 1903–77) (Jover 2002). Songs made popular by Machín include, among others, "El manisero" (The peanut vendor), "Dos gardenias" (Two gardenias), and "Angelitos Negros" (Black little angels), which are regular staples on the radio, country fairs, and *verbenas*, as depicted by José Luis Cuerda in his well-liked film *La lengua de las mariposas* (Butterfly) (1999), set in 1936 Spain at the brink of the Civil War and whose title pays homage to one of the three short stories adapted from the collection *¿Que me queres, amor?* (1995) by Galician author Manuel Rivas (1958–).

However, we are not to confuse Spain's enjoyment and passion for this music in the first half of the twentieth century and, in particular, during Franco's lengthy dictatorship, with the attempts at musical hybridization carried out by Radio Futura. For one, thought timidly at the beginning, the band actually incorporates melodic motives from jazz and Afro-Cuban music into their compositions (Tango 2006). These attempts at musical cross-fertilization are not at work when Spaniards consumed – as exotic objects of desire – Afro-Cuban music and jazz during the 1930s and onwards. Indeed, it is the lack of musical cross-pollination that prompts Santiago Auserón's to produce *Semilla del son* in 1992 since, according to him, Spain needs to learn from the *son* and Cuba's tradition of great *soneros* as made clear in the lines of his "Coplas añadidas a Semilla Negra." There the poetic voice states: "Aquí te traigo la semilla / *De este son para ti* / *Que me la dió Beny* [*sic*] *Moré* / *Y Miguelito Cuní*" (*Canciones de Radio Futura*, 1999, 115; emphasis mine). As I explain later on in the chapter, Santiago Auserón establishes a direct lineage between the poetic voice, we can assume it is Auserón himself, and these two musical titans from Cuba – Benny Moré, born Bartolomé Maximiliano Moré Gutiérrez (1919–63), and known as "El Bárbaro del Ritmo" (The Wildman of Rhythm), and Miguel Arcángel Cunill (1917–84), known as Miguelito Cuní – who metaphorically also infuse Spanish rock/pop with the rhythms of the Cuban *son*.[4]

Rock and *son* share many similarities since, according to Santiago Auserón both musical forms are borne out of the "semilla negra" (black seed) of African music and in both rhythm takes precedence over harmonies. Auserón continued to explore musical cross-pollination in his 2011 self-published CD *Río negro* (Black River), produced under his artistic name of Juan Perro, which became Santiago Auserón's musical persona when he launched his solo career in 1996. *Río Negro* is inspired by New Orleans and the devastation brought on by Hurricane Katrina, where Auserón further investigated musical genres such as blues and jazz. In 2012, as already mentioned, he published *El ritmo perdido: Sobre el influjo negro en la canción española*, a thorough exploration of Arab and African musical influences in Spanish popular music with a second edition in 2015.

Radio Futura released "Un africano por la Gran Vía" in 1984, in the early stages of experimenting with musical hybridization. The project was further developed in the 1987 album *La canción de Juan Perro* (The Song of Juan Perro) (Ariola 1987, in creations such as "La negra Flor" (Black Flor), the precedent to "Paseo con la negra Flor" (A Stroll with black Flor) – a rap version infused with reggae rhythms that was first launched as the B-side of a maxi-single published in 1987 and then listed as track four in their final album, *Tierra para bailar* (Land for dancing) (BMG Ariola 1992); it is this poem I study here from *Canciones de Radio Futura* (1999). The increasing incorporation of Afro-Caribbean and Latin American rhythms by Radio Futura leads Tango (2006) to conclude that the band had finalized its learning process by the time Radio Futura released their fourth album, *La canción de Juan Perro* (84–7).

To discuss "Un africano por la Gran Vía" and "Semilla negra" we first need to consider that the album in which these texts appeared, *La ley del desierto, la ley del mar*, surpassed all sales expectations rising to number two on the best-seller list during the summer of 1984 (Lesende and Neira 2006, 207). The album's success was due in part to songs such as "Escuela de calor" and "Semilla negra." In fact, "Semilla negra" was such a hit that, in 1985, was re-released as a maxi-single and launched internationally with the incorporation of the great flamenco guitarist Raimundo Amador (1959), one of the pioneers, with Paco de Lucía, of the cross-breeding of flamenco with other musical genres. Amador had a leading role in the founding of the groups Veneno (1977) (with his brother Rafael and performer Kiko Veneno) and Pata Negra (1981) (with his brother Rafael), and is recognized as one of the early promoters of flamenco fusion.

The band's commitment to Afro-Hispanic rhythms infused musical hibridity into Spain's postmodern urban reality, thus making a significant contribution to the musical landscape of the 1980s (Guillot 1992; Villamandos 2007). Songs such "Un africano por la Gran Vía," "Semilla negra," and "Paseo con la negra Flor" attested to the vibrancy of the Spanish musical scene. They also confirmed the nation's changing social landscape as per the arrival of migrant newcomers mostly from Latin America – in particular the Caribbean – and from North and sub-Saharan Africa at that stage of the migratory processes. The impact on the Spanish culture of *La ley del desierto, la ley del mar*, which includes "Un africano por la Gran Vía" and "Semilla negra," needs to be underscored since, almost ten years after it first came out, it was once again made massively available to a new generation of Spaniards in the summer of 2003 by the daily newspaper *El Mundo*. The CD, which could be purchased with an extra 5.50 euros, came as a supplement to *El Mundo*'s 20 July 2003 Sunday edition and as part of the newspaper's promotion of Spanish pop music of the 1980s.[5] Given the album's reissue, "Un africano por la Gran Vía" doubly resonates, first in 1984 and then in 2003, as one of the first songs to "document" the presence of black African subjects in the Spanish territory and as constitutional Spain was seeking to solidify its status as a European nation.

Black African men, as desired and feared subalterns, are not new to Spanish popular music since songs such as "Madre, cómprame un negro" (Mother, buy me a black man) (1929) and the 1930s "Al Congo" (To the Congo), both inscribed in the ragtime jazz rhythms of the charleston, rely on the stereotyping of African men as sexually potent and promiscuous (Marí 2007).[6] In the case of "Madre, cómprame un negro" there is more than mere stereotyping taking place. The command by which the female speaker orders the mother to "buy" her a black man so she can dance with him – not a subtle metaphor for sexual encounter – makes light of the horrors of slavery. As such, the request is embedded in a colonial desire in which the transactions of slavery are reified. The song did transgress the rigid social paradigms of sexual conduct of 1920s Spain by voicing the desires of an independent woman, unfortunately it did so by dismissing the horrors of slavery and by participating in the epistemic violence such representations perpetrate against black persons.

A crucial distinction needs to be made between the songs from the early twentieth century and those produced since the early 1980s. For one, the latter were produced within the spatial reconfigurations of the globe brought about by neoliberal policies and transnational capitalism whereby Spain begins to experience migration as a host nation and not as a sending nation. Second, the literal and metaphorical distance inscribed in the earlier songs – as in the desire to travel to Africa to dance, as in "To the Congo" – mark the historical and social distance by which black African men are no longer distant exotic objects of desires, but actual subjects perceived as invader "strangers" whose immediacy is met with apprehension and concern. In their evaluation of the album, Tito Lesende and Fernando Neira highlighted "Un africano por la Gran Vía" as a song with "great sociological value" (2006, 207). I believe that, in part, this value derives from the semantic and symbolic reverberations of the term *africano*. A Spanish word that has as its first meaning a place of origin – a man from Africa (see Moliner 1977) – but also implicitly refers to a specific racial phenotype, a notion from biology that relies on outward, physical manifestations to determine racial identity (Appiah 2005). The semantics of *africano* (African man / black man) cannot be overlooked when assessing the song's participation in racialized naming. If, as Frith argues when discussing "songs as texts" in *Performing Rites*, "song language is used to say something about both the singer and the implied audience" (Frith 1981, 166), in "Un africano por la Gran Vía," language "says something" about what the term *africano* denotes, and it is not merely a geographical place of origin.

That *africano* also means "black" is in part determined by the complex colonial past Spain shares with Morocco and the Sahara region. Therefore, when discussing nationals migrating from Africa, a linguistic distinction is made between those arriving from North Africa – either derogatorily called *moros*, or more correctly *magrebíes* – and those arriving from sub-Saharan Africa, called either *africanos* or *negros*. Significantly, Juan de Vicente's study evaluating migratory flows to Madrid identifies migrant workers from sub-Saharan Africa with the term *negroafricanos* (black-Africans) (1993, 251).

I call attention to the term *negroafricano* since it is suggested though never actually enounced in "Un africano por la Gran Vía." This, and other aspects of the poem written by Santiago Auserón, do not provide an easy interpretation of what, by 1984, was becoming a new social development: black African persons, mostly men, arriving as migrant subjects and settling throughout the Spanish territory, particularly in Madrid (de Vicente 1993, 251–336). In discussing the presence of a (black) African man in one of Madrid's most emblematic of boulevards, "Un africano por la Gran Vía" speaks to an anxiety over the presence of black African immigrants in the capital of the Spanish kingdom. As one of the early musical manifestations of a Spanish racial imagination at the end of the twentieth century, I include, along with the evaluation of its lyrics, the melodic analysis of "Un africano por la Gran Vía" courtesy of musicologist Eduardo Viñuela. I quote the poem from *Canciones de Radio Futura*; the song's chords are included:

Musical Introduction:
G – A – G
F – A – G – A

G A	
Con un suave balanceo voy por ahí	With a smooth swagger there I go
G A	
a la hora en que cierran los clubs	when the clubs close
F A	
con un suave balanceo, sin sonreír	with a smooth swagger,
G - A	
más de lo necesario.	smiling just enough.
G A	
tras algún signo de vida voy	I´m chasing some sign of life
G A	
no sé quién soy ni donde nací	I do not know who I am or where I was born,]
F	
pero llevo un africano	but I have an African

A G - A	
dentro de mí, oh sí.	inside of me, oh yes.
G A	
Y todavía estoy oculto en la maleza	And I am still hidden in the bushes
G A	
el colour rojo me hace perder la cabeza	the colour red makes me lose my mind]
G A	
soy capaz de arrastrarme por el suelo	I could start crawling on the floor
G A	
y sólo tiemblo cuando tiembla el cielo.	and I only tremble when the skies tremble.
G	
Con un traje nuevo	With a new suit
A	
entra en la cafetería	an African
G	
un africano	enters the Cafe
A	
por la Gran Vía.	on the Gran Via

(Auserón 1999, 46)

Ambivalence and ambiguity are at the core of who this African man may be. The gender marker of the Spanish language unambiguously establishes that the protagonist of this musical story is a man, by the "o" ending of the word *africano*. What it is less clear is who he may actually be since he simultaneously appears to be the confused speaking subject – no sé quién soy ni dónde nací / pero llevo un africano dentro de mí (I do not know who am I nor where I was born / But I have an African inside of me) – and hence a Spaniard of the *movida* enjoying the club scene. Yet, he also appears to be an actual African man, a black man wearing a new suit whose mere presence inscribes a racialized sense of place in a Gran Vía café.

The urban setting of after-hours swagger and postmodern indifference – "sin sonreir más de lo necesario" (Without smiling more than needed) – is contrasted with a jungle setting that makes the postmodern *flâneur* lose his composure and behave like an animal, as in the line "[t]he color red makes me lose my mind." The transformation from postmodern nightlife urban dweller to savage is prompted by the expression of a desire – "[t]ras algún signo de vida voy" (I am chasing some sign of life) – and the recognition of a lack of subjectivity or national identification – "no sé quién soy ni donde nací" (I do not know who am I nor where I was born). It is within the trope of the urban wilderness, and only after desire and lack are enunciated, that the speaking subject recognizes the presence of an (Other), and this Other is none other than a black man from Africa: "pero llevo un africano dentro de mí" (But I have an African inside of me). This confusion of self and other, driven by the (usually) unconscious desire to be the Other, allow us to address the issue of identity and identification in psychoanalytic terms.

Indeed, the song becomes a site in which identity is no longer homogeneous and absolute, but needs to be understood within the lived social text of the moment: Spain's desire to finally be recognized as a full-fledged European nation. Spaniards will come to see integration into the *Comunidad Ecónomica Europea* (CEE, European Economic Community), which happened in 1986, as the culmination of a modernization process by which Spain was finally no longer considered the beginning of Africa – as in the popular saying "Africa begins at the Pyrenees" – but part of Europe. Thus, we can see how the identification of the lyric voice with an African man in "Un africano por la Gran Vía" is not without symbolic consequences since on the one hand the identification embodies one of Spain's worst fears and anxieties: the equation of Spain with Africa, because "Africa, more closely than any other area of the world, haunts contemporary Spain" (Epps 2005, 114).[7] On the other hand, it signals how the presence of black African nationals in the Spanish territory was considered a throwback in Spain's efforts to join the CEE.

Behind the song's anxiety lurks fear, which, as Slavoj Žižek (1991) argues, is nurtured by the stereotyping of black persons as figures of unrestricted jouissance – the racialized Other "has access to some specific enjoyment" that escapes the speaking subject (187). Indeed, the African man described in "Un africano por la Gran Vía" appears to be the emblem of jouissance, and as such, and as per the stereotype, capable of indulging every sexual desire and aggressive impulse, so much so that he metaphorically loses his head upon seeing the colour red – "the color red makes me lose my mind." The *africano*, thus, is literally depicted as "seeing red," as someone whose drive energies are intact: "I could start crawling on the floor."

Confusion and ambiguity are also at the heart of the song's melody. According to the musical analysis provided by Viñuela (e-mail message to author, 19 April 2010), the introductory tones reinforce the confusion from the beginning since first the bass becomes the protagonist in the early musical compasses, but then an oppositional tension is generated by the entrance of the guitar. Thus, while the melody of the guitar aims to establish a regular structure for the tonality and rhythm of the song, the bass *escapes* through progressions that question the stability of the parameters established by the guitar. In sum, the introduction constitutes a *mise en abîme* of what will comprise the song's total tonality. In regard to the vocals, Santiago Auserón moves within the range of an octave with ascending and descending intervals that, along with the bass's fugues, prevent fixing a clearly defined melodic structure. Moreover, the constant anticipations and delays related to the metric irregularity of the lines clash with the regularity of the guitars, generating a rhythmic ambiguity that comes to question the pulse of the entire song (Viñuela, e-mail message to author, 19 April 2010).

Tension also arises between this rhythmic ambiguity and the regularity present both in the bridge and the brief chorus of the song. The style of "Un africano por la Gran Vía," close to funk in the guitar, drums, and bass, but with hints of soul in the tonal structure and the use of winds, shows a clear connection with the dance music that was popular in the Madrid club scene of the mid-1980s. Finally, one of the song's main musical features is the counterposition between the rhythmic and harmonic ambiguity of the stanzas with the progressive regularity of the bridge and chorus, giving it an ethos that can be said to musically represent the coexistence and struggle of a subject that is simultaneously African/*Madrileño* (from Madrid), native/postmodern, and rural/urban (Viñuela, e-mail message to author, 19 April 2010).

Both in terms of melody and lyrics, the song voices extra-textual matters – the anxiety generated by the presence of a well-dressed black man in a Gran Vía café. Thus, I argue that "Un africano por la GranVía" is one of the earliest manifestations of discomfort, guilt, and even racist attitudes with which Spaniards came to deal with cultural and racial diversity in late twentieth-century Spain.[8] The very emphasis on highlighting the presence of this African man – marked as a "gendered black body," wearing a suit – signals the emergence of anxieties over the racial make-up of Madrid. These anxieties appear to respond to a fear about identity that can be best articulated as a question: whose city, whose place is Madrid if we now see *Africanos por la Gran Vía* (African men in the Gran Via)? One possible answer to this question came in 1985, a year after the publication of the song, when Felipe González's Socialist government passed and enacted the *Ley orgánica sobre derechos y libertades de los extranjeros en España* (Organic Law about Rights and Liberties of Foreigners in Spain) on 1 July 1985. Immigration came to be used by the PSOE as a political tool to win the presidential elections of 1986 and the passing of this law was a decisive factor in being able to join the ECC since Spain was considered, up until the 1985 law, to have "one of the most lenient and passive immigration policies in all of Europe" (Roy and Kanner 2001, 247).

A postcolonial response to the restrictive effects of the 1985 Law and to Radio Futura's "Un africano por la Gran Vía" is offered by Francisco Zamora Loboch's poem "El prisionero de la Gran Vía" (The Prisoner of Gran Via). First published in Donato Ndongo's 1984 *Antología de la literatura* guineana, the poem was also included in Zamora's *Desde El Viyil y otras crónicas* (From El Viyil and other chronicles) (2008). A journalist and musician, Zamora Loboch has resided in Madrid since the early 1970s when he left Equatorial Guinea to pursue a college degree in the metropolis. Along with thousands of other exiled Equatoguineans, he has not been able to return because of the brutality of the Macías Nguema regime in power since 1979 (Ugarte 2010). The author of *Cómo ser negro y no morir en Aravaca* (How to be a Black man and not to die in Aravaca) (1994), a caustic denunciation of Spanish racism discussed in chapters 2 and 3, he has also published the poetic collection *Memoria de laberintos* (Memory of labyrinths) (1999) and the novel *Muerte en el green (El informe Abayak)* (Death in the green [The Abayak File]) (2009). In "El prisionero de la Gran Vía," Zamora Loboch offers a countermemory to the secondary position and fetishization carried out by Radio Futura's song.

The poem works within and against fetishization – as in the transfer of erotic interest to an object or subject perceived as an object – by regaining personhood and subjectivity. Both are inscribed through the figure of the mother as moral compass and the use of the dramatic monologue. The monologue relies on the ethical judgment implicit in two modalities of a popular expression – "si me viera mi madre" (if my mother could see me) or "si te viera tu madre" (if your mother could see you) – to narrate the processes by which the speaking subject, an African man, loses his identity markers as he becomes enslaved to the cultural practices of Spain:

Si supieras
que no me dejan los días de fiesta
ponerme el taparrabos nuevo
donde bordaste mis iniciales
temblándote los dedos de vieja.
Si supieras
que tengo la garganta enmohecida
porque no puedo salirme a las plazas
y ensayar mis gritos de guerra.
Que no puedo pasearme por las grandes
  vías]
el torso desnudo, desafiando al invierno.
y enseñando mis tatuajes,
a los niños de esta ciudad.
Si pudieras verme
fiel esclavo de los tendidos,
vociferante hincha en los estadios,
compadre incondicional de los mesones
Madre, si pudieras verme.

If you only knew
That, on holidays, they do not let me
Wear the new loincloth
Where you embroidered my initials
Your old lady fingers trembling.
If you only knew
That my throat feels mossy
Because I can't go out into the plazas
And practice my battle cries.
That I cannot stroll on the boulevards.

With naked chest, defying winter.
And showing my tattoos,
To the children of this city.
If only you could see me
Faithful slave of bullrings,
Screaming fan in the stadiums,
Loyal buddy in the taverns
Mother, if only you could see me.

(Zamora Loboch 2008, 39)

Turning the expression "going native" upside down, Zamora's poem uses several strategies to question the stereotyping and misrepresentation that define certain cultural practices as "savage" and others as "civilized." For one, the references to "taparrabos nuevo" (new loincloth), "gritos de guerra" (battle cries), and "torso desnudo" (naked torso) present the gendered image of an African warrior, the personification of masculinity through a series of synecdoche that could be easily misconstrued as merely reinforcing a patriarchal imaginary. The poem asks us to be attentive to the ways in which so-called Third World cultures (whether from Africa, the Caribbean, or Latin America) become "feminized by an imperial, colonizing gaze" (Aparicio 2000, 96). Unable to perform his battle cries or to show his tattoos, this African man has become feminized and thus turns to his mother for validation. Only she, as the person that gave birth to him, can comprehend the depths of what has happened to him – "Si pudieras verme / fiel esclavo de los tendidos" (Faithful slave of bullring fights). Only she, as an African woman, can more readily understand what it means to be ethnified – a process defined as "to be constructed and displaced as Other, as 'heathen alterity'" (Aparicio 2000, 96).

Zamora's poem foregrounds masculinity as it works against cultural transactions that ethnify and feminize African men. First, by reclaiming the figure of the African male subject as a warrior, then by representing his transformation into a Spanish male indistinguishable from those that go to bullfights, attend soccer games, and hang out at bars.[9] Both modes are contrasted to expose how, while the masculine rituals practiced by African warriors – battle cries – are culturally marked as "primitive" and "tribal," the hegemonic masculine cultural practices, all reinforcing Spanishness, that now occupy this African male subject are considered civilized. The poem longs to embrace the African practices that have been left aside in the acculturation process by which this African man has become a Spanish man. In so desperately seeking to assimilate, the poetic subject appears to want to escape being noticed or pointed at, as in the case of the African man in Radio Futura's "Un africano por la Gran Vía."

Zamora's poem and Radio Futura's *La ley del desierto/La ley del mar* share being defined by contradictory impulses. In the case of Zamora's "Prisionero de la Gran Vía" the contradiction resides in lamenting a loss that occurs at the expense of the poetic subject's embracing Spanishness. In the case of Radio Futura's "Un africano por la Gran Vía," it is in the double gesture by which the song embraces African rhythms while racially containing African nationals. Notwithstanding its contradictions, Zamora's poem does work against containment by reinserting material activities connected with dance and performance – wearing a loincloth, the activities of screaming, walking half-naked – that have been culturally marked as savage and primitive. Against the fear and anxiety expressed by the song over the presence of an African national in Madrid's most well-known boulevard, "El prisionero de la Gran Vía" offers a first-person *testimonio* of what it means to be a transnational, exiled, black man in 1980s Madrid. The poem, ultimately, can help us understand "Semilla negra," the last track of *La ley del desierto, la ley del mar* since it addresses the possibility of cultural diversity.

"Semilla negra," while presented within the premises of a colonial gaze, is a song that moves beyond the anxiety of "Un africano por la Gran Vía" by fully embracing hybridization, particularly when five more stanzas were added in 1992 in the production titled *Tierra para bailar* (Land to dance). I first consider the poem from *Canciones de Radio Futura,* which, when listening to it as a song, engages us with the African roots of Latin American music. "Semilla negra" in its musical format is one of the first attempts to bring salsa rhythms into Spanish rock by using the bass to play the *clave* and as a substitute for percussion. Here is the 1984 poem:

Ese beso entregado al aire es para ti	That kiss blown to the air is for you
fruta que has de comer mañana	Fruit that you are to eat tomorrow
guarda la semilla porque estoy en él	Save the seed because I am in it
y hazme crecer	And make me grow
en una tierra lejana	In a far away land
si me llevas contigo	If you take me with you
prometo ser ligero como la brisa	I promise to be light as the breeze
y decirte al oído	And whisper in your ear
secretos que harán brotar tu risa.	Secrets that will make your laughter sprout]
Esos ojos detrás del cristal	Those eyes behind the glass
son dos negros cautivos cruzando el mar	Are two enslaved Blacks crossing the sea
por la noche estaré solo en la selva	At night I will be alone in the jungle
¿Qué voy a hacer?	What will I do?
esperando a que vuelvas	Waiting for your return
si me llevas contigo	If you take me with you
prometo ser ligero como la brisa	I promise to be light as the breeze
y decirte al oído	And tell you
secretos que harán brotar tu risa.	Secrets that will make you smile.
Yo tengo un pensamiento vagabundo	I have a wandering thought
voy a seguir tus pasos por el mundo	I will follow your path around the world
Aunque tú ya no estas aquí	Although you are no longer here
te sentiré	I will feel you
por la materia que me une a ti	Through the matter that links me to you

(Auserón 1999, 48)

When one listens to the song, the transatlantic movements of people comes to mind since "Semilla negra" opens up with the sound of seagulls chirping in the background. Hence, the ocean, first metonymically evoked by the seagulls, and then clearly named in the action "cruzando el mar" (crossing the sea), becomes the incessantly moving site that allows for the tepid inscription of hybridization in the 1984 version of the song. This process is called upon by the action of "crossing the sea," directly linked to the slave trade through a metaphor by which the eyes of the object of desire are emblematized as "dos negros cautivos cruzando el mar" (two enslaved blacks crossing the sea). An unfortunate metaphor, this "slip of tongue" – a so-called Freudian slip that reveals an unconscious belief – speaks of an embedded colonial gaze that minimizes the brutal enterprise by which millions of black Africans were displaced to Europe's New World colonies as part of the Atlantic slave trade.

The imprecise and often deliberately incomplete documentation produced during the Atlantic slave trade prevent us from accurately assessing its demographics (Lipski 2005, 45).[10] Lipski ventures the figure of 9.6 million for the entire period of the trade (45), but according to Jerome C. Branche, more recent estimations place the number at 36 million, (2006, 11). It is in light of these numbers and the actual predicament of the slaves who were robbed of human dignity and had to experience the trauma of exile and degradation that the line "dos negros cautivos cruzando el mar" (two enslaved blacks crossing the sea) reveals a repressed way of thinking and looking at the world inherited from centuries of enslaving Africans.[11]

But one cannot overlook that the musical project driving "Semilla negra" is to plant the seeds of Afro-Cuban music in the Spanish cultural landscape to further hybridization. It is in this sense that Santiago Auserón's enterprise goes beyond the mere enjoyment and appreciation of Afro-Cuban music as evidenced by the 1920s songs already mentioned or Spain's fascination with *sonero* Antonio Machín whom, in 1935, left for Europe to tour settling finally in Madrid – where he resided until his death in 1977 (Moore 1997, 179). Racial hierarchies are at work when assessing Machín's popularity in Spain, described as "one of the first Afrocubans of the thirties to perform with a white jazz orchestra and also the first to play at the exclusive Casino Nacional" (Díaz Ayala quoted by Moore, 179). However, despite Machín's popular performances – consumed as "exotic-other" products – and his extensive recording musical career, Spanish music did not embrace any of the rhythms or melodies of the *son*. Thus, though wildly popular, Antonio Machín did not transform Spanish music from within. This is why Radio Futura's "Semila negra" is considered to be a song that actually inscribes rhythms associated with Afro-Cuban music in the sounds identifying a patently Spanish band of the Movida.

"Semilla negra" dramatizes the difficulty inherent to hybridization processes since the original version works within contradictory impulses that pit the music against the lyrics. Hence, on the one hand, we have a literal "planting" of the seed of African music by having the bass dabble as the percussion instrument marking the salsa rhythms, while, on the other, we have lyrics sustaining a colonial gaze. And, in spite of this colonial gaze, "Semilla negra" is truly invested in narrating the musical hybridization processes taken place as shown by the stanzas later added by Santiago Auserón in the section listed under the title of the 1992 album (see Auserón 1999, 115). Thus, the one-sided expression of desire presented in the original version of 1984 has been transformed, in the 1992 version, into a narrative that has the singing subject and his desired object, a woman addressed as *china*, involved in a conversation by which she is inviting him to follow her. The context here indicates that the term *china* means "girl," as used by Argentinians, underscoring linguistic hybridization.

The added stanzas pay homage to the Cuban *son* with direct references to that musical genre and to two of Cuba's greatest *soneros*, Beny Moré and Miguelito Cuní, further emphasizing the relevance of Afro-Cuban music for Radio Futura. These are the added stanzas:

Semilla negra (chorus)	Black Seed (Chorus)
Me dijo; vente conmigo	She said; come with me
si quieres tú compartir	If you wish to share
me dijo; vente conmigo	She said: come with me
si quieres tu compartir	If you wish to share
la fruta del porvenir	The fruit of the future
seremos buenos amigos.	We will be good friends.
Semilla negra	Black seed
y en un barquito de ensueño	And in a wonderful little boat
alcanzaremos la orilla.	We will reach the shore.
Y en un barquito de ensueño	And in a wonderful Little boar
alcanzaremos la orilla.	We will reach the shore.

Plantaremos la semilla
en una tierra sin dueño.
Yo me voy contigo donde tú quieras ir.

Que yo me voy contigo, china, donde tú quieras ir]
que aquí te traigo la semilla de este son para ti]
que me la dio Beny Moré. y Miguelito Cuní.]
Semilla negra.
Ya me voy, me voy,
me voy, me voy
Así.

We will plant the seed
In a land with no lord
I will go with you wherever you want to go.]
I will go with you, China, wherever you want to go]
I bring you here the seed of this son for you]
It was given to me by Beny Moré and Miguelito Cuní.]
Black seed.
I am leaving, I am leaving,
Leaving, leaving
Like this.

(Auserón 1999, 115)

Adding more to the song, the extra stanzas open the song to hybridization processes by, first, refocusing the way in which the lyric subject looks at the object of desire, the *china* of the 1992 version. They also highlight that Spanish musicians from the Movida period have much to learn from the great tradition of Cuban *soneros* about rhythm in speech, sound, and motion. The learning process leads Santiago Auserón, as I pointed out at the beginning of this chapter, to the study, production, and dissemination of the Cuban *son* throughout the Spanish territory not only with the album *Semilla del son* but also with his active participation in roundtables and academic discussions on Afro-Cuban literary and musical traditions. The masterful dramatization of a rite of passage in which the singing subject directly receives the *son* from the masters Beny Moré and Miguelito Cuní, allows Radio Futura to inscribe themselves within the lineage of Afro-Cuban musicians that have made an art – and even in some cases a quasi-religious experience – of singing popular songs.

One such song is Radio Futura's smash hit "La negra Flor" from their 1987 *La canción de Juan Perro* (Ariola) and where the musical topic of the erotic-exotic Caribbean woman is revisited by Juan Perro, the central character/narrator of the 1987 album and Santiago Auserón's alter ego. The original "La negra Flor" was so successful that a longer version was produced as a maxi-single later in 1987. The

B-side of the maxi-single included an eight-minute rapped song titled "Paseo con la negra Flor," which relied on long-established rituals of using insults and put-downs. Imbued with racial, sexual, and class implications (Villamandos 2007), this long version uses the culturally complex figure of the black/mulatta Caribbean woman to dramatize the desire of a low-life man for a fetishized Other, "la negra Flor" (Black Flor). That Flor is a Caribbean woman is suggested by the reggae rhythms in which the song is inscribed, although we cannot identify her national origins. As a dancing lioness – con tu cola de gato y tus ojos de leona" (With your cat's tail and your lioness eyes) (*Canciones de Radio Futura* 77) – she joins an iconic musical tradition – that of the black/mulatta woman dancing, walking, or moving in songs such as "La negrita Concepción" (Little Black Concepción) and "La negra Tomasa" (Black Tomasa) (composed by Cuates Castilla and Guillermo R. Fife, respectively). This tradition, "ever present in Latin Salsa, Dominican *merengue*, and Afro-Latin rap … permeates the discourse of male composers and musicians as well as of male Caribbean writers, from turn-of-the-century essays to … contemporary postmodern renderings" (Aparicio 2000, 95). It could be argued that Radio Futura's fascination with African rhythms and Caribbean music is such that it mirrors the discourse of Caribbean composers, musicians, and writers and, in that sense, the song is involved in the same ethnifying and gendered articulations to which Aparicio has called our attention.

And despite all these, la negra Flor is presented as a complex character with the ability to respond to the insults and advances of the male suitor – she is not a mere sexual object to be looked upon. In part, this complexity is due to the fact that the figure of the mulatta or black woman dancing or walking – in the song, Flor is strolling down the beach – is not a fixed discursive figure and can be invested with potentially oppositional meanings (Kutzinski 1993; Aparicio 2000). Such is the case with la negra Flor, represented as a subaltern subject resisting being controlled by the desiring male subject by both rebuffing his advances and putting him down by sending him back to his Mamma – "Oye muchacho, ¿qué tal tu mamá? / ¿Por qué no vas a verla que ya debe estar / esperando por ti y te va a regañar?" (Listen, kid, how is your Mamma? / Why don't you go and see her because she must be / waiting for you to scold you?) – and by telling him to go and find a girlfriend willing to listen to him: "y te buscas una novia / que te quiera escuchar" (And find yourself a girlfriend /

who is willing to listen to you) (Auserón 1999, 77). Here, the song's lyrics need to be considered as rhetoric, since "Paseo con la negra Flor" relies on performative strategies to convey its meaning. Indeed, we have a dramatization where the actual characters of the story – the unnamed low-life young man and negra Flor – are the ones calling attention to their mismatched encounter, to the social and racial issues they narrate, and ultimately, to the misleading title of the song, since negra Flor does not agree to take a stroll with the unnamed young protagonist.

The story takes place in *Las Ramblas*, an iconic space of the city of Barcelona, and at a particular time – during the redevelopment of Barcelona's docklands, waterfront, and decaying urban zones in preparation for the 1992 Olympics (Sánchez 2002). In fact, the lower part of *Las Ramblas* – named in the song as "[a]l final de la Rambla – ended up being transformed into a gentrified area in which the two characters of the song could no longer be welcomed. This transformation is suggested in the song, both explicitly and implicitly, with the specific reference to the social and economic hierarchies that allude to the Catalan bourgeoisie in the lines "señora con un piso puesto con un chalet / con piscina privada y un salón de té" (a lady with a furnished flat, with a chalet / with a private swimming pool, and a tea room). The lyrics suggest that the two principal characters of the story, involved in a mutual and very witty put-down, could never belong to social circles that enjoy such residences. Flor is a prostitute, "y si quieres yo te quiero / pero págame primero" (And if you want me to I can love you/ But pay me first), while the male suitor is a sort of a low-life pulling "a trabajito" – maybe a small-time robbery? – that is yet to be paid: "Si tú quieres dinero yo te voy a dar, / porque hice un trabajito / y me lo van a pagar" (if you want money I will give it to you, because I did a small job / and it will get paid) (Auserón 1999, 78). Economic issues are further stressed by a play on the popular Catalan saying: "Barcelona es bona si la bolsa sona." The song calls attention to how "having money" helps to enjoy the city – "Si la bolsa 'sona', si la bolsa 'sona' / te pones los zapatos y te vas a Barcelona" (If the purse chimes, if the purse chimes / You put on your shoes and go to Barcelona) (Auserón 1999, 77). At the end, "Paseo con la negra Flor" attests to how Radio Futura imagined race in constitutional Spain by developing urban narratives that moved from the certain anxiety expressed in "Un africano por la Gran Vía" to the recognition and attempt at negotiation dramatized in "Paseo con la negra Flor."

Let's Talk about the *Guerra de Cuba*, Race, and Slavery in 1980s Spain: Mecano's "No es serio este cementerio" and "El blues del esclavo"

One of Spain's biggest selling bands, Mecano posted over twenty-five million wholesale records all over the world (Adrados and del Amo 2004; Lesende and Neira 2006). During their heyday, the trio enjoyed unrivalled appeal throughout Latin America and Europe – particularly in Italy and France with recorded versions in French and Italian of several of their songs. And while much has been written about Mecano's success and their place in the history of Spanish pop music and the Spanish cultural imaginary, not all of it is laudatory or positive. Controversies aside, Mecano is a fixture of the Spanish cultural landscape, and as with other groups and performers of the 1980s, enjoyed a revival in the first decade of the twenty-first century fueled by nostalgia and by the unparalleled success of the first ever Spanish pop musical, *Hoy no me puedo levantar* (Today I cannot get up), created by Nacho Cano and, originally, the title of Mecano's 1982 debut single (Fouz-Hernández 2009).

Two songs by Mecano attested to racialization processes in 1980s Spain, but they did so by displacing racial hierarchies and references to distant pasts. Both "No es serio este cementerio" (This is not a proper cemetery) from the 1986 album *Entre el cielo y el suelo* (Between heaven and earth), and "El blues del esclavo" (The slave's blues) from the 1988 album *Descanso dominical* (Sunday's off), bring back the ghosts of history to tell stories that were relevant to Spain's rapidly changing social landscapes in the last two decades of the twentieth century. The terms *negro* and *negrito*, used respectively in each song, point to the activation of racial taxonomies as Spain became a multiethnic and multicultural nation beyond the multilingual and multicultural identities imagined by the newly minted Spanish Constitution of 1978 – as in the so-called historic nationalities Basque, Catalan, and Galician. Indeed, while the "No es serio este cementerio" narrates the comings and goings of ghosts from the *Guerra de Cuba* (War in Cuba) in a Spanish cemetery precisely when there is an influx of migrant newcomers from the Caribbean, Latin America, and Africa, "El blues del esclavo" brings the history of slavery in the United Stated and its Civil War, borne out of the Secession of seven Southern slave states, to bare relevance on the rapidly changing labour conditions in 1980s Spain.

The ghosts of history, as Jo Labanyi (2002) argues, are hard to lay to rest. Spain's particular colonial ghosts – those of Cuba's lengthy War of Independence – and, more significantly, black ghosts, are evoked in "No es serio este cementerio," at a time when the media increasingly paid attention to the presence of black and mulatto Caribbean migrant newcomers in the Spanish territory. Another spectre of the past – a dictatorship – loomed large in 1986 since only five years earlier, on 23 February 1981, Spain's nascent democracy had to deal with the *Tejerazo* (one of the names given to the failed coup d'état of 23F). Moreover, Spaniards were experiencing *desencanto*, a sense of loss and confusion produced by the experience of not fulfilling the high expectations for social and political achievements after Franco's death. This sense of loss and confusion is displaced in "No es serio este cementerio" to the 1898 loss of Empire, the so-called Disaster [*Desastre*] by which Spain was defeated by the United State in the Spanish-American War, another time when Spaniards also experienced much sense of failure and confusion during a transitional period.

At a time when Spain was at a crossroads – negotiating a European identity while still dealing with the spectre of the 23F failed military uprising – the 1986 song revisits an apparently forgotten past since, as per the lyrics below, one of the *héroes de Cuba* (heroes of Cuba) narrates the ghostly comings and goings taking place in this cemetery. Lyrics and chords are quoted from Eduardo Viñuela's *El videoclip en España (1980–1995). Gesto audiovisual, discurso y mercado* (2009):

Stanza I	**Stanza I**
Dm Bb A	
Colgado del cielo	Hanging from heaven
Dm Bb A	
por doce cipreses	By twelve cypresses
Dm Bb A	
doce apóstoles de verde	Twelve green apostles
Dm Bb A	
velan doce meses	Watch over twelve months
a la tapia en ruinas	The wall in ruins
que lo delimita	That demarcates it
le han quitado algunas piedras	They have taken some stones
para hacer la ermita	To build the chapel

Bridge

Dm Bb A Dm
tiene mi cementerio una fosa común
Dm Bb A Dm
donde estamos los héroes de Cuba
los domingos los negros no dejan dormir
pues les da por cantar misa luba

Chorus

D A Bm F#m G
y los muertos aquí lo pasamos muy bien
A
entre flores de coloures
D A Bm F#m G
y los viernes y tal si en la fosa no hay plan

nos vestimos y salimos
D A G A
para dar una vuelta
D A G A
sin pasar de la puerta eso sí

D A Bm F#m G
que los muertos aquí es donde tienen que estar]
A Dm
y el cielo por mí se puede esperar

Stanza II

Este cementerio no es cualquiera cosa
pues las lápidas del fondo
son de mármol rosa
y aunque hay buenas tumbas
están mejor los nichos
porque cuestan más baratos
y no hay casi bichos.
Luego en plan sensorial,
el panteón familiar
de los duques Medina y Luengo

Bridge

My cemetery has a common grave
Where we, the heroes of Cuba, are
On Sundays Blacks do not let us sleep
Because they are singing Luba Mass.

Chorus

And we the dead here have such fun
Among colourful flowers
And on Fridays, you know, if there is no party in the common grave]
We dress up and go out
For a stroll
Without, of course, going beyond the entrance]

Since the dead here is where they have to be]
And heaven for me can wait

Stanza II

This cemetery is not just any cemetery
Since the tombstones at the end
Are made out of pink marble
And though there are good tombs
The niches are much better
Because they are cheaper
And have not too many insects
Then, more stately,
the family pantheon
Of the Dukes Medina and Luengo

que aunque el juicio final
nos trate por igual
aquí hay gente de rancio abolengo

And though the Final Judgment
Is to treat us equally,
There are people here of noble ancestry

(2009, 100)

The poem relies on performative strategies that call attention to the characters of the story – ghosts from Spain's lengthy colonial war with Cuba, among which there are Spanish soldiers, black subjects, and a few aristocrats. The speaking subject, one of the heroes of the Spanish–American War, identifies himself as part of a particular military group with great significance in the history of modern Spanish culture. The popish song, with its repetitive musical format – its hooks and its chorus – cannot be easily dismissed since, by letting one of the ghosts of the 1898 Disaster "speak" in the social and cultural sphere of 1986's Spain, the song enacts what Labanyi (2002) calls "the return of the past in spectral form" (8). The speaking subject brings to the fore the ghosts of black men that, as per the context provided by the song, cannot be but Cuban nationals. And, while there is no accounting for why any black Cubans fighting against the Spaniards would be buried in a Spanish cemetery – we are discussing the "return of the past in spectral form" here – it is the presence of black ghosts and the reference to Afro-Cuban religious practices in "No es serio este cementerio" that trace racialization processes in postmodern Spain.

In his analysis of the music video done for the television program "La bola de cristal," musicologist Eduardo Viñuela underscores that "No es serio este cementerio" presents a musical format very common in pop songs of the 1980s: stanza, bridge, chorus, and coda (2009, 100). The music video was filmed in a junkyard – a literal cemetery for old and totaled cars – and serves as an apt metaphor for a song narrating Spain's crushing defeat in 1898 at the hands of a recently modernized US naval fleet. And while the video invites us to visit a more modern scenario – that of the junkyard – the song also asks us to revisit a loss that took place almost a hundred years earlier; that is, Cuba the jewel of a tattered Spanish Crown.

In particular, and given the reference to blacks and *Misa luba*, we are required to revisit the racial tensions connected with Cuba's becoming the world's leading sugar producer in the 1820s – a development that required increasing the numbers of African slaves brought to the island, a population that reached approximately 430,000 slaved by 1840. This continuation of slavery and colonialism made Cuba a pariah among the other Spanish American nations since all but Puerto Rico had achieved their independence from Spain during the 1820s. By 1868, Cubans considered the situation to be unsustainable and, on 10 October 1868, their lengthy battle for independence began. The so-called "Ten Years' War" would end with a "no-victors" peace agreement in 1878. That there were racial concerns to the *Guerra de Cuba* is highlighted in part VI, section I of Pío Baroja's *El árbol de la ciencia* (1911) when Dorotea, the servant, sings what appears to be a popular song of the times: "Parece mentira que por unos mulatos, estemos pasando tan malos ratos" (It is hard to believe that because of a few mulattos, we are having such bad times) (Baroja 1937, 229).

Such historical matters are not addressed in Mecano's "No es serio este cementerio." However, the song does consider the social landscape of that period by having different groups share the pantheons, tombs, and niches. Thus, the ghosts of the heroes of Cuba stroll along those of "people of noble ancestry" and those of the black African slaves brought to Cuba, the latter now buried in Spanish soil along the same Spaniards they fought against. The Atlantic connection that joins Africa, the Spanish Caribbean, and Spain is not only highlighted by the implicit reference to the Spanish–American War – which originated as the *Guerra de Cuba* – but also by the hierarchical distinctions that reproduce, in death, the social classes of the world of the living. Tellingly, the heroes of the 1898 Disaster lack a pantheon, the kind of monumental recognition granted to those of noble ancestry. Placed all in a mass grave, the nondescriptive space highlights their being history's losers.

And, however fleetingly, it is through music that these ghostly traces are remembered. By giving voice to one of the ghosts of the *Guerra de Cuba*, Mecano's "No es serio este cementerio" provides a space, within the cultural narratives of a new democratic Spain, for the past to be recognized as past. But, if the ghosts of the *Héroes de Cuba* lack a proper burial ground, a fitting monumental recognition, they are not the ones making trouble in the cemetery. The song makes a point of noting that the noisy ghosts, the ones preventing the rest of everyone else on Sundays, are those of black persons: "los domingos los negros no dejan dormir / pues les da por cantar misa luba" (On Sundays blacks do not let us sleep / Because they are singing *Luba* Mass). Involved in cultural practices that evoke the African continent, black ghosts are brought to the centre of attention as that which has been most repressed about the *Guerra con Cuba* – the fear that Cuban independence was going to signify the taking over of the island by the blacks who were brought to Cuba by European slave ships to work mostly in the sugar cane plantations. In the end, slavery, as a horrifying social practice that looms large in human history, remains colonialism's ghostly legacy, a legacy that sustains present-day racial hierchization and racist ideologies and, as such, remains undead in Mecano's "No es serio este cementerio."

It is against this ghostly historical background – where the transatlantic history of Spain's involvement in the slave trade has yet to be thoroughly assessed – that we need to read Mecano's "El blues del esclavo," the 1988 song from *Descanso dominical*. A successful production, the album gave the trio their first transnational hit, "Mujer contra mujer" (Woman against woman), a song narrating a lesbian relationship that was also recorded in French, English, and Italian. In considering *Descanso dominical* vis-à-vis processes of racialization we need to take into account that the album is released the same year that *SOS Racismo* is first established in Madrid with twenty-seven centres within the Spanish territory. The non-governmental organization is created with the purpose of helping migrant newcomers with problems of acculturation but also to promote anti-racist levels of social consciousness and to denounce and report any racist and xenophobic activities in the Spanish territory. The creation of *SOS Racismo* indicates that by 1988 racism and xenophobia have become serious social problems. Indeed, the articulation of immigration as a menace and the xenophobic reaction to the presence of migrant newcomers had been made apparent to Spaniards by the 1985 enactment of the *Ley Orgánica de Extranjería* under Felipe González's first presidency (Lozano 2002).

To contextualize the 1985 Immigration Law, let us not forget that between 1985 and 1988 Spain's political and labour landscapes changed dramatically. For one, the so-called honeymoon between the labour unions and the PSOE came to an abrupt end on 20 June 1985 with a general strike protesting pension reductions. The second general strike of 14 December 1988 was a hard political blow to Felipe González and his government. The unions protested the PSOE's economic plan, particularly infuriated by the "Plan de empleo juvenil" (Plan for the employment of young workers) that further facilitated the hiring of temporal workers – a younger workforce that could be paid less and required little or no contributions to the pension system. The strike paralysed the Spanish territory and was successful in forcing the government to shelve the Plan.

All of these events, as well as the conflicted relations between the labour unions and the PSOE-led governments of 1982 and 1986, are relevant to my analysis of "El blues del esclavo," though none of the economic anxieties worrying many Spaniards were relevant to Mecano due to their unprecedented commercial success. Moreover, they were fast becoming a transatlantic cultural phenomenon, with legions of adoring fans in Latin America. It is within this transatlantic paradigm that a poem such as "El blues del esclavo" resonated with all of its racial and postcolonial significance:

El ser negrito	Being black
es un colour	Is a colour,
lo de ser esclavo	Being a slave
no lo trago	I can't swallow
me tiene frito	I am fed-up
tanto trabajar de sol a sol	With working from sunrise to sunset
las tierras del maldito señorito.	The damned master's land.
Los compañeros	My comrades
piensan igual	Think the same
o hay un Espartaco	They'll either be a new Spartacus
que entre a saco	To destroy all this
y esto cambia	And there will be change
o 'tos pa' Gambia	Or everyone goes to Gambia
desde Kunta Kinte a nuestros días	From Kunta Kinte to our time
pocas mejorías	There have been few improvements
a ver si ahora con la Guerra de secesión]	Let's see if whether with the War of Secession]
se admite nuestro sindicato del algodón	Our cotton Union is recognized
que a saber	Which, let everyone know
quiere obtener	Wants to secure
descanso dominical, un salario normal	Sundays off, a decent salary
dos pagas, mes de vacaciones	Two paychecks a month, a one-month vacation
y una pensión tras la jubilación	And a retirement pension

que se nos trate con dignidad	And that they treat us with dignity
como a semejantes	as fellow
emigrantes	immigrant subjects
que se terminen	For the end
las pasadas,	Of hazing
los derechos de pernada.	And the "droit de seigneur"
Y el que prefiera que se vuelva	And whoever wants to, can return
al Senegal	To Senegal
correr desnudos por la selva	To run naked through the jungle
con la mujer y el chaval	With the wife and kid
ir natural	To go natural
"erguiendo" cuello y testuz	With neck and chin high
como hermana avestruz	Like sister ostrich
para que no digan	So they can't say
que somos unos Zulús	That we are a bunch of Zulus
hemos hecho este blues	We have created this blues.

(José María Cano at www.grupomecano.com/EL_BLUES_DEL_ESCLAVO.php)

Framed within popular culture narratives – the film *Spartacus* (1960) and the book and TV series *Roots* (1976, 1977) – of revolt against slavery, the song forces us to consider diverse labour conditions ranging from slavery (as in the references to "Spartacus," "The War of Secession," and "Kunta Kinte") to wage labour (with is references to "labour union" and "Sundays off"). Hence, listeners are asked to consider the intersection between class and race in a global and Atlantic context, where there are imperialist references to ancient Rome and the United States; albeit the information comes filtered through two popular culture realms – television (Kunta Kinte) and film (*Spartacus*). In the latter with the reference to Spartacus, the Thracian gladiator that revolted against his Roman captors in 71 BC; in the former, with its allusion to the history of slavery and their note in regard to Martin Luther King and the civil rights movement. Noteworthy in the song is the insistence on the depiction of the physical and territorial suppression suffered by black persons in the history of slavery. A historical anachronism is used to acknowledge the intricate forms of slavery and to expose both the social issues relevant to labour in late 1980s Spain and the reality that social injustice knows no national boundaries or historical contexts. In fact, the narrating voice of the song – that of a black male slave who speaks also in the name of his comrades – demands the array of social benefits that were slowly being taken away from union workers by the new economic policies of the González's government. The demands – "two paychecks a month," "a one-month vacation," "and a retirement pension" – could by extension also be from the immigrants that were working in Spain under almost slavery conditions.

The allusion to "being treated like other fellow immigrants" reverberates in the Spanish context of the late 1980s since the speaking voice asks for the granting of equal status to everyone now residing in the Spanish territory. A parallel is established between those forced to migrate because of slavery and those immigrants arriving into Spain by the late 1970s: they were too forced to leave their countries either to escape political persecution or because of economic needs. I am not trying to equate slavery to exile, the two processes addressed by the song, but to point out that the request of the speaking subject – the black slave – to be recognized as a "fellow immigrant" acquires significance only in the context of the political and social history of late twentieth-century Spain and not in the complex history of black persons in the United States.

In fact, Mecano was so aware of the implicit social and historical problems of writing such a song that they felt compelled to add a disclaimer in the CD's liner. Listed last, after the presentation of the lyrics, the note clarifies that "'El blues del esclavo' aims to be a historical disfiguration – *desfiguración histórica* – of the historical event of the end of slavery in the US without any relation to the actual racial vindication of blacks, which we deeply respect as we admire the figure of Martin Luther King" (my translation). This "historical disfiguration" is at work in the very title of the song since blues were not musically born during slavery. Black men developed blues in the Deep South sometime after the United States Civil War (Pratt 1990). There is also much "musical" disfiguration at play since "El blues del esclavo" is not actually blues; it does not have the twelve-bar structure and harmony of the blues, nor the AAB structure of blues lyrics. Hence, both the song's title and the reference to "go on singing these blues" need to be understood in terms of the denunciatory values assigned to this musical genre.

The "historical disfiguration" claimed by Mecano can be more readily understood in the context of the history of labour relations in late 1980s Spain. A kind of "historical disfiguration" was being promoted by the new labour laws of the González's Socialist government since, against its historical alliance with the Unión general de trabajadores (UGT) and other labour unions, they had embarked in a neoliberal economic project that openly benefited business by taking away hard-fought social benefits from the Spanish workers. The PSOE's betrayal of the UGT – whose union members, along with those from Comisiones obreras (CCOO) (Worker's Commission) and Confederación nacional de trabajadores (CNT) (National Confederation of Worker's), helped Felipe González win the elections of 1982 – was not to remain without consequences and, as I pointed out earlier, the unions pounded Spain's streets in strike after strike throughout the 1980s.

By inscribing the song in a socially charged musical tradition such as the blues, Mecano bears witness to the denunciatory origins of this manifestation of black culture in the United States. It is in the early African-American cultural criticism on the blues, as Houston Baker argues in his seminal study *Blues, Ideology, and Afro-American Literature* (1984) that we find the linkages between the musical and the racial. Taking into consideration the role played by slavery in the birth of the blues, along with the economic issues that contributed to its urban development, it seems only fitting for Mecano to articulate a song that discusses labour issues, asks for social equality, and rejects slave wages within the demands for equal and just treatment emblematized by the blues.

The song's liberatory strategy is highlighted by the calling of a new Spartacus to revolt and by the reference to the character Kunta Kinte, created by Alex Haley in his *Roots: The Saga of an American Family* (1976). It is only after the enunciatory stance evokes the images of the television miniseries that the allusion to the War of Secession and the defeat of a powerful slaveholding class resonates with cultural meaning. Kunta Kinte's resistance to being (un)named speaks to his resistance to slavery and his refusal to be stripped of his own cultural identity, while *Roots* as a whole can be understood as a postcolonial narrative speaking against the legacy of slavery and its aftermath. The *Roots* television miniseries produced by ABC in 1977 attracted worldwide attention, and was, therefore, a cultural reference clearly understood by the Spaniards of the late 1980s: Radio Televisión Española (RTVE) had aired the miniseries in 1979. The reference to Spartacus, the Thracian gladiator who led a slave revolt against his Roman rulers, brings this fact home very early on in the song. His contemporary image comes to us mostly from Stanley Kubrick's 1960 film in which an erotically appealing Kirk Douglas plays the leading role and serves as an emblem for the abolition of slavery. Both names, Spartacus and Kunta Kinte, resonate within popular culture paradigms and acknowledge the power and relevance of television and cinema on the ways in which Spaniards became familiarized with these two emblems of resistance.

There is no small irony in the fact that the story told by Mecano's slave is narrated in terms of its direct relevance to the labour situation of the late 1980s in Spain. In this sense, the song operates within the paradigms of racial containment by which actual themes of African agency and resistance are eclipsed so that the story has meaning in direct relevance to the labour situation of late 1980s Spain. But, racial containment is also openly inscribed in "El blues del esclavo" by the "going native" ending of the song perpetuating stereotypes of the good savage: "correr desnudos por la selva / con la mujer y el chaval/ ir natural" (to run naked through the jungle / With the woman and the kid / To go natural). Racial containment is also operative in the matter-of-fact reference to *ser negrito* alongside the very derogatory use of *Zulu* – a coded term for savage.[12] *Negrito*, a common racialized epithet in Spanish speaking countries that contextually can be used as a term of endearment, as in the song "Duerme negrito" (Sleep little black baby), does not escape its infantilizing and patronizing connotations in Mecano's "El blues del esclavo." All these discourse strategies work to racially contain migrant newcomers by (mis)representing immigrants as coloured subjects that by being labelled as "savages" – as in *Zulu* – are symbolically pushed back to the African continent. The song bears witness to immigration's hardship and unfair labour conditions, but does not abandon Spanish racial anxieties.

Muslim Migrants in the Catalan Maresme: Joan Manuel Serrat's "Salam Rashid"

Black persons were not the only group subjected to deep-rooted degrading clichés in late twentieth-century Spain. Muslims, in general, and Moroccans, in particular, also withstood much denigration. This is not just the result of migratory patterns that began in the early 1970s "but a substantive feature of Spanish tradition" (Zapata-Barrero 2004,

145; see also Martín Muñoz 2000, Martín Corrales 2002). The attitudes against, and (mis)perceptions of, the Moroccan community are imbedded within the complex and lengthy history between the two nations and within Spain's centrality in the history of Islam between 711 and 1492. Laden with hegemonic significance, 1492 marks the conclusion of the *Reconquista* and the beginning of the global expansion of Spanish Catholicism promoted by Queen Isabella and King Ferdinand. The *Reconquista* leads to the 1492 expulsion of Muslims, Jews, and Gypsies, a series of homogenizing processes that further cemented the demonization of these groups in the construction of a "Spanish" national identity (Tofiño-Quesada 2003). In regard to Muslims, the expulsion will come to reify one of the prejudices attached to the iconography of the Moors (*moros*) – that of invaders – very much at work in the (mis)representation of Moroccan immigrants in present-day Spain. This particular iconography is also at the heart of how Spaniards enact two contemporary prejudices, *Maurophobia* (phobia of the Moors) and Islamophobia, both of which rely on ethnic, cultural, and religious racism to promote negative images of Muslims in general and Moroccans in particular.

The conflictive Spanish-Moroccan relations of the past century and a half – from the Spanish Moroccan War of 1859–60 to the beginning of the second decade of the twenty-first century – have further contributed to reinforce biases and negative representations.[13] Given the intertwined history of the two nations, it is certainly telling that this migrant community has been mostly rendered in Spanish pop music. More so if we consider that by 1991, two years after Serrat released "Salam Rashid," Moroccans constituted the largest immigrant group in Spain. In his 1992 *La inmigración en España: 1980–1990*, Antonio Izquierdo Escribano assesses distribution of work permits between 1980 and 1988 to measure the influx of migrant workers according to geographical areas of origin and establishes that, "*Africa: Is the migratory flow that registers the highest increase*" with Morocco contributing 60 per cent (1992, 79, emphasis in the original). Instead of differentiating between North African migrant workers and sub-Saharan ones, Izquierdo Escribano evaluates the African continent as a whole but makes sure to clarify that Moroccan migrant workers surpass all other African countries combined (1992, 82). In fact, by the mid-1990s, the Moroccan immigrant community residing in Catalonia is "the oldest and largest of those residing in Spain" (Colectivo Ioé 1996, 146).

In light of the data and the entwined histories of Morocco and Spain, why such scarcity of songs narrating the presence of Moroccan migrant workers in late twentieth-century Spanish pop music? Two symbolization processes may help us account for this omission. First, the omission is but another manifestation of the "fear of the Moor" where migrant newcomers from the Maghreb region, and Moroccans in particular, are represented as the embodiment of the return of "'invaders' of Spain" (Flesler 2008, 9). What's more, the exclusion is operative within what Edward Said referred to, in 1981, as "covering Islam" – a play on how the media provides information on Islam, but also conceals and hides other facts, thus perpetuating the series of clichés that currently go along with a spectacular reading of Islamic events.[14]

It is against and within these symbolic and cultural narratives that Serrat's "Salam Rashid" needs to be assessed. The song's compelling lyrics openly work against the concealing represented in the "covering of Islam" by, first, rendering visible the term "Salam" – short for "Salam alaykum" and the Arabic greeting often translated as "peace be upon you." And second, by depicting the hardships of this Muslim migrant worker enticed by market forces to migrate to areas where capital is abundant. Unfortunately, and as we shall see, the song also revalidates the imagery of "invader" assigned to Maghrebi/Muslim migrant newcomers:

T'ho havien dit,	They'd told you
allà baix a la terra dels teus pares,	Down there in the land of your parents
t'ho havien dit	They'd told you
que Europa era molt gran,	That Europe was very big,
per això hi anardes	And that is why you went.
del gran Sud,	From the grand South
on l'ombra de les palmeres és dolça	Where the palm trees' shade is sweet
i l'aigua dels rius	And the rivers' waters,
camina de puntetes, cautelosa.	tip-toe cautiously
T"ho havien dit	They'd told you
de nit les passes lentes de les dunes.	The slow passages of the dunes at night.
T"ho havien dit,	They'd told you
que el desert es va fent gran a mesura	That the desert becomes vast step by step
que els rics del Nord	That the rich people of the North
hi trenquen els seus rellotges de sorra	Break their hour glasses
a contracor.	Half-heartedly.
I tu només tenies ganes de córrer.	And you only wanted to run

¿Què hi fas, Rashid, perdut a la frontissa

d'un Nord poruc i un Sud que es
desespera?]
T'han estripat l'honour i la camisa

i un cop aquí no tornaràs enrera.
Pell de colour de dàtil o de sutge
que sempre està fent cua a Laietana,
no ets innocent sigui qui sigui el jutge

Ets el pecat, el camell, la fulana.

Dècim trencat, propina d'urinari
ets tot allò que el fariseu rebutja.

Trinca la creu i puja al teu calvari.

Salam Rashid.
Ja ni saps quant
fa que camines per ciutats llogades
la sensació que a tot arreu sobraves.]

Et coneixem.
Ets carn de soterrani i de conquesta,
la falca justa perquè
no trontolli la taula de la festa.
Bulls al perol
somnis del Sud contra la incerta ràbi

de morir sol.
Volies volar, i Europa és una gàbia
i vas perdent
a poc a poc records per les voreres

feixugament,
però et sents viu i esperes com les feres.
El món es mou pels qui com tu caminen
més del que volen. Mà d'obra barata.

What are you doing, Rashid, lost in the
hinges]
Of a scary North and a South that
despairs?]
They've ripped your honour and your
shirt.]
And once here you will not turn back
Skin colour of date or soot
Always lining-up in Laietana
You are not innocent, no matter whom the
judge is.]
You are the sin, the mule (drugs), and the
whore.]
Broken lottery ticket, bathroom tip
You are everything rejected by the
Pharisee.]
Break the Cross and walk up to your
suffering.]

Hello Rashid
You no longer know how long you have
been walking through rented cities
with the nagging feeling that where ever
you went you were not wanted]
We know you.
You are meat of tunnels and conquests
The party table not to wobble

You boil in the pot
Dreams of the South against the uncertain
anger]
Of dying alone.
You wanted to fly, and Europe is a cage
And you go on losing
Little by little your memories through the
sidewalks]
Awkwardly,
But you feel alive, and wait like the beasts.
The world moves for those like you that walk
More than they want to. Cheap labour.

Sobrevivents de presons i pallisses	Survivors of prisons and beatings
que han decidit que els guiïn les sabates.	Who have decided to be guided by their shoes.]
Demà per tu somriurà la Mona Lisa.	Tomorrow the Mona Lisa will smile for you.]
Faràs servir el Louvre de nevera.	You'll use the Louvre as a fridge.
Les catedrals alternaran la missa	Cathedrals will alternate masses
amb l'Alcorà i les danses barbaresques.	With the Koran and Berber dances.
Però mentres tant Europa va fent d'esma.	In the meantime, Europe continues with its routine.]
Ha embolicat les porres amb banderes	Has wrapped-up the stick with flags
i a tu et reserva un jardí del Maresme.	And holds a reservation for you in a garden in the Maresme]
Salam Rashid.	Hello Rashid

(Catalan version transcribed by Silvia Bermúdez
from the CD with permission from Joan Manuel Serrat)

Co-author of the poem with Joan Barril, when listening to the album one immediately notices that Serrat sings "Salam Rashid" in a low voice that conveys the seriousness of the matter. The presence of violins and a cello also lends the song *gravitas*, while bass and percussion speak to musical hybridization. The singing subject, Joan Manuel Serrat himself according to the discursive rhetoric defining the productions of *cantautores*, addresses Salam Rashid in his mother tongue, which highlights the heartfelt nature of his appeal to fellow Catalans. The use of Catalan also reaffirms Serrat's alliances to the *Nova canço catalana* since it is in this language that he launched, in 1965, a successful transatlantic musical career spanning now over four decades (see Serrat's web page for a complete discography of the artist). Committed to defending Catalan against Franco's repressive linguistic policies, SerraXt joined the group *Els Setze Jutges* (The Sixteen Judges), the driving force, along with the label Edigsa, for the development, expansion, and promotion of the *Nova canço* in the late 1960s (García-Soler 1976; Vázquez Montalbán 1969).[15] In his alliance to Catalan and Catalan identity matters, Serrat questioned and rejected the repressive linguistic policies where Catalan, Galician, and the Basque languages were prohibited and persecuted (see figure 2). It is in Spanish, however, that Joan Manuel Serrat is known

2. Serrat at Palau dels Esports de Barcelona (Barcelona Sports' Palace). Copyright Manel Armengol, 1976.

the world over as a leading *cantautor*, by songs such as "Mediterráneo" (Mediterranean Sea), "Aquellas pequeñas cosas" (Those Small things), and "Señora" (Madam), among others, that have become embedded in the sentimental landscapes of legions of fans in Spain, Latin America, and the Lusophone worlds.

In 1989, Serrat returns to Catalan to produce *Material sensible* (Sensitive Material), and by so doing signals his commitment to give testimony to fellow Catalan citizens of the plights of migrant workers coming from the South – in this case the South that is northern Africa. Catalan is thus used to show solidarity with this migrant worker, identified as a Muslim man coming from northern Africa. In so doing, the song gives testimony but is not a *testimonio*, since Rashid, the actual fictional agent of the migratory process, is not singing or producing either the music or the album. However, given the discussions on Latin

American *testimonios* (see Gugelberger 1996; Beverly's 2004, among others), this musical production must be incorporated into the genealogy of testimonials. In this case, the Other is represented as an immigrant and as a geopolitical and economic subject; at the same time, he is contained as racially marked and therefore Other in what can be considered an "anxious *testimonio*" where the subaltern does not speak (to use Spivak's term) but is represented and thus, ultimately, witnessed.

There is no denying that Serrat seeks to work against the racist attitudes that compound Rashid's suffering. For one, the use of individualization – this migrant newcomer is a person with a name – and the direct form of address is used by Serrat to commiserate with Rashid about his present situation as an undocumented migrant worker. In fact, several points are made to expose the brutality of clandestine migration. First, the reference to "Laietana" – the name of the boulevard in Barcelona where the Central Police Station is located and where immigrants wait in long lines to seek all legal papers – renders visible the brutal process by which the migrant worker wandering through Europe in search of a job suffers abject poverty, humiliation, but, more poignantly, persecution and police brutality. Second, by calling attention to the endless wandering that being a migrant worker entails: "You no longer know / how long you have been walking through rented cities." This wandering should not be mistaken with that of the *fláneur* or the tourist since the undocumented migrant worker is forced into this incessant displacement because, as a supposedly "*failed citizen*" – the term belongs to Thomas Nail – s/he is constantly experiencing all forms of social expulsion (2015, 3, emphasis in the original).

In 1989 Serrat already thematizes how Rashid, as undocumented migrant, is subjected to territorial, economic, political, and juridical forms of social expulsion. The singer-songwriter also brings to the fore that the border crossing of subjects, money, material goods, cultural practices, ideologies, and symbols is tied to globalized capitalism – a point that the singer-songwriter further develops in his 1992 "Disculpe, el Señor," as I discuss in the next chapter. Indeed, transnational capitalism is central to Rashid's wandering since the reference to "the rich people of the North," "Cheap labour," and the reservation in a garden in the Maresme – the fertile agricultural region where undocumented migrants harvested mostly flowers in the late 1980s – highlights how immigration, racism, and xenophobia need to be addressed within the global labour movement. Also in chapter 2, Moroccan/Catalan musician

Chad Samir and his band will bring several of these issues to the fore when addressing the crossing of the Strait of Gibraltar in *pateras*.

Conclusion

All of these songs prefigured the racialization of migrant workers as one of the central issues to shape Spain's social and political agendas in the 1990s and well into the second decade of the twenty-first century. It was only after these early songs by Radio Futura, Mecano, and the 1989 single by Joan Manuel Serrat that other artists came to participate in the articulation of a Spanish racial imagination vis-à-vis migration. It is in this sense that "Un africano por la Gran Vía," "Semilla negra," "Paseo con la negra Flor," "Coplas añadidas a Semilla Negra," "No es serio este cementerio," "El blues del esclavo," and "Salam Rashid" serve as musical thresholds where the anxieties over race and ethnicity are first inscribed in Spanish pop music. These first manifestations of the racialization processes taking place in democratic Spain are to be understood as soundtexts where music and discourses about race intersect. The poems, songs, by Radio Futura, Mecano, and Joan Manuel Serrat cannot be said to combat the enduring nature of a racist vocabulary and cultural background; by offering challenging meanings, though, as problematic as the social circumstances they narrate, all of these artists signal popular music as one of the spaces where the negotiation of Spain's new social reality was taking place. Ultimately, because these songs include problematic representations, they are just as complex and in flux as the culture and social milieu they aimed to represent.

2

The 1990s, Take One: Fortress Europe, Racism, Apologies, and Contestation

The 1990s brought its own set of problems to racialization processes in late twentieth-century Spain. For one, "race" openly became a structuring principle when discussing migration and was constantly used in media outlets to describe the presence of transnational migrant subjects, particularly when referring to those from the Maghreb, particularly from Morocco, sub-Saharan Africa, and the Caribbean. The imagery of the printed press – black letters / white pages – is used by Octavio Vázquez Aguado in his "Negro sobre blanco: inmigrantes, estereotipos y medios de comunicación" (1999) (Black over white: immigrants, stereotypes, and mass media) article to expose the ways in which Spanish newspaper media transmitted prejudiced beliefs about migrants using a "black" versus "white" discourse. In the case of the pejorative term *moros* (Moors), employed to describe newcomers from the Maghreb region, and in particular those from Morocco, a series of conflations take place since Islamic practices and many different nationalities were and continue to be collapsed under said term. It comes as no surprise, then, that this was the decade that witnessed an alarming increase of racist attacks against black migrant subjects and those from the Maghreb.

Indeed, violence against migrant workers in the 1990s found its most tragic symbol, first, in the assassination of Lucrecia Pérez, the black Dominican woman killed in Aravaca in November 1992 and to whom singer-songwriter Carlos Cano offers an apology in "Canción para Lucrecia" in 1994 and Ska-P remembers in their 2000 piece "Lucrecia." Efforts to foster *convivencia* with Muslims – on 10 November 1992 the *Comisión Islámica de España* (Spain's Islamic Commission) signed a cooperation agreement with the Spanish state (law 26/1992) establishing the protected rights of Muslims and their places of worship henceforward in the Spanish territory – appeared not to be of much help in fighting xenophobia. In fact, after an anti-migrant demonstration with some 1,300 people turned violent on 14 July 1999, the end of the decade finds Maghrebi Muslim migrants residing in Terrasa – a city twenty-eight kilometres to the west of Barcelona – in harms ways. Maghrebi-owned cars and shops, as well as their owners, were subjected to three days of attacks, foreshadowing the violence against Moroccan migrants that took place seven months later, in February 2000, in El Ejido, in the province of Almería. Significantly, as Spain became increasingly racist and xenophobic, notorious efforts were made by non-governmental organizations such as SOS *Racismo* to step up projects extending and promoting ethnic solidarity and increasing awareness about the ills of racism.[1]

In geopolitical terms the decade marked several milestones for democratic Spain, beginning with the three major events that showcased the 1992 commemoration of Columbus' 1492 voyage – the expo in Seville, the Olympic Games in Barcelona, and Madrid being named Cultural Capital of Europe. If internationally 1992 was ripe with symbolic significance celebrating "Spain's Year," nationally the year signalled a milestone for Felipe González's government – the culmination of the Socialist decade that oversaw major makeovers of the nation's economic and social infrastructure, as self-celebrated in the 1992 volume *La década del cambio: Diez años de gobierno socialista 1982–1992* (1992) (The Decade of Change: Ten Years of Socialist Government 1982–1992). One such innovation was the renovation of the Atocha train station – site of the 11 March 2004 train bombings and across which since 2007 rests the Tribute Monument to the Victims of 11-M – that on 21 April 1992, freshly restored, welcomed the high-speed train linking in less than three hours the 471 kilometres separating Madrid from Seville. Known as AVE by the company's initials – *Alta Velocidad Española* – the high-speed trains motioned Spain's fast-forwarding towards the future, while the renovated grand passenger hall echoed past imperial grandeur.[2]

The sense of accomplishment for Spain's rapid transformation was such that none other than Alfonso Guerra, then PSOE's vice-secretary general, and Felipe González's right hand, along with José Félix Tezanos, then secretario de dormación de la comisión ejecutiva federal del PSOE (secretary of education of the federal executive committee of the PSOE), co-edited *La década del cambio: Diez años de gobierno socialista*

1982–1992 (1992) (The decade of change: Ten years of Socialist government 1982–1992).[3] The volume touted the Workers' Party's achievements throughout 779 pages highlighting innovations in several areas, such as infrastructure and public works, education, technological modernization, and women's issues. Tellingly, migration is mentioned in passing in Manuel Navarro's "Cambios sociales en los años ochenta" (642–83) (Social Changes in the 1980s) when assessing how Spain, known until the 1970s as a major exporter of labour, transformed itself from a sending to a receiving society in the 1980s, "with a tendency to increase, though for now within reduced dimensions" (1992, 642). This conspicuous presentation of migration, already contradicted by the PSOE's enactment of the 1985 Immigration Law, was but forgotten in 1993 when the party campaigned under a "controlling immigration" banner for the general election. The successful strategy allowed the PSOE to secure power one last time before the Partido Popular (PP) became the governing party from 1996 to 2004.

In tune with the nation's preoccupation on migration and, in some instances, with the racialization processes attached to the transnational movements of people, songsters Joan Manuel Serrat (1943–), Carlos Cano (1946–2000), Joaquín Sabina (1949–), and Pedro Guerra (1966–), as well as the Barcelona housed raï band Chab Samir, and rapper El Chojin (born Domingo Edjang Moreno, 1977–), turned their attention to transnational capitalism, postcolonial ties, and to Spain's racist discursive and cultural practices. In songs published between 1992 and 1999, legendary figures Joan Manuel Serrat and Joaquín Sabina, as well as popular performers Carlos Cano and Pedro Guerra, focused, in varying degrees, either on the materiality of migration, on ethnic diversity, or on xenophobia and racism. The most powerful anti-racist stance came from a musician publishing his first album: rapper El Chojin. The son of an Equatoguinean father and a Spanish mother, in his 1999 "Mami, el negro está rabioso" (Mama, the Black man is mad), El Chojin rhythmically denounced Spain's long-standing racism. Also publishing his first album in 1999, seven years after his arrival to Barcelona, was Moroccan/ Catalan artist Chab Samir. To voice the treacherous, many times fatal, clandestine journeys by Moroccan migrants across the Mediterranean and the plight of the undocumented, Samir relied on raï, the main pop genre throughout the Maghreb and an important protest song in France among the Maghrebi communities. Both artists introduced two new musical genres – rap and raï – to the landscape of Spanish popular music.

For his part, Joan Manuel Serrat continued to show concern for the situation of migrant workers with the release of "Disculpe el señor" (Pardon sir) from his 1992 *Utopía* (Utopia). Poking fun at the securitization of migration and to the relevance of transnational capitalism, Serrat's song was released not a moment too soon since Lucrecia Pérez's murder tragically demonstrated how pervasive and rampant xenophobia was in 1990s Spain.[4] The slaying also served as a reminder of how little the 1985 Immigration Law had done to either decrease the number of migrant newcomers to Spain or to improve the situation of the migrant workers already living in the Spanish territory. In fact, the law was used by the Felipe González's Socialist government to embrace the nation's role as gatekeepers and to prove to the European Union that Spain could serve as an effective border control of Fortress Europe. In his "Disculpe el señor," Joan Manuel Serrat appears to question Spain's role in the securitization of Fortress Europe – basically serving as Germany's and France's gatekeepers – since that is precisely the role of the butler enouncing the phrase serving as the song's title. Serrat underscored this very point in many concert and television performances when coming to the stage wearing white gloves and a butler's waistcoat.[5]

"Fortress Europe," a phrase used at different times in history, is generally employed to describe the fortification of Europe in some fashion, to prevent entry from the outside. In its current incantation, the term has been used within debates about migration from the Global South and East to Europe to refer to the ever-changing policies as well as the militarization of the EU's frontiers – mostly the southern ones, as in Spain, Italy, and Greece – to prevent the entry of so-called economic migrants. Serrat, Cano, Guerra, and Sabina turn their attention to these perilous crossings in the decade that sees "something of a revival in the popularity of *cantautores* (singer-songwriters)" (Allison 2000, 270, emphasis and parenthesis in the original). This popularity may have helped them sell albums – we cannot forget that *cantautores'* songs function within a popular music paradigm that aims to sell records and entertain – but *cantautores'* music is defined by the emphasis in the telling of a story that the public is invited to connect with. In the songs by these four artists we are compelled to respond to the denunciation presented against the politicization of migration and to racist ideologies and practices. We are also obliged to respond to how rap, the other genre that gains momentum in Spain in the mid- to late 1990s, foregrounds "the story." This is central to El Chojin's vigorous denunciation of Spanish racism when narrating the experience of growing up black in late twentieth-century

Spain in his "Mami, el negro está rabioso." Speaking in Arabic to the migrant Moroccan communities living in Spain, Chab Samir's uses raï to offer fellow uprooted compatriots the possibility of constructing new transnational identities while also addressing the perils and physical risks of being an illegal migrant. But before turning our attention to El Chojin and Chab Samir, we need to first consider, in order of publication, the songs by Joan Manuel Serrat, Carlos Cano, Joaquín Sabina, and Pedro Guerra within the musical landscape of *cantautores*.

Cantautores in the Spanish Cultural Imaginary

Explicitly lyrical, songs written by singer-songwriters appear to derive their power and allure mostly from their verbal qualities. In fact, songsters are considered poets since, according to Roy Shuker, "an emphasis on lyrics has resulted in such performers being referred to as song poets" (2005, 277; see also González Lucini 2006). And poetry has always been a primordial component of the musical trajectories of Serrat, Sabina, Cano, and Guerra. Joaquín Sabina is a published poet with several poetic collections under his name who, along with Carlos Cano and Luis Eduardo Aute, contributed to the *Poesía 70* journal published in Granada (1968–9) under the leadership of Juan de Loxa.[6] Joan Manuel Serrat is well known for his musical homages to canonical Spanish poets such as Antonio Machado – *Dedicado a Antonio Machado, Poeta* (1969, Zafiro/Novola) – and Miguel Hernández – *Miguel Hernández* in 1972 (Zafiro/Novola) and the 2009 *Hijo de la luz y de la sombra* (Sony Music), the latter of which celebrated the poet's 2010 centenary. In 1998, Carlos Cano turned into songs Federico García Lorca's *Diván del Tamarit* (EMI) with the help of, among others, singer-songwriters Paco Ibáñez and José Antonio Labordeta, flamenco singer Navajita Plateá, and performers Santiago Auserón and Marina Rossell.

Specific performative strategies – the ability to sign about experiences common to all in a "direct" and "frank" manner – need also to be considered when discussing the figure of the *cantautor*. Simon Frith argues that singer-songwriters, while working within the commercial medium and institutions of popular music, use "frankness, musical irony, and paradox as their artistic insignia" (1981, 53). Ultimately, "authenticity" – as a trademark connected to the ability of being frank – serves an important social function. One that, as Dino Pancani and Reiner Canales describe, requires a testimonial vent given that a songster is someone always in tune with what is happening in his time and place (1999, 14). It is from this authorial and privileged position that Serrat, Cano, Guerra, and Sabina call attention to the connection between transnational capitalism and immigration (Serrat, Sabina), the need for solidarity and ethical stances for Spain's racism and xenophobia (Cano), and the challenge placed on existing notions of identity nationality and citizenship by the changing religious, cultural, and ethnic landscapes in present-day Spain (Guerra, Sabina). In fact, as developed later in the chapter, this challenge is represented by Pedro Guerra as a desire to know and be possessed by the feared newcomer through the metaphor of "contamination." A revealing symbol, "contamination" explicitly articulates migration and migrants as primary sources of contagious diseases that speak to bodily insecurity where violent migrant men are feared as security threats and migrant women and children are potential sources of cultural alienation that also could undermine the social system of European welfare states.

All four songsters are major musical and cultural figures – arguably Joan Manuel Serrat leads the group – sharing symbolic imageries and true social concern when addressing immigration. They also share close publication dates in the 1990s, since between 1992 and 1995, and beginning with Serrat, each published songs centred on migration. There are also close musical and personal ties that, in the case of Serrat and Sabina, were established long before 2007 when they first joined forces for their successful transatlantic tour "Dos pájaros de un tiro" (Two birds with one stone). Since then, the two renowned artists have become inseparable performing around the globe in joint ventures such as the tours "Serrat & Sabina: Cuenta conmigo" (Serrat & Sabina: Lean on me) (2011), "Dos pájaros contraatacan" (Two birds strike again) (2012), and "Serrat & Sabina: La orquesta del Titanic" (Serrat & Sabina: The Titanic's orchestra) (2012), among others.[7]

Early on, in 1996, Sabina musically expressed his admiration for Serrat in "Mi primo, el Nano" (My cousin, the Kid) from the album *Yo, mi, me, contigo* (I, mine, me, with you). Through a familiarizing strategy by which the poetic subject – we are to understand Sabina himself – claims Serrat as a blood relative, the song serves as a personal genealogy where Sabina, the apprentice embracing his anxiety of influence, positions Serrat as the master and the model to follow. Recognizing Serrat's Catalan identity with the use of the familial *Nano* – Catalan for "the kid" and Serrat's actual nickname since 1967, given to the artist by Lasso de la Vega after becoming his manager – the lyric voice praises the Catalan's mastery in creating unforgettable songs: "Tengo yo un primo que es todo un maestro / de lo mío, de lo tuyo, de lo nuestro, un lujo para el alma y el oído" (I have a cousin that is a master / Of that which is mine, yours, ours, / A delight for the soul and the ear). Sabina establishes Serrat's towering presence over the world of *cantautores* by naming him "a master" in the art of transforming the minutiae of everyday life into musical delights providing pleasure and solace. Serrat's much-praised attention to detail leads Manuel Vázquez Montalbán to establish two identities for the songster: one focused on poetry – a "Serrat lírico" (lyric Serrat) – and another on social issues – a "Serrat cívico" (civic Serrat) (1972, 6).

Joan Manuel Serrat's 1992 "Disculpe el Señor": Postcolonial Returns, Poverty, and Fortress Europe

In 1965, with the publication of *Una guitarra* (A Guitar), an extended play (EP) in Catalan with four songs, Joan Manuel Serrat launches a successful transatlantic musical career spanning over five decades and a production that includes the penning of over three hundred songs (see http://jmserrat.com/). Serrat's towering stature in the diverse cultural and musical landscapes he criss-crosses – Catalonia, Spain, and Latin America – needs to be taken into consideration when assessing "Disculpe el Señor," a text that functions as a political act since it is positioned at the "dangerous crossroads" where a song operates as a "political act while being sold as 'commodity in a capitalist market structure'" (Lipsitz 1994, 11). Clearly political in its presentation of poverty and colonial legacies as forces driving migration movements of the 1980s and 1990s, "Disculpe el Señor" is track 4 out of 10 that constitute *Utopia* (Ariola), published in April of 1992. The song's focus on the postcolonial returns brought by the legacies of empire building and capitalist expansion distinguishes this musical piece from all those studied in *Rocking the Boat*. First, this is the only song that articulates migration within the historical and epistemological backgrounds of coloniality. Second, it is also original in that it does not racialize the migrant subject. Furthermore, by considering the colonial legacies, already in 1992 Serrat advances migration theories and conceptualizations offered by contemporary social scientists later that decade (see Grosfoguel and Cervantes-Rodríguez 2002; Cervantes-Rodríguez, Grosfoguel, and Mielants 2009).

Utopía can be considered a political production since the *cantautor* expresses much concern throughout the album with the state of affairs in Spain – the accelerated progress of some done at the expense of many – while advancing the need to recover utopian ideologies to promote social justice. These high expectations did not sell well due in part to lack of promotion given that Serrat embarked on a lengthy tour throughout Latin America immediately after launching the CD in Madrid. The ideological premises are unequivocally set by the album's title and are further emphasized in "Disculpe el Señor" by the direct reference to Karl Marx in the lyrics' closing line. In fact, the notion of "utopia" resonates in unexpected ways when addressing migration in 1990s Spain: "[i]n spite of all the problems and difficulties associated with immigration, it is perhaps reassuring for many to see Spain represented no longer as a country of emigrants but as *somebody else's Utopia*" (Santaolalla 2002, 62, emphasis mine).

As we shall see, "Disculpe el Señor" dramatizes the consequences of "being somebody else's Utopia" in its representation of a metonymically named house – primarily an emblem for Spain but also for Europe, with references to the vestibule and pantry – that serves as the migrant workers' utopia. But the song also advances the notion that the so-called "invasion" is due, in part, to having Spain's former utopian and material spaces – Spain's former colonies, those former *El Dorados* – return to claim what was taken during the colonial enterprise. Indeed, Serrat's use of the spatial metaphor of the house as the emblem of a contested and conflictive space refers, at one signifying level, to the Spanish national territory as it is perceived to be invaded by migratory movements from some of the poorest nations of the globe. It also points to Fortress Europe, the homely spatial configuration created by the Schengen Agreements – originally signed in 1985 and subsequently transformed as more EU states were included – and now by Frontex whereby subjects from Africa, Latin America, and other troubled geopolitical regions of the globe are prevented the free movement granted to the signatory states.[8] Significantly, Spain and Portugal are granted free movement in 1992.

It is within this colonial/postcolonial framework that the characters of the story are presented in oppositional terms within the economic categories of "the haves," emblematized by the singular figure of *El Señor*, and "the have nots," *los pobres*, in plural, a plural that exponentially grows from the pair of the first stanza to the indeterminate "los pobres" (the poor) of the last one. The voice introducing these characters is that of an unnamed butler, addressing his master in regard to the arrival of the unwelcome visitors. In many concerts, Serrat performed the song wearing white gloves and a butler's waistcoat, to represent – in a theatrical manner – the voice of this waged worker. The chords for "Disculpe el

Señor" are provided by David Thurmaier (e-mail message to author, 15 August 2009). He explains that some of the chords are placed approximately because some do not occur in words but between words.[9] Below are the lyrics and chords for "Disculpe el Señor," which I have transcribed from http://jmserrat.com/ with permission from the artist:

Introduction: Em, D, Bm, D

A section
Em
Disculpe el señor
D Em
si le interrumpo, pero en el recibidor
D Bm
hay un par de pobres que
Em
preguntan insistentemente por usted

B section
G D/F#
No piden limosna, no
E Bm/D C
Ni venden alfombras de lana.
Bm C
Tampoco elefantes de ébano.
D Em
Son pobres que no tienen nada de nada.
D Em
No entendí muy bien

C section
Am Bm C
si nada que vender o nada que perder
D Em
pero por lo que parece
D Em
tiene usted alguna cosa que les pertenece.

B section
¿Quiere que les diga que el señor salió…?
¿Que vuelvan mañana en horas de visita…?

¿O major les digo, como el señor dice:
'Santa Rita, Rita, Rita,
lo que se da, no se quita'…?
Interlude: Soprano Saxophone solo

A section
Disculpe el señor
se nos llenó de pobres el recibidor
y no paran de llegar
desde la retaguardia, por tierra y por mar.

B section
Y como el señor dice que salió
y tratándose de una urgencia,
me han pedido que les indique yo
por dónde se va a la despensa,
y que Dios se lo pagará.

C section
¿Me da las llaves o los echo? Usted verá
que mientras estamos hablando
llegan más pobres y siguen llegando.

B section
¿Quiere usted que llame a un guardia y que revise
si tienen en regal sus papeles de pobre…?
¿O major les digo como el señor dice:
'Bien me quieres, bien te quiero,
no me toques el dinero'…?
Interlude: Soprano Saxophone solo

A section
Disculpe el señor
pero este asunto va de mal en peor.
Vienen a millones y
curiosamente, vienen todos hacia aquí.

B section
Traté de contenerles pero ya ve,
Han dado con su paradero.
Éstos son los pobres de los que le hablé.
Le dejo con los caballeros
y entiéndase usted…

C section
Si no manda otra cosa, me retiraré.
Si me necesita, llame...
Que Dios le inspire o que Dios le ampare,
que ésos no se han enterado
que Carlos Marx está muerto y enterrado
Outro: Alternates between D and Em[10]

(transcribed by Silvia Bermúdez from http://jmserrat.com/, with permission from Joan Manuel Serrat).

The realities of migration are presented to the audience by the singing voice of the song, the butler positioned between the *Señor* and the *pobres*. He is the waged worker occupying the sphere of the *Señor* in more ways than one since he serves both as filter and buffer to the *pobres*, the newcomers wanting to enter the house, those who are literally invading the familiar space as the song progresses. As the in-between subject,the butler's voice echoes those representing migration as an invasion – "y no paran de llegar / desde la retaguradia, por tierra y por mar" (And they do not stop arriving / From the rearguard, by sea and by land). That the newcomers are migrant subjects is conveyed by the reference to the activities of street vendors all over Spain selling all kinds of ethnic products – "alfombras de lana" (wool carpets) and "elefantes de ébano" (ebony-made elephants), and that Donato Ndongo poignantly narrates in his 2007 novel *El metro* (The subway). And while the economic paradigms presented in the song do refer to class issues – the clash between the poor and the wealthy – in the context of the symbolism of 1992, and the legacies of colonialism, they also point to the processes of globalization where transnational capitalism and migratory flows constitute a global cultural economy described by Appadurai as "the shifting world of immigrants, refugees, exiles, and other moving groups" (1996, 222).

Through the questions "Do you want me to call the police / So they can check if they have legal papers?," the song brings to the fore the dire reality that "law and order" is the immediate solution offered by the Spanish Government and the European Union to the "immigration problem." The reference to the police exposes the securitization of migration by which "first, migration is a threat; and second, migration is a security issue" (Gebrewold 2007, 173). The solution, as in the questions posed by the butler, is simply to just get rid of the poor and forget that migratory flows are the result of economic and social forces unleashed by transnational capitalism and coloniality. However, the material bases of the problem are unambiguously stated by the butler in the lines "son pobres que no tienen nada de nada" (they are poor people that have nothing of anything) and when he explains that these poor newcomers are at the house not to sell the goods usually associated in Spain and the EU with illegal migration – rugs, ebony-made elephants. In fact, a hint of sarcasm is present in the butler's apparent confusion in understanding the reasons why all are asking to see the man of the house: "I did not understand quite well, if nothing to sell or nothing to lose." The irony is evident and cleverly used to introduce the crucial point of the "but it seems / That you have something that belongs to them" further emphasized by the popular saying "Santa Rita, Rita, Rita / lo que se da no se quita" (Saint Rita, Rita, Rita / What's been taken away, cannot be given back) and "Bien me quieres, bien te quiero, / no me toques el dinero" (You love me, I love you, / but do not touch my money). In "Disculpe el señor," Serrat's frames the migratory flows to Spain within the colonial, postcolonial, and neocolonial relations that tie together the historical process and economies of Africa, Spain, and Latin America.

To conclude, I bring to your attention some of David Thurmaier comments since they underscore the relevance of the refrain – identified as B in the chords – in reiterating the song's overall ideological message. Thurmaier explains that the song, tonally in the key of E minor, features a lot of "modal inflections" and does not follow a traditional verse-chorus form found in most popular music (e-mail message to author, 15 August 2009). The refrain occurs five times and alternates with the other sections (A and C), which repeat three times each. The A section contains the title of the song, and occurs three times, while the B section features a descending bass line and chord progression and happens five times. The C section has a faster paced chord progression and occurs three times. In the above-cited e-mail message, Thurmaier highlights that the B section seems to be the most important because of its frequency and its position in the form and because the singer always comes back to it. In regard to the "modal inflections" stressed by the musicologist, those of us who have been Serrat's long-time followers know that vocal inflections are one of his trademarks. The vocal inflections are, I argue, one of the ways Serrat uses to remind Spaniards of the real and actual legacies that were being celebrated in 1992. In hindsight, the song was foretelling that the situation was becoming increasingly untenable, and Lucrecia Pérez's racist murder in November 1992, and the racist attacks in Terrassa in 1999 and in El Ejido in 2000 would, sadly, prove Serrat right.

1994: The Ethics of Apology in Carlos Cano's "Canción para Lucrecia" and Denunciation and Stereotyping in Joaquín Sabina's "La casa por la ventana"

Carlos Cano's untimely death in December 2000 brought much consternation to his fans and the Spanish musical landscape. Born José Carlos Cano Fernández, he joined the ranks of Spanish *cantautores* after penning his first song "Miseria" (Misery) in 1968. Cano contributed to the articulation of an Andalusian identity with the 1975 hit "La verdiblanca" (The green and white), in reference to the colours of the Andalusian flag (Téllez 1999). He is also considered one of the radical innovators of the *copla* for, among others, albums such as *A la luz de los cantares* (1977), *Crónicas granadinas* (1978), *Cuaderno de coplas* (1985), *Quédate con la copla* (1987), and *La copla, memoria sentimental* (1999), the latter of which reached platinum (Ramos Espejo and Téllez 2004, 260).[11]

"Canción para Lucrecia" was not the author's first show of solidarity with Latin American migrants since he had already paid attention to migration and racialization issues in his 1992 CD *Mestizo* (Mixed heritage) with songs such as "Mestizo" and "Me llaman *sudaca*" (They call me *sudaca*), the belittling expression was reappropriated by the Che Sudaka band formed in Barcelona in the early 2000s and discussed in chapter 4. In 1992 Cano released *Mestizo* "para reivindicar algo muy distinto a la Exposición Universal de Sevilla" (to vindicate something very different to the Seville's World Fair) (Ramos Espejo and Téllez 2004, 236). His 1994 *Forma de ser* signals a new level of commitment from Cano, as producer, songwriter, and performer, he controlled all levels of production. The album was a success; "[f]ue disco de oro y ganamos mucho dinero" (it went gold and we made lots of money), stated Antonio Peña, Cano's financial partner (quoted in Ramos Espejo and Téllez 2004, 233).

Lack of means is what prompted Lucrecia Pérez, a black Dominican woman with no education, to come to Madrid to seek employment as a maid. And to fully assess the implications of Cano's musical redress, his desire to make amends, we must first consider the crime's impact on the social fabric of the nation as well as in its imaginary. Extensively documented in mass media outlets and sociological and legal studies, the misdeed shook Spaniards to the core because, at one level, the tragic event was perceived as an anomaly, the action of isolated groups that did not reflect the actual sentiments of the whole of Spanish society. However, as Tomás Calvo Buezas indicates in *El crimen racista de Aravaca* (1993), Lucrecia's murder forced Spaniards to collectively realize that racism was a real, national problem that was not limited to a marginal few (1993, 14, see also Bermúdez 2007, 240–1). Indeed, many acts of denunciations against racism took place in the months preceding and following Lucrecia Pérez's murder attesting to the severity of the problem. With "Canción para Lucrecia," Carlos Cano aligned himself with all those protesting and working against racism's ills.

An elegy sustained by anaphoric repetitions, the song cannot be considered mere entertainment; it is, foremost a denunciation against racism and the enunciation of a public apology seeking to provide some moral and practical redress for the wrong done to Lucrecia Pérez by Spanish men. To accentuate this aspect, Cano is joined by leading Catalan singer-songwriter Marina Rossell (1954–) on the CD (see www.marinarossell.com). The gesture underscores that the songster's apology is not just an individual act but a shared one that speaks of the collective. Furthermore, in "Canción para Lucrecia," Cano brought to the fore the relevance of migrant women to Spain's twentieth-century history of migration. The lack of musical representation of women migrant workers is a telling void since, as Carmen Gregorio Gil has argued, if we had to search for the single face to represent migration in 1990s Spain "it will have to be that of a woman from the South" (quoted in Bermúdez 2001,188). Cano's song counteracts how "political as well as media discourses consistently deny or minimize female protagonism" in migratory movements (Ballesteros 2015, 65; see also Nash 2005, 26). "Canción para Lucrecia," along with Las Hijas del Sol's "A ba'ele' (The foreigners) and "Tirso de Molina" – discussed in chapter 3 – are the only songs studied in *Rocking the Boat* where the migrant newcomer is represented as female.

In regard to Lucrecia's murder Cano points to race (she was black) and class (she was poor) as the real reasons behind such violence.

And it is against said violence that Equatoguinean author Francisco Zamora Loboch published *Cómo ser negro y no morir en Aravaca* (1994) to lay bare the social and cultural paradigms legitimizing aggression and brutality against black persons in Spain. For Zamora Loboch, Lucrecia Pérez's murder was not an isolated incident but the most extreme consequence of centuries of verbal aggression against black persons legitimized through racial naming, jokes, and the Spanish literary canon. The importance of race naming needs to be understood within the history of "modern race making," argues Jerome C. Branche, since "modern race making ... was consonant with the colonial enterprise and with the international development of capitalism ... and integral to national discourse both in the metropoles and in their colonial and ex-colonial areas of influence" (2006, 4). These points are forcefully and ingeniously argued in *Cómo ser negro y no morir en Aravaca* as Zamora Loboch exposes the little acknowledged history of Spanish racism, "so rarely detailed in traditional historical texts" (Martin-Márquez 2008, 343).

To reinforce that Lucrecia Pérez's murder took place within a cultural tradition that has been exerting epistemic violence against black persons through jokes, Zamora Loboch brings Lucrecia to the fore in a chapter ironically titled "Humor negro" (Black humour). Duplicity and equivocation are at play in the title since "humor negro" refers simultaneously to a "genre" within humouristic productions ever-present in Spanish arts as well as to humour about black persons. Through this strategy the author calls attention to the fact that "[e]n España, descojonarse de los negros es vieja y secular costumbre que data, más o menos, del siglo XVI" (In Spain, to fucking laugh out loud at blacks is a centuries-old tradition dating, more or less, to the sixteenth century) (1994, 41). It is within this tradition that Zamora Loboch, under the heading "Jódete, Lucrecia" (Fuck You, Lucrecia) (1994, 48, bold in the original), subtitles the section "Humour negro." This "Fuck You, Lucrecia" is a direct quote of graffiti painted in many streets of Madrid after Lucrecia's murder, showing not everyone was appalled by such racist violence. The brief section – pages forty-eight to fifty – does not comment on Lucrecia Pérez, but questions the cultural tradition of *descojonarse de los negros* (laugh the fuck out about blacks). Zamora Loboch reproduces some of the most racist jokes – no longer funny when contextualized in its advocation of violence – to finally call to task those involved in the telling of such jokes. Ultimately, the author chastises journalist Ignacio Carrión for using the prestige and power of his column in *El País* to print a racist joke against blacks precisely "cuando las cosas ya amenazaban con desmadrarse" (when things were already threatening to explode) (1994, 50).

It is against this epistemic violence, also responsible for the actual violence exerted on Lucrecia Pérez, that "Canción para Lucrecia" resonates as a poetic text bringing to light the brutality and violence of racism. More importantly, Cano's moral apology transforms the song into an important historiographical document, one that offers the "ethics of apology" argued by Joseba Gabilondo following Roy L. Brooks (Gabilondo 2003, 247–66; Bermúdez 2007, 245–6). However, Cano's heartfelt apology needs to be assessed alongside the many instances of racial containment at work in the song. The Dominican Republic is metonymically presented with stereotypically sensual references to "rum," "palm trees," and "cinnamon," a paradise for drinking, eating, and dancing. The sensual references and the emphasis on dancing – *bolero, merengue, rumba,* and *merecumbé,*[12] the latter of which is a musical product of Caribbean Colombia combining the rhythms of *merengue* and *cumbia* – are not insignificant when assessing the song's racial containment. As a preferred sexual tourist destination for Spaniards, the Dominican Republic is symbolized in the Spanish imaginary as a "fantasy island" populated by erotic-exotic black and mulatto men with endless sexual energy. But, as Beverly Mullings suggests, the time has come to face the consequences of having the Caribbean function as a paradise in the collective European and North American imaginations since "40 years of tourism has threatened the social and environmental foundations upon which these fantasies have been built" (2004, 97).

Among the social foundations of the Dominican Republic, the song highlights "voodoo," the religious practice most emblematic of the Africanness of the nation and what most expresses the fact that they are "the black Other" – witchcraft practitioners. Despite its repression, Dominican voodoo is an important cultural referent in the world view of Dominicans. And by choosing to exert his revenge for Lucrecia's murder by performing voodoo, the lyric voice – implicitly Cano himself by the description of "a man from Andalusia" – further identifies with Lucrecia Pérez's nation. Yet, the significant colonial ties between the Dominican Republic and Spain are silenced in the song. This is a most revealing suppression since the Dominican Republic was the first Spanish colonial site established by Christopher Columbus during his first voyage; it was Columbus who gave the island the name of *La Española*. The lyrics do bring to the fore the articulation of "the South" – Andalusia, the south of Spain, and the Dominican Republic to the south of Spain – as the geopolitical location of the "dark Other" and of what is, supposedly, the source of the nation's maladies: the poor and the hungry who have come to take away the riches of the North.[13]

Despite its racial containment, Cano embraces the Caribbean literary canon by placing the song within the transatlantic paradigms of black Latin American poetry as in the anaphoric repetition "merecumbé, merecumbé, merecumbá" echoing Nicolás Guillén's creative use of onomatopoeia in "Sensemayá: Canto para matar una culebra" (*Sensemayá*: Song to kill a snake) (Guillén 1979, 256). There are also traces of Luis Palés Matos's "Intermedios del hombre blanco" (White man's intermissions), a poem that, as does Cano, connects *tambores*, *aguijón*, and music: "¡Ahí vienen los tambores! / Ten cuidado, hombre blanco, que a tí te llegan / para clavarte su aguijón de música" (Here they come, the drums! / Be careful white man, that they will get you / to stick in you their musical sting) (1988: 170). Both Palés Matos and Cano mark "the sting" as an emblem of the fear with which Afro-Caribbean cultural manifestations are generally perceived.

In its valorization of Caribbean cultural productions, with its references to *bolero*, *merengue*, and *rumba*, "Canción" aligns itself with Palés Matos. First, by having the poetic voice command the drums to angrily produce their music and, then, by asking the Caribbean *compadre* to drive the white man crazy by performing a rumba. In contrast with these lyrics, the song begins, as per David Thurmaier's musical analysis, with an introductory violin solo that consists of small intervals and some long notes that sound mournful (e-mail message to author, 15 August 2009). According to Thurmaier this is an effective melodic strategy setting the mood for the lyrical content of the song (e-mail message to author, 15 August 2009). I argue that it also sets the mood for the enunciation of Cano's apology, which, notwithstanding the song's racial containment, does serve an ethical and social function in the Spanish public sphere by denouncing racism and by acknowledging responsibility for the crime.

Joaquín Sabina's "La casa por la ventana": Going for Broke, the Ethics of Denunciation and the Problems of Stereotyping

Beloved by legions of fans, Sabina's impact on the Spanish cultural imaginary rests, according to Luis García Montero, on his ability to produce songs "[capaces] de emocionar y de definir sentimentalmente la historia de tres generaciones" (able to move and sentimentally define the history of three generations) (2001, 10). Born Joaquín Ramón Martínez Sabina (1949–), he started performing as Joaquín Sabina in the early seventies when living in London and, from the very beginning, as if to serve as emblem of Frith's definition of the singer-songwriter, Sabina used frankness as his artistic insignia (1981, 53). Frith also mentions "musical irony and paradox" (1981, 53) and both, along with "authenticity," are Sabina's artistic trademarks (see de Miguel 1986 and 2005; Menéndez Flores 2000). Early albums such as *Malas compañias* (Bad company) (CBS 1980), *Mentiras piadosas* (White lies) (Ariola 1990), *Física y Química* (Physics and chemistry) (Ariola 1992, which sold over one million copies worldwide), and *Esta boca es mía* (This Mouth is Mine) (BMG/Ariola 1994), along with his 2009 triple platinum *Vinagre y Rosas* (Vinegar and roses) (Ariola, the 2009 bestselling album in Spain), and several poetry collections attest to Joaquín Sabina's enduring and successful artistic career (see www.jsabina.com for complete discography).

For Sabina, authenticity is the driving force behind his creations, vocals, and concert persona. Indeed, there are many examples of his resolve on producing albums that sound "homemade" (Lesende and Neira 2006, 358). As we shall see, "authenticity" will serve an important ideological function in "La casa por la ventana," where Sabina ironically advances a postcolonial critique of Spanish migration policies. However, the song also contributes to the perpetuation of stereotypes and serves as a discursive form of racial containment since, as in Serrat's "Pardon sir," the house metaphor is used to convey a certain anxiety with the "abundant" presence of migrant workers. A master in using contemporary urban discourses and slang as well as sayings, Sabina recurs to the saying "Tirar la casa por la ventana" – literally "throwing the house out through the window" but meaning "going for broke" or "going whole hog" – to represent how the migrant workers "get wasted." By (mis)representing a diverse population of migrant workers as underpaid subjects that overspend their meager salaries on drinking and dancing, Sabina further contributes to the stereotyping of the migrant communities he clearly wants to defend and support as per the lyrics transcribed by me, by permission, from the CD *Esta boca es mí*:

Quemaron todas las naves
para iniciar una nueva vida
pagaron cara la llave
falsa de la tierra prometida.
Pero, en lugar del Caribe,
con su bachata, con sus palmeras,
la madre patria recibe
al inmigrante por peteneras.
Y no es bona Barcelona
cuando la bolsa, primo, no sona
y gana el cholo en Madrid
menos que un perro sin pedigrí,
y el mestizo por Sevilla,
va dando cantes por pesadillas,
y, si dos vascos atracan
a un farmacéutico en Vigo
jura el testigo que eran sudacas.
Y cada fin de semana
tiran la casa por la ventana
marcándose un agarrado
en El Café del Mercado
que no es lo mismo que el Tropicana.
Se matan haciendo camas,
vendiendo besos, lustrando suelos
si pica el hambre en la rama
la tortolita levanta el vuelo.
Y, en plazoletas y cines,
por un jergón y un plato de sopa,
con una alfombra y un Kleenex
le sacan brillo al culo de Europa.
Y, el cuerpo de policía
viene con leyes de extranjería
y, al moro de la patera,
corta el rollo una patrullera,

They burnt all their ships
To begin a new life
Paying a hefty price for the false
key to the Promise Land.
Instead of the Caribbean
With its *bachata* and palm trees,
The motherland greets
The immigrant skewedly
Barcelona is not good,
My friend, when pockets don't chime
And the *cholo* in Madrid earns
Less than a mixed-breed dog
While the *mestizo* in Sevilla
Works to fulfill his nightmares.
If two Basque men hold-up
A pharmacist in Vigo,
The witness swears they were *sudacas*
And every weekend
They go for broke
doing a slow-dance
in *El Café del Mercado*
Which is different from Tropicana.
They kill themselves making beds,
Selling kisses, polishing floors,
And if hunger strikes
The birds migrate again
In city squares and movie theaters,
For a straw mattress and a plate of soup
They help shine Europe's ass
With a carpet and a Kleenex.
And the police force
Applies Immigration Laws.
The Coast Guard chases like a panther
The Moor hiding in the *patera*

y, al mulato sabrosón,	While the hot mulatto's inquisition
le dan en toda la inquisición,	Gets hit with great precision
y, al gitanito, la ola	And the Little Gypsy suffers,
malaje y paya le quema	The mob of non-Gypsy punks,
el tejadillo de la chabola.	Who burn the roof of his shack
Y cada fin de semana	And every weekend,
tiran la casa por la ventana	They go for broke,
chilabas y desayuno	*Chilabas* and breakfast
de kifi con té moruno	Of Hashish with mint tea
y escriben cartas a la sultana.	While their write to their *sultanas*.
Y cada fin de semana	And every weekend
con sus caderas dominicanas,	With their Dominican hips,
compadre, una guarachita,	My brother, a *guarachita*,
candombé, samba o rumbita	*Candombé*, samba or a little rumba,
¿o es que nunca estuvo en la Habana?	Or haven't you ever been in Havana?
Y el coreano currela	And the Korean sweats
vendiendo rollos de plimavela [*sic*],	Selling "Spling" [*sic*] rolls
y, en bares porno el paquete	While a Guinean dong
de guineano cuesta un billete,	Costs a bundle in the Porn Bars.
y, al almacén del judío,	And, in the Jew's grocery store
van seis niñatos buscando lío,	Six punks look for trouble.
y el ingeniero polaco	While the Polish Engineer,
que vino huyendo del frío	Who came fleeing from the cold
ya es mayordomo del tío del saco.	Is now the butler of that guy with a suit.
Y cada fin de semana	And every weekend
tiran la casa por la ventana	They go for broke
y, mientras planchan un traje,	While they iron a suit,
su corazón de viaje	Their traveling heart,
se va cantando La Varsoviana.	Goes aways as it sings a polka
Y cada fin de semana	And every weekend
queda el negrito	That "Blackie" goes out
con la ucraniana,	With the Ukrainian woman
y bailan polca y pasito,	And they dance polka and *pasito*
y soplan vodka y mojito	And drink vodka and *mojito*
y vuelven trompas por la mañana.	And come back wasted in the morning[14]

In this salsa song, recorded as a duet with Pablo Milanés, the legendary singer-songwriter from the *Nueva Trova Cubana*, migration is clearly presented as a traumatic transnational experience through the two images first alluded to in the song, "las naves" (the ships) and the "tierra prometida" (promised land). The *naves* are an important syntagm simultaneously signifying the ships of the mighty empire that colonalized the Americas, the slave boats of the transatlantic trade, and the infamous *pateras* of present-day transoceanic endeavours. Displacement and diaspora are the only real gains of the Caribbean migrant workers mentioned early in the song as they are caught in postcolonial exchanges that bring nothing but suffering to them. Framed within neocolonial and postcolonial paradigms, the song represents immigration as a direct consequence of both processes (see Grosfoguel, Cervantes-Rodríguez, and Eric Mielants 2009: 1–17).

Sabina's penchant for authenticity resonates, even more loudly, in the graphic lines describing how migrant workers fill unskilled and poorly paid jobs in the service sector: "Y, en plazoletas y cines, / por un jergón y un plato de sopa, / con una alfombra y un Kleenex, / le sacan brillo al culo de Europa" (In city squares and movie theatres, / for a straw mattress and a plate of soup, they help shine Europe's ass / with a carpet and a Kleenex). The unequivocal statement "they help shine Europe's ass" showcases the placement of migrant newcomers in the lowest social strata, while the references to "cleaning" and "city squares" – usual meeting places for female domestic workers – point to the feminization of migration during the 1990s. Between 1993 and 1999, the Spanish government responded to the high demand for migrant women to perform domestic service by establishing a policy of annual quotas where, in 1993 for example, "84 percent of the favorable quota decisions corresponded to domestic work" (Oso Casas 2009, 211).

Along with recognizing migration as a legacy of coloniality, "La casa por la ventana" denounces racist ideologies and practices by exposing the many ways in which different ethnic communities – Jews, *Gitanos* – are subjected to violence and harassment. Racist ideologies and practices are also operative when migrant workers from South America – identified by the pejorative term *sudacas* – are criminalized. In dramatizing the instance by which Latin American migrants are accused of a crime actually committed by "two Basques" – it is not irrelevant that Basques, because of ETA and the lengthy disputes between the Spanish state and the Basque government, are also construed as "feared Others" – Sabina wants the audience to be aware of how easily migrant workers are falsely identified as "challenges" and "threats" to crime control and national security. In fact, national security is the foundation for the categories "legal" and "illegal" conveyed in the song by references to "Immigration Laws" and the "moor of the *patera*." Presented in plural as *leyes de extranjería*, the line appears to make reference to the fact that by 1994, the 1985 Law had been revised once – in 1991 – with a series of provisions that included, among other changes, the modernization of border installations and reducing the number of asylum visas granted. The stipulations further criminalized migrants and offered no respite for asylum seekers.

And for all of its denunciations, stereotyping is still at work in Sabina's salsa song as per the detail of reproducing the linguistic difficulties Korean migrants have in pronouncing the Spanish "r." But, the undermining of the very denunciation expressed by the song is most salient when perpetuating the supposed irresponsibility of migrant workers. Bent on the repetitive motion – every weekend – of "drinking" and "dancing" their miserable lives to oblivion, the song concludes by underscoring an interracial couple as "they dance polka and *pasito* / Downing vodka and *mojito* / And get back wasted in the morning." And while the deterministic presentation of migrants cannot be overlooked, neither can we obviate Sabina's keen socio-economic description of globalization: population displacements from former colonies to the metropolitan centre – Madrid – to be structurally placed within the "'underdeveloped' residue of industrialism," doing personal service jobs, low-skill construction jobs, and/or prostitution (Quintero-Rivera and Márquez 2003, 219). Through the rhythms of salsa music – born in the United States "largely [as] a response of (im)migrant youth of Latino-Caribbean culture to rock and roll" – Sabina lyrically explains what social scientists do using complex theoretical models; that is, globalization is linked to inequality in industrialized and developing economies (Quintero-Rivera and Márquez 2003, 219).[15]

Pedro Guerra's "Contamíname" and the Fear of ContamiNation

A *cantautor* with close ties to the tradition of the Latin American *nueva canción* (New Song), Pedro Guerra spent his early years in Tenerife working to create an authentic and relevant musical form for the Canary Islands.[16] He founded the *Taller canario de canción* in 1985, when he was but nineteen years old. In the *Taller* he participated in the collective album titled *Nueva canción canaria* (New Canarian song), and in 1993 moved to the multicultural neighbourhood of *Lavapies* in Madrid, an experience that inspired Guerra to write "Contamíname" (Contaminate Me) (Lozano 62–3), included in his album Golosinas (Sweet Treat) (BMG-Ariola 1994). The song's title demonstrates how by the mid-nineties, the notion of the migrant as "pollutant" was imbedded in Spain's symbolic imaginary. Thus, the song reifies the dominant assumptions about migrants in 1990s Spain lending to the interpretation that migration is a serious threat to the "health" and survival of the nation. The metaphorical representation of migrants as contaminants is a tried strategy that continues to operate transnationally as J. David Cisneros demonstrates in his discussion of the visual rethoric of immigration in the United States and the (mis)representation of the "immigrant as pollutant" (Cisneros 2008, 570).

Highly successful, "Contamíname" (Contaminate me) earned the award for "Best Song" at the 1995 *Premios Ondas* (Ondas Award), and was first performed by Ana Belén and Víctor Manuel in Asturias in April 1994 in a two-day concert titled "Mucho más que dos" (Much more than two). The successful musical extravaganza, which included acts by Joan Manuel Serrat, Joaquín Sabina, and Antonio Flores, was subsequently transformed into a tour throughout the Spanish territory also resulting in Ana Belén's 1994 release of the *Mucho más que dos* CD. Pedro Guerra originally wrote "Contamíname" for Ana Belén – well known to Spanish and Latin American audiences as a famous singer in her own right and as a well-respected actress – and it was Ana Belén's and Víctor Manuel's rendition of the song that first captivated audiences. In fact, originally, the song became more identified with Ana Belén and Víctor Manuel than with Pedro Guerra, prompting Víctor Manuel to state, "fue muchos años el tema que más me pedían en los conciertos" (it was during many years the song most requested in concerts) (quoted by Lesende and Neira 2006, 314).[17]

In its third incarnation the song was recorded in 1996 in a version done by Ana Belén and Víctor Manuel along with Miguel Ríos and Joan Manuel Serrat for their album *El gusto es nuestro* (The pleasure is ours), the result of the tour "El gusto es nuestro," which took Ana Belén, Víctor Manuel, Miguel Ríos, and Joan Manuel Serrat throughout the Spanish territory. In its 2016 variation, the four artists joined forces once more to tour again all over Spain under the banner "El gusto es nuestro: 20 años después" (The pleasure is ours: Twenty years later). Thus, "Contamíname" is an unusual song in that its lifespan in terms of massive exposure and popularity lasted for several years and was interpreted with much success, first by the artistic duo of Ana Belén and Víctor Manuel, then by the artist himself (see note 17), and finally by four of the most recognized Spanish performers in 1990s Spain. The song dramatizes the encounter between an autochthonous subject addressing two postcolonial migrants; first a person from the Maghreb for the stereotypical references to "desert," "dates, " and "palm trees"; and then a person from sub-Saharan Africa for the metonymical reference to slavery through the term "chains." In the 1994 version, Ana Belén and Víctor Manuel take turns to address, respectively, each migrant subject. But the possibility of establishing any kind of dialogue in the fiction of the story is erased by the series of demands each speaking subject requests from the migrant newcomers.

Grounded in a hermeneutics of desire that appears to want to know the Other as Other, "Contamíname" most tellingly reveals an anxiety with the presence of migrant newcomers from North Africa, sub-Saharan Africa, and the Latin American Caribbean by first validating the notion presented in news discourse that migrants are harmful, destructive pollutants. Second, that anxiety is expressed though the use of the command form that orders the migrant subject to provide the singing voice with the desired knowledge. (Mis)representing migrants through metaphors of "pollution" is a tried and successful strategy as Cisneros demonstrates when discussing media representations of migration in the United States (2008). In his discussion of how the discourse of California's Proposition 187 campaign accomplished presenting migration as dangerous, Cisneros points out that this was done through the use of metaphors such as "'pollution,' 'infection,' and 'infestation'" that "created images of biological invasion or contamination that ... fueled the Proposition 187 movement" (2008, 572).

In "Contamíname," Spaniards appear to have surrendered to the "biological invasion" of the feared Others by requesting to "be infected." Thus, Ana Belén and Víctor Manuel, two musically powerful and authorial Spanish voices – one female, one male – "stand-in" for the nation in the oxymoronic gesture of surrendering to the contamination process but keeping authorial control by instructing the two subaltern subjects to produce meaning. Both "knowledge" and "meaning" are at the core of such requests because the singing subjects reveal an orientalist desire to know of that to which s/he is simultaneously foreign and familiar – Islam, as emblematized in the request to "hear" about "las mezquitas de tus abuelos" (your grandparent's mosques). The familiar/unfamiliar dynamics of the uncanny appear to be at work in this particular request since Spain's Muslim heritage seems to have been forgotten by the "natives" who need for the "newcomers" to explain to him/her – depending on whom is singing the song – a historical past shared through seven centuries. The insistence on uncovering that which has been kept concealed – there is allusion to secrets – appears to be a manifestation of the uncanny.

Significantly, concealment was at work in the silencing or hiding of Spain's Islamic past in 1990s school textbooks. In *El Islam en las aulas: contenidos, silencios, enseñanza* (1997) edited by Josep María Navarro, the erasure of Islam is explained as a consequence of Spain's desire to belong to what Juan Goytisolo has described as "club de los países ricos" (club of rich countries) (Goytisolo 2003, 23). For this reason, Navarro argues "no debe extrañar a nadie ... que en España tratemos de abominar de nuestras raíces islámicas ... por cuestiones de prestigio internacional. ¿Cómo vamos a entrar en el club de los 'países VIP' con ese pasado tan poco europeo?" (It should come as no surprise ... that in Spain we try to abominate of our Islamic roots ... for reasons of international prestige. How are we to enter the club of the 'VIP countries' with such an un-European past?) (Navarro 1997, 20). It is, then, the perceived "ContamiNation" brought by the fear of Islam that drives "Contamíname," which cannot escape its longing and desire for the "contaminating subject," as the theme of contamination is musically dramatized by the infectious melody with salsa overtones.

It is within the double axes of fear and desire that the singing voices express a longing for "mixing" with the migrant-Other – metonymically reduced to body parts – while simultaneously fearing and rejecting him/her for bringing into the open the repressed in the form of anger and bad dreams. Moreover, by minimizing and sentimentalizing the violence of slavery, the song actively participates in the epistemic violence exerted on black persons by a cultural and literary canon that makes light of the horrors of slavery and its aftermath. Once again, racial containment is at work and no amount of valorization of diverse musical world views – when referring to *boleros* and musical instruments such as *bouzukis* – can erase the denigration the lyrics enact.

But, if the lyrics betray Guerra's commitment to diversity and multiculturalism, then music itself, as an inclusive realm of production, embracing and engaging diverse and multicultural musical instruments, becomes the central focus in "Contamíname." This diversity is inscribed in the song through a melody that includes tonalities and musical instruments from Africa, the Arab world, and Latin America. It is also inscribed lyrically with the reference to *darbukas*, North African/Latin American drums, and *bouzoukis*. At the end, it is music that "saves" the *cantautor*, for all of its problems and contradictions; "Contamíname" is the impulse that drives Pedro Guerra to commit to diversity and multiculturalism with the creation, in 2000, of *Fundación Contamíname* (Contaminate me foundation). Focused on combating racism from within the musical arena, the Foundation was operative between 2000 and 2009. It promoted intercultural dialogue to fight racism and defended human rights while questioning and contesting globalization's homogenizing tendencies, its push to obliterate cultures.

Rap and Race: El Chojín's Anti-Racist Stance in "Mami, el negro está rabioso"

Rapper El Chojin (Domingo Edjang Moreno, 1977) takes his name from the anime *Urotsukidōji*.[18] *Chōjin* means "super-deity" and he is to bring peace to the three worlds battling in the anime. If not peace, El Chojin is committed to bringing awareness to many of the social ills plaguing present-day Spain, such as racism, discrimination, and gender-based violence (see http://elchojin.net/site/index.php/en/). He is considered one of the most prolific MCs in Spain and the practitioner of what in Spain is called "rap conciencia" (Awareness raising rap) (Bermúdez 2015). Relevant to my discussion of migration and racialization processes is his collaboration with rappers Krazé (Marcos Ela Edjang) and Meko for the Spain Amnesty International's anti-racist campaign based on Krazé's song "Ponte en mi piel" (Walk in my shoes), included as track 14 on El Chojin's 2002 album *Cuando hay obstáculos…* (When there are obstacles…) (Boa). His talents are not limited to music having co-authored, with Paco Reyes, *Rap: 25 años de rimas, un recorrido por la historia del rap en España* (2010), the first official history of Spanish rap. In 2011, at the request of Espasa-Calpe, he published *Ríe cuando puedas, llora cuando lo necesites* (Laugh when you can, cry when needed), a collection of personal reflections in the format of a diary (sold under the "self-help" category). The book's title reproduces a rap from El Chojin's 2007 album *Striptease* – a version of which, in a duet with songster Luis Eduardo Aute, was also included in his 2009 album *Cosas que pasan, que no pasan y que deberían pasar* (Things that happen, that do not happen, and that should happen) (Boa).

To appreciate the impact of "Mami, el negro está rabioso" (Mama, the black man is mad), we first need to consider rap's history in Spain. Born in the 1970s in New York's South Bronx, rap, musically speaking, is a term interchangeable with hip hop. In part because "rapping" is one of the four key stylistic elements that define hip hop; DJing/scratching, sampling (or synthesis), and beatboxing are the other three. It is in the mid-1980s that hip hop arrived in Spain through films such as *Beat Street* and *Breakdance*, both from 1984. Under their spell and the influence of young black Americans residing in Spain, some young Spaniards took to breakdancing. In Madrid, youngsters began meeting to dance to the new beat in the area of *Nuevos Ministerios*, a section of the city's financial district in the Chamberí neighbourhood and with a metro station of the same name. Simulatneously, the music of Run DMC, LL Cool J, and other rappers was being heard on radio stations such as Radio Torrejón – El Chojin was born and grew up in Torrejón de Ardoz – and Radio 3. The action exploded in Madrid's working-class peripheral neighbourhoods such as Torrejón, Móstoles, and Alcorcón as well as in Barcelona's El Prat de Llobregat. In 1989, the independent label Troya produced the hit *Madrid Hip Hop*, which included music by groups such as Sindicato del Crimen, Estado Crítico, DNI, and QSC (El Chojin and Reyes 2010, 77–80). Most critics and rappers, including El Chojin, mark the birth of Spanish rap in late 1996 (El Chojin and Reyes 2010, 164–6). He arrived to this musical scene in 1998 with his single *100% = 10,000 mi estilo* (Revelde), releasing his debut album *Mi turno* (My turn) a year later, also by Revelde, a subdivision of Fonomusic that published *Spanish Hip Hop*.

"Mami, el negro está rabioso" (Mama, the black man is mad) is track 7 of *Mi turno* and the rapper borrows a few of the well-known lyrics from the popular *merengue* "El Africano" (The African) to both title his song and make statements against Spanish racism. The *merengue*'s question, "Mami, ¿qué será lo que quiere el negro?" (Mama, what is it that the black man may want?), as well as the hook "mami, el negro está rabioso" (Mama, the black man is mad), were made famous throughout the Spanish speaking world by Dominican star Wilfrido Vargas (born Wilfrido Radamés Vargas Martínez, 1949–), in a song written by Calixto Ochoa. It has been sampled in the United States by two well-known Cuban-American rappers. In 1991, rapper/producer DJ Laz (Lázaro Mendez, 1975–) paid homage to the original by titling his debut album *DJ Laz featuring Mami El Negro*. In 2007, global star Pitbull (Armando Christian Pérez, 1981–) revisited the song in "The Anthem" from his album *The Boatlift* (Pitbull 2007). The song features Lil' Jon and samples the hook from Vargas's "El africano" and the beat from Rune RK's "Calabria."

Musically, DJ Laz updates the original but does not change the lyrics, whereas Pitbull plays into the prejudices of the *merengue* by furthering the racial stereotyping of "oversexed" black men and, in his version, black/*mulata* women. El Chojin's 1999 version is the only rap questioning the *merengue*'s blatant racism. If we compare the three raps it becomes apparent that Pitbull's 2007 "The Anthem" reifies racist stereotypes of black male sexuality while further sexualizing the black/*mulata* woman. On the contrary, and by calling attention to the power of music to perpetuate and disseminate prejudices and racist ideologies, El Chojin's "Mami, el negro está rabioso" stands as a pivotal anti-racist denunciation, making an unequivocal statement about how tired and angry the author is, as a black Spanish man, of hearing racist comments and jokes.

In his denunciation of racism, El Chojin pays particular attention to the Spanish cultural motifs and symbolization processes that have promoted racist attitudes. Indeed, he has much to say about TV commercials, jokes, and how he feels about being constantly compared with two well-known African-American men of the 1990s – Michael Jordan from the world of sports and Eddie Murphy from the Hollywood industry. When listening to "Mami, el negro está rabioso" we first hear how it opens with breakbeats reminiscent of funk where the bass and a melodic element produced using a synthesizer are the backbone to the lyrics that follow. It ends with the similar musical sequence and no rhymes. According to the analysis by musicologist Eduardo Viñuela, the song follows a constant succession of the sequence IV-V-I in Fa major in which Sib functions as the support for Do major, a strategy that reinforces a sense of progression throughout the song (e-mail message to author, 31 July 2010). We also appreciate that melody has been reduced to a minimum pointing to El Chojin's prioritizing the beat and the lyrics. In fact, as soon as the beat begins we are told, in no uncertain terms, that what El Chojin has had to endure as a black person growing up in late twentieth-century Spain is nothing but unadulterated racism.

The rhyming of "mismo" (same) and "racismo" (racism), where the two terms share the same four final letters in "ismo," helped El Chojin underscore the pervasive nature of this social ill. This "mismo racismo," which cannot be captured in English when stating "the same racism," serves as an introduction for the narration that follows. The rapper immediately calls attention to the experience of growing up in Spain listening to two immensely popular and racist promotional songs used to sell the products *Conguitos* (from Lacasa) and *Colacao* (from Nutrexpa). The musical references expose how racism is lodged deep in daily discourses and cultural practices. El Chojin's powerful denunciation renders visible how racist images and ideologies are promoted through music and media advertisement. Indeed, we cannot ignore that these two cocoa-based products were made popular to generations of Spanish children through promotional songs, which, in this case, were reinforcing racist ideologies. The lyrics demonstrate that the marketing was done using well-established stereotypes that, as El Chojin's rap shows, were insulting and offensive to black Spanish children. The artist used hip hop's raw power of denunciation to deconstruct the racist imagery and ideologies promoted through these two songs – blackface stereotyping in the case of the "Conguitos" and packaging design and hard labour conditions for black persons in the case of "Cola Cao." Ultimately, "Mami, el negro está rabioso" served as a countermemory to the hegemonic perception of the two songs since what may appear to be either funny or appealing to the majority of "white" Spanish children, was not so to Spanish children like El Chojin.

"Conguitos", with its obvious allusion to Africa as per the name of the nation formerly known as Zaire, are peanuts coated in milk chocolate – there is also a white chocolate version now – and were heavily promoted on TV during the 1980s. The original logo of the product used one the most patently racist archetypes: the image of the happy-go-lucky darky (see figure 3).[19]

In the case of Cola Cao – powdered cocoa to drink with milk – we have a product with enduring symbolic relevance since generations of Spaniards have been drinking the product since 1946, when it was created by the Catalan group Nutrexpa. It was in the 1950s when the infamous "La canción del negrito" (The little black boy song), also known as "La canción del Cola Cao" (Cola Cao's song), began to be heavily promoted on the radio becoming part of the cultural references of the nation.[20]

3. Image of Spanish candy. Copyright by Manel Armengol.

Cola Cao's massive appeal was at work when sponsoring the 1972 and 1992 Olympic Games – in Munich and Barcelona respectively – when the product was promoted as "alimento olímpico" (Olympic food). Cola Cao's staying power has not waned in the twenty-first century since one of Spain's most globally recognized elite athletes, tennis start Rafael Nadal, has sponsored the ready-to-drink version.

Cola Cao's song and its many racist reverberations – the use of the word "negrito," the slavery evoking images of black persons singing while harvesting – concern El Chojin since he makes reference to this particular product twice in his rap. First, he implicitly alludes to Cola Cao when mentioning the infamous promotional song and its reference to *negro* and *negrito*. Then he names the product in one of the three angriest instances of the song – made evident in each case by the use of swear words like "cagarse" to indicate El Chojín's level of frustration and justified anger. To deal with both, El Chojin does not subscribe to multiculturalist redefinitions of citizenship – implicated and promoted by Pedro Guerra's "Contamíname" and by the band Ska-P I discuss in chapter 4. On the contrary, following a Malcom X approach – the CD cover features a picture of El Chojin at the corner of Malcom X Blvd and Lenox Ave in New York – he rejects integration by maintaining that there is no such thing as equality and by arguing that there is no need to pretend that we are all equal. He defends self-reliance in his music and closes "Mami, el nergro está rabioso" by establishing the power of music to promote new ideas. It would be ten years later with "N.E.G.R.O," studied in chapter 4, that El Chojin deploys identity politics strategies to establish a black Spanish identity to combat racism.

Spanish/Moroccan raï: Perilous Mediterranean Crossings and Transnational Communities in the Music of Chab Samir

As per the *Garland Encyclopedia of World Music*, raï is a musical form originating in western Algeria at the turn of the twentieth century as rural, folk music combining Bedouin folk forms and Arab love poetry (Mazouzi 2002, 269). It thrives in the port of Wharan (Oran) during the first decades of the twentieth century as rural migrants flowed into the laissez-faire port town. It is, since this stage of development, migrant music, first brought to Oran through internal Algerian migration. It ceased to be "regional music" through the modernization of sounds, recording techniques, and instrumentation in the early 1980s, when it gradually became a genre "with a nationwide appeal led by a new generation of rai singers, known as chebs (young men) and chabas (young women)" (Swedenburg 2003, 190). Raï's pull transcended Algeria when it grew to be relevant to the Maghrebi communities in France – especially the *Beurs*, the bi-cultural, socially excluded children of North African parents – as they demanded cultural recognition and political rights as in the 1983 *Marche pour l'égalité et contre le racisme* (March per equality and against racism) from Marseilles to the centre of Paris, which gained national visibility for the *génération Beur* (Beur generation). In France, "pop" raï turned into "one of the chief means of cultural expression for a minority struggling to carve out an identity in a racist environment" (Gross, McMurray and Swedenburg 1992, 13). The term "raï" means opinion but is best idiomatically translated as "'my way,' 'tell it like it is' and even 'oh, yeah!'" (Mazouzi 2002, 269).

All of these aspects intrinsic to "raï" – being migrant music, the cultural expression of identity in a racist environment, and the "telling it like it is" – are found in the Spanish/Moroccan modality of raï produced by Chab Samir and his mixed Moroccan/Catalan group in their 1999 self-titled CD *Chab Samir*, produced by Afro-Blue Records. The songs are in Arabic, peppered with words or comments in Spanish and/or Catalan. 1999 was a productive year for Samir since it also saw the movie premiere of *Saïd* (Said), the film by Llorenç Soler, where he plays the role of Ahmet, one of the main protagonist's friends. *Saïd* tells the story of the main character's clandestine arrival in Barcelona via *patera* to look for a better life to only have his aspirations crashed by being sent back to Morocco at the end of the film. Through the application of multiple perspectives, Llorenç Soler's intent was to document "the experience of a community of Moroccan male immigrants in Barcelona and the racial and ethnic discrimination and physical aggression they suffer" (Ballesteros 2015, 41). And one of the means these migrants cope with blatant racism, discrimination, and constant harassment by the police is by creating a raï playing band named "Baraka," which Saïd joins. The film mirrors, in more ways than one, Chad Samir's own personal experience, except for the arrival by *patera*, as we shall see below.

In my comments on the social function of the song "Patera," I take into account the CD, a number of press releases and concert announcements (see RedAragon.com 2005), and the interviews conducted by Parvati Nair in April 2001 in Barcelona (Nair 2006), to evaluate the role this music plays in the voicing of the exclusion and marginalization of Moroccan migrants in late twentieth-century Spain. Nair interviewed Samir, the group's lead singer and songwriter, his band members, and Driss and Hasan, two male followers of the band only identified by these names, to examine the impact of the publication of the first raï CD in Spain in 1999 but also that of the weekly club performances taking place in districts like Sabadell, in Barcelona's outer reaches. These particular performances "provided the group with their core, socio-cultural function," more importantly, and much in tune with the social function of raï, they offered Moroccan migrants "a spatial and temporal affirmation of specific socio-economic and political positions" (Nair 2006, 75).

Chab Samir, whose CD cover has the baby-faced Samir wearing a white jacket with a black polo shirt against a nightlife background, consists of eight songs, all written by Samir except track 2, "Zidni Zidni," which is co-written with Ginesa Ortega. The song "Sabare," which shares a title with a piece by well-known raï artist Khaled (formerly known as Cheb Khaled), is presented twice, once in trance version (track 4) and once in club (track 8) – indicating how Samir's raï, in his invitation to the Moroccan community to dance and sing, despite their tribulations, fulfills a social function.[21] Chab Samir's migrant followers, the ones attending his live performances in clubs, emphasize the social function the band's music plays in providing a sense of community despite and against their illegal status. Music also allows Samir's Moroccan followers the voicing of an emergent double identity delineated by the "there" and the "here" distinctions presented by Driss when explaining to Nair why he follows Samir:

> I do not just go because I miss my village or my family, but because being in the club *means something to me.* You know, I feel I have to be there, to listen, to dance, to sing along. It is important because it is our music, it is about us and we are here and we are doing it here, and all the time we are without papers. *We have no papers, who knows, maybe no future, but we are singing and we are dancing … You understand?* (quoted by Nair 2006, 75, emphasis mine).

Driss' comments point to the ways in which music evokes deeply felt emotions and has the power to touch upon important social identities; this is marked by the change from the individual experience ("I feel I have to be here") to the communal ("it is our music, it is about us"). Also, and central to the discussion of music and migration, Driss precisely explains how music also helps people express insights into their own lives by twice insisting in the Moroccan shared experienced of being undocumented – "and all the time we are without papers" and "we have no papers, who knows, maybe no future." The insights shared by Driss with Parvati Nair also expose how, while attending a performance, listeners recognize, categorize, and reflect on the music while listening (Cox 2012).

In "Patera," a 6:01-minute song (track 5), Samir sings of the perilous crossings of the Mediterranean Sea through the Strait of Gibraltar via an inflatable dinghy, an experience actually not familiar to him. As stated in the introduction, Samir arrived in Barcelona by plane in 1992 to attend the Olympics Games in Barcelona and he overstayed his visa due to a relationship with a Catalan woman that became his wife. The change in his status – from illegal to legal – does not prevent him from singing about "the cultural memory of migration as risk, possible death, and certain fear" (Nair 2006, 77). But while "Patera" may appear a more relevant song for all the obvious reasons when discussing clandestine migration to Spain and to Fortress Europe, including its association with death, Samir in his interview with Nair revealed that he seldom performed the song in the live concerts for fellow Moroccans, providing a detailed explanation of his reasons:

> Why should I sing to them of dying in the sea? They all know about it. I sing that to people who wouldn't think of it otherwise. Almost all of us who are here know of someone who came that way (via *patera*). Can you imagine what it must be like to spend fourteen hours drifting on a raft in the windy seas? Those fourteen hours are not just fourteen hours, there is no measure for them (cited by Nair 2006, 80, the clarification and parenthesis mine).

Samir's ability to understand the group's distinct audiences allows him to negotiate new musical spaces that simultaneously speak to those that "know all about" *pateras*, clandestine migration, and liminal spaces as lived experience, and to "people who wouldn't think of it otherwise." In all instances, as he has stated, his music "is a bridge across the Strait, like the *pateras*, it makes its crossings" (quoted by Nair 2006, 80 emphasis in the original). [22]

Conclusion

The productions studied in this chapter render visible the entrapments of good intentions and the depths of Spanish racist attitudes. There is no doubt that Joan Manuel Serrat, Carlos Cano, Joaquín Sabina, and Pedro Guerra use their cultural status as beloved and trusted *cantautores* to impact the public sphere and call attention to the hardships and risks suffered by migrant newcomers to Spain, an experience musically voiced by Chab Samir's Spanish/Moroccan raï. Nor is there any question that all of these artists sought to impact the social sphere by showing solidarity with all migrant communities by exposing the alliance between colonial legacies and transnational capitalism (Serrat, Sabina), the ills of racism (Cano), and the rich cultural diversity brought by the migrant newcomers (Guerra). However, their texts cannot escape the coloniality of power and contribute to the racialization processes taking place in late twentieth-century Spain by subjecting the fictional migrant newcomers they seek to support to the treatment of racialized colonial subjects. More importantly, and as El Chojin's powerful "Mami, el negro está rabioso" has rendered visible, racism is so imbedded in Spanish everyday cultural practices that combating it requires much more than just mere "good intentions." At the end, and despite their massive diffusion – less so in the case of Serrat's "Disculpe el Señor," El Chojin's "Mami, el negro está rabioso," and Chab Samir's "Patera" – the songs did little to diminish Spanish racism since the end of the 1990s and the racist attacks of July 1999 in Terrasa, a most troubling prelude to the ones to occur in El Ejido in early 2000, as we shall see in the following chapter.

3
The 1990s, Take Two: The Racial Profiling of Black and Maghrebi Migrant Subjects

The contradictory tendencies that defined the treatment of migrant newcomers in 1990s Spain – rising xenophobia along with the creation of hundreds of NGOs to combat racism and foster integration – did not operate in a vacuum. They thrived within the legacies of a "colonial imaginary, colonial knowledges, [and] a racial/ethnic hierarchy linked to a history of dominance" (Grosfoguel, Cervantes-Rodríguez, and Mielants 2009, 8). It was within these complex processes that, in the last decade of the twentieth century, migration was mostly assigned a "black face" and that "blackness" was articulated as a racial category threatening Spain's materialization as a "true" European nation because its supposedly racially homogenous (white) identity was being disrupted by the presence of postcolonial (non-white) subjects. Indeed, and in relation to the six songs studied in this chapter, it is instructive to return to Francisco Zamora Loboch's *Cómo ser negro y no morir en Aravaca* (1994) and his denunciation of the legacies of colonial knowledges. In particular, Zamora Loboch's unveiling of how race naming, established as a primary indicator to mark difference, was inscribed and perpetuated in the Spanish cultural imaginary through a weighty literary tradition.

According to Zamora Loboch, to understand how black persons became assigned to radical otherness in 1990s Spain, one must first identify Spain's heavy involvement in the slave trade where "[v]ascos, catalanes, cántabros, gallegos y asturianos se dieron con verdadera vocación y dedicación completa a la trata de esclavos" Basques, Catalans, Cantabrians, Galician, and Asturians dedicated themselves with true vocation and complete devotion to the slave trade) (20). Zamora Loboch's detailed enumeration of the diverse cultural and national identities engaged in slave trading exposed the connections between the assertion of an "essential" Spanish identity and the articulation of racism, where the warring sections of the nation became unified in a joint project ultimately benefiting the motherland. A similar assessment is offered by Ignacio Tofiño-Quesada when discussing Spain's colonization of Africa and the external relationships that shaped the configuration of the state. He argues that "when the time came to go abroad and colonize, Catalan, Basques, and Galicians went hand in hand with Castilians, as nationals of the metropole" (2003, 142).

Tellingly, Zamora Loboch's discussion of Spanish racism in *Cómo ser negro y no morir en Aravaca* begins with a reference to Boabdil's expulsion from Granada by Isabella and Ferdinand, and to the Immigration Law of 1985: "El primer moro a quien España aplicó la Ley de Extranjería se llamaba Boabdil" (The first Moor to whom Spain applied the Law of Foreignness was named Boabdil) (1994, 11). Zamora Loboch's insistence on Boabdil's right to consider himself a legal resident points precisely to one of the fears that appeared to fuel the racist attacks against Moroccan Muslin immigrants during the 1990s, the centuries-old discourse of the "threatening and invading" moors – with new and present-day connotations because of the globalized rise of Islamic fundamentalism since the 1970s. The most palpable outcome of this fundamentalism resulted in the ghastly attacks of 11 September 2001, and, in the particular case of Spain, in the bombings of commuter trains in Madrid on 11 March 2004. These attacks, along with the insistence with which Al Qaeda's leaders and followers refer to the loss of al-Andalus, have fueled a discourse of the reverse reconquest of Spain by which Arabs/Muslims are to reclaim their lost paradise through either conquest or migration.

In adhering to this rhetoric Spain appeared to display, much like the rest of Europe, an "Eurocentric and paranoid vision" (Bensaad 2007, 53) that fomented the opening of its internal borders for Europeans while reinforcing the notion of Fortress Europe through exclusionary migration laws and the closure of its external borders to non-Europeans from the Global South and East. Six songs, five in Spanish and one in Bubi – one of the languages of Equatorial Guinea – attest to how this paranoid vision resorted to the articulation of migrant newcomers as racialized non-white counterparts to a seemingly homogenous (and white) Spanish identity. As per their release date the songs are: The 1991 "Africanos en Madrid" (Africans in Madrid) by the male-female duo Amistades Peligrosas, the 1992 "Oveja negra" (Black sheep) by the hard rock/heavy metal band Barricada, and the 1994 "Alí, el magrebí" (Ali, the Maghrebi) by the punk-ska band Ska-P. Also, the two 1995 songs by the

Equatoguinean aunt and niece duet Las Hijas del Sol, "A ba'ele" (The foreigners) and "Tirso de Molina," as well as the 1996 "Que se te escapa el negro" (The *Negro* is getting away from you) by another female duo, Ella Baila Sola.

The Imagination of Race in "Africanos en Madrid" by the Duo Amistades Peligrosas

Ahead of the 1992 celebrations, the Felipe González government signalled Spain's political relevance on the world stage by hosting the first Middle East peace conference in November 1991. It is in this social and cultural climate that Amistades Peligrosas, a pop music duo formed by Cristina del Valle and Alberto Comesaña, released "Africanos en Madrid" from their album *Relatos de una intriga* – a song that, despite its title, aimed to call attention to the suffering of a single black African migrant newcomer. Comesaña and del Valle collaborated from 1990 to 1998, producing four albums and a compilation of best hits with the EMI label.[1] Well known in the musical milieu of the 1980s because of his participation in the Galician "rock-erotic" group called Semen Up, Alberto Comesaña was also a recognized figure, as a host and as an actor, on Galician television. Before Amistades Peligrosas, Cristina del Valle was part of the group Vodevil, and since the duet's dissolution she has dedicated herself more fully to diverse social causes; in 2000, she founded the *Plataforma Mujeres Artistas contra la Violencia de Género* (Women artists platform against gender violence). For her fostering of diversity and multiculturalism she has received many awards (see www.cristinadelvalle.com).

As Amistades Peligrosas, Comesaña y del Valle were famous for songs such as "Me quedaré solo" ("I'll be alone"), which won the 1996 *Organization Générale des Amateurs D'Eurovision* Song Contest, and "Estoy por ti" ("I am here for you"). They had a successful run in South America, going platinum in Chile and Argentina. In Spain, they managed to sell an impressive number of records – over one million copies altogether in the Spanish territory – and had a following receptive of their eclectic musical style that hoped for a "reconciliation." Indeed, fans rejoiced when the duet reunited in 2003 to produce *La larga espera* (The Long Wait) with the independent label Vale Music. This was a short-lived project focused on the objective of the album, which was to raise awareness about the plight of the Saharawi people, the inhabitants of the former colony of the Spanish Sahara, annexed to Morocco in 1979.[2] Aptly titled, *La larga espera* simultaneously makes reference to how long the Saharawi people have been waiting for independence and the right to self-determination, as well as to how long Amistades Peligrosas's fans had to wait – fifteen years – for Alberto Comesaña and Cristina del Valle to reunite, if only briefly. That they came back together to work on a project with clear ideological and political objectives is one more indication that, even though consumer capitalism is inherent in producing popular music, there is always the possibility of articulating resistance politics.

The 1991 song, with a title that places the presence of migrant newcomers in the nation's capital – "Africanos en Madrid" ("Africans in Madrid") – readily invites a comparison with Radio Futura's "Un africano en la Gran Vía." For one, the change from the singular "Un africano" (An African) in Radio Futura's song to the plural – "Africanos" (Africans) – in the Amistades Peligrosas piece, both literally and metaphorically, calls attention to what by the 1990s was perceived as an invasion of migrant workers from sub-Saharan Africa. The progression from singular to plural foregrounds this perception since, in actuality, the lyrics of "Africanos en Madrid" only describe the experience of a single black African man. The title also indicates a spatial change signalling that the presence of the postcolonial subject is no longer limited to one boulevard – the Gran Vía, as in the song by Radio Futura – but is now evident throughout the entire city of Madrid, as in Amistades Peligrosas' song. Significantly, the racial meaning attached to the term *africano* did not change since the plural form used by Amistades Peligrosas maintained the double semantic meaning – a man from Africa, a black man from Africa – attached to *africano* in the song by Radio Futura. Amistades Peligrosas privileged the second meaning when describing the migrant subject as being made of ebony and ivory, very much in tune with the 1982 single "Ebony and Ivory" by Paul McCartney – performed with Stevie Wonder – which emblematized the black person.

Inscribed, among other musical styles, in calypso rhythms that speak musically more of the Caribbean than of sub-Saharan Africa, the song, despite is title, narrates the everyday struggles facing one African man who embarked on the transnational search for work. By focusing on the trials and tribulations of an individual African man, the lyrics aim to humanize this liminal subject. The singing voices – the third person narrators – stand as a witness to the transnational experiences of this African migrant subject. The witnessing function is also highlighted since the singing subjects address both the audience and the African man who is trying to reach Madrid's Gran Vía without having the police ask for identification – and indication that the migrant subject is being catergorized as undocumented. Throughout the song, Amistades Peligrosas function as *de facto* witnesses giving testimony to Spanish audiences on the trials and tribulations of this particular migrant subject. This individualization feature is one of the song's contributions to combat the generalization of the title of the song and against the strait-jacketing images of racism that represent black persons from Africa as lacking humanity.

Personhood is articulated in the second stanza with references to emotions and sentiments in the lines that describe how the narrators are familiar with the comings and goings of this migrant newcomer as he searches for work throughout the nation's capital. By touching on the familiar – the lyrics clarify that this person has a hometown – the song allows for a complex political and social transnational process such as migration to be presented in a personal, experiential vocabulary. Also, it relies on empathy and solidarity as emotions with which to connect with the plight of this migrant subject. In so doing, "Africanos en Madrid" appears to have aimed to generate some kind of resistance to the prevailing social order, not only by exposing the abuse to which African immigrants were subjected by the police, but by presenting the dire conditions – such as homelessness – they confronted in Madrid. Actually, the song sought to get to core of the matter by resorting to the equation "sameness in difference": despite our ethnic/racial differences we all have a beating heart. The "heart," as the basic metaphor to allude to the humanity in all of us, is used to bring home in uncomplicated terms a message of solidarity with the migrant community. Though simple, the message was relevant since Lucrecia Pérez was to be murdered just a year later.

At the heart of "Africanos en Madrid" is also the issue of boundaries as per the reference to the *Plaza de España*. It is within the *Plaza* that we observe how deterritorialization, as a central force within global flows, was at work in 1990s Madrid since the song underscores the presence of "laboring populations in the spaces of relatively wealthy societies" (Appadurai 1996, 225). Under deterritorialization, Madrid's emblematic spaces such as the *Gran Vía* and *Plaza de España* became sites of contention where the new social and political landscape of Spain was constantly drawn and redrawn. Radio Futura foreshadowed this deterritorialization in their 1984 song "Un africano por la Gran Vía" by expressing uneasiness at seeing a black person – the African man described in the title and chorus – in a business suit in a café on one of Madrid's emblematic boulevards. In Amistades Peligrosas's narration of this foreign presence, the African nationals populating the semiotic architectural space called the *Plaza de España* have displaced Spaniards from the now uncannily and unfamiliar affect of this most familiar place (I emphasize here the presence of African nationals because of the song, but the *Plaza* functioned as a gathering place for immigrants of many nations and ethnic origins).

Located at the heart of one of Madrid's historic, business, and tourist districts, the *Plaza de España* was built – most of it between 1925 and 1930 – to emblematize Spanish national identity. Designed by architects Rafael Martínez Zapatero and Pedro Muguruza, and by sculptor Lorenzo Coullaut Valera, the monumental sculptural design of the Square has the lofty figure of Miguel de Cervantes gazing upon the bronze sculptures of his creations, Don Quixote and Sancho Panza. Though most of the monument was built between 1925 and 1930, it was only finished between 1956 and 1957 by Federico Coullaut-Valera Mendiguitia, the son of the original sculptor, during Franco's dictatorship. The identification of Spain – as per the name *Plaza de España* – with Cervantes and his creations, appears to echo, in a most imperial manner, Nebrija's "language is the empire's helper" motto (see figure 4). The three figures are spatial examples of sheer cultural immensity and stand as physical and concrete proof of the linguistic and literary turns of Spanish nationalism. The cultural shock to the Spanish social imaginary by what is perceived as an appropriation by black Africans of the *Plaza de España* cannot be underestimated, since what is at stake here is how the grandiosity of the physical space and its symbolic national meaning appears to be "devalued" by the presence of (non-white) postcolonial subjects.

Indeed, space is a site of racial anxiety in the song. By equating the urban spaces of Madrid with the new global and Atlantic order triggering so-called Third World migration, and the rural village with the African point of origin of the migrant, the song once again displaces the black subject to a rural territory from which Spain itself emerged in the 1970s. The reference to the migrant's village in the lyrics of the song is one of the most widely shared historical memories of Spanish culture of the 1960s and 1970s, when large groups of villagers emigrated to northern Europe and the Americas. By displacing the village to the other side of the globalized migration divide, once again, the song contains

4. Madrid's *Plaza de España* (Spain's Square).
Copyright Javier Lafora, 2014.

anxiety about sharing a historical and economic experience – rural migration. In this manner the lyrics relocate Spain and its capital as a First World, transnational, white space that does not share any historical relation with past migration experiences that now – according to the song – have become solely African and black. In this case, then, race also becomes a way to rewrite Spanish history and exorcise its own anxieties about being considered the "Africans" of Europe.

Ultimately "Africans in Madrid" proposes a shift on perspective that allows us to gain some insight into social relations framed by race and class and brought about by transnational capitalism. More specifically, the song calls attention to the fact that the global motions of peoples resulting from transnational capitalism are dependent on the actual exploitation, for the most part, of people like the African man of the song. Deemed "the salt of the earth," the migrant of the song is presented in constant motion looking for any kind of job. He is also presented in constant fear of being harassed by the police and it is to this policing and persecution that Barricada turns its attention in the 1992 album with the telling title of *Balas blancas* (White bullets).

Barricada: Violence and Misrecognition in "Oveja negra" (Black Sheep)

Barricada, a hard rock/heavy metal band from Pamplona (Navarra), appeared on the musical scene in 1982, the same year as Mecano, and disbanded in 2013 after thirty-one years together. The members were Enrique Villareal "El Drogas" (bass and vocals), Javier Hernández "Boni" (guitar and vocals), Alfedro Piedrafita (guitar and vocals), and Ibon Sagarna (Ibi), and their explosion on to the musical scene brought attention to how the so-called historical autonomous communities were sites of intensive creative energy. The group originated in the feisty neighbourhood of *La Txantrea* – located at the north end of the city of Pamplona and very committed to grass-roots enterprises – and was granted the title of "Best Group of Navarra" in 1984 by the readers of the Basque newspaper *Egin*. Very prolific and politic, Barricada even released a work focused on the Spanish Civil War titled *La tierra está sorda* (The earth is deaf) (Dro East West) in 2009; the group also contributed to the musical discussion to the criminalization of migration in 1990s Spain with "Oveja negra" (Black sheep). The song is the second track on *Balas Blancas* (White bullets), the album released in 1992 that went platinum leading radio station "*Los 40*" (The forty) to name Barricada the "most important rock band" (Zarata 1992).

Balas blancas established a paradigmatic moment in the racialization processes taking place in late twentieth-century Spain since it detailed the brutal violence racism exerted on black persons. It also exposed how this violence – real and symbolic – was justified, and continues to be justified, by a racist discourse of misrepresentations. Any discussion of "Oveja negra" must be framed within the already discussed historical significance of 1992, the year *Balas blancas* was released. For one, the series of staged public and international events served to mark Spain's coming of age as a postmodern democracy. However, the speed and complexity of the changes taking place between 1975 and 1992 had a disorienting effect on the Spanish nation leading to what at the time was termed as "social schizophrenia" by the media. The expression aimed to capture the bafflement experienced by the majority of Spaniards and the negative effects produced by the riches of late capitalism. Indeed, writers Juan Goytisolo and Rosa Montero point to racist and xenophobic attitudes as one of the most negative effects produced by Spain's sudden wealth (see Bermúdez 2001, 178; Flesler 2008, 30–1). And while Montero argues that, "pretentiousness, ostentation, superficiality, selfishness, and a rejection of the poor worthy of the newly converted" manifests itself "in an increased xenophobia and racism" (Montero 1995, 319), Goytisolo takes Spanish politicians to task in *El peaje de la vida* for not promoting civility and ethical concerns for migrant workers in "nuestro país de *nuevos ricos, nuevos libres, nuevos europeos*" (our country of new rich, new free people, new Europeans) (2000, 214, emphasis in the original).

Barricada's "Oveja Negra" deploys an ethnographic fixation on teeth to render evident that the desire to see "difference" requires paying attention to the body as a marker of social difference. Hence the need for establishing features that supposedly allow for the instantaneous recognition of such a difference. Racism is also operative in the misrecognition implicit in the naming of black persons as "cerdos" (pigs) by the policeman speaking in the song, and as such needs to be understood as an integral part of racism. Étienne Balibar ventures the idea that "the racist complex inextricably combines a crucial function of *misrecognition* (without which the violence would not be tolerable to the very people engaging in it) and a 'will to know,' a violent *desire* for immediate *knowledge*" (Balibar 1991, 19, emphasis in the original). Barricada's use of the dehumanizing metaphor "black sheep" foregrounds how racism collapses the distance between the signifier and the referent in the construction of persons as "black."

The objectification principle subsiding the distinct categories of "human" and "animal" is a discursive strategy that, according to Jerome C. Branche, can be traced back, in the Luso-Hispanic cultural tradition, to Gomes Eanes de Zurara's *Crónica dos feitos de Guiné* completed in 1453 (Branche 2006, 35, translated as *The Chronicle of the Discovery and Conquest of Guinea* by Charles Beazley and Edgar Prestage). In his evaluation of Zurara's *Crónica,* Branche highlights how this royal chronicler's account, "in recording an early instance of exploration-associated plunder, trade, and capital accumulation, prior to colonization proper, labels blacks and other colonized people as inferior, under various rubrics" (2006, 35) and, in so doing, establishes justifications for their subjection and "a discursive precedent for subsequent colonial writing" (2006, 35). The lyrics of "Oveja negra" make patently clear that this early (mis)representation of black persons is very much operative in 1990s Spain having survived slavery and the European colonial enterprises.

In fact, by alluding to hunting images, as in the Spanish police going after black migrant subjects, the song can be said to participate in a historiographic exercise that reminds us of all the expansionist narratives (mis)representing black persons as mere animals – as sheep and pigs in the song – that are to be "hunted down."[3] The hunting metaphors serve the purposes of institutionalized discrimination since the violence exerted on black persons is justified within the structures of power and as a necessary means to supposedly keep the social order. The high degree of violence in "Oveja negra" cannot be overlooked since it represents racial difference and anxieties such that both are simultaneously contained and canceled. Thus, while "Balas blancas" attests to the epistemic and corporeal violence exerted on black persons, the song is not exempt from racial containment. However, by exposing how the exertion of violence on black persons is justified to prevent a change in the power structures, Barricada offers an unequivocal questioning of racist discourses and ideologies. This is not an irrelevant gesture since it is within a racist discourse – articulated through a very complex shared historical past – that North Africans, particularly Moroccans, had "become the immigrant group most ill-regarded by Spaniards" (Martín Muñoz 2000, 32; Flesler 2008, 2). It is to them, and to all migrants from the Maghreb region, that Ska-P turned their attention in 1994.

Ska-P and the Plight of North African Migrant Workers in Fortress Europe

Transnational capitalism is also at the core of Ska-P's "Alí, el magrebí" (Ali, the Maghrebi), a song narrating in two voices – that of Alí, the migrant subject, and that of the band commiserating with his plight – the comings and goings of a North African Muslim migrant subject. A ska-punk band formed in the working-class neighbourhood of Vallecas (Madrid) in 1994, Ska-P, pronounced [ɛs ka pe], played together from 1994 to 2005 and then from 2008 to 2014, with the possibility of joining forces again in the future. The band members were Roberto Gañan Ojea (Pulpul), Ricardo Delgado (Pipi), José Miguel Redin (Joxemi), Julio César Sánchez (Julitros), Alberto Javier Amado (Kogote), and Luis Miguel García (Luis Mi). Their nonconformist attitude is musically reflected by their eclectic affiliations to hard rock and ska-punk, among other hardcore musical styles. The band name is a play on the Spanish word for escape and ska p(unk). The name further takes advantage of the letter k common to ska, and, since the early 1980s, also closely associated with the spelling of Vallecas as Valle*k*as.

"Alí, el magrebí" – written by Tony López and Roberto Gañan Ojea and with music by López – belongs to their self-titled 1994 album *Ska-P* (with the label Balboa Recording Corporation) and narrates the trials and tribulations of this particular migrant newcomer. In the song, Alí, emblematizing the feared Arab-Muslim world of the Global South, wanders through several rich and (mostly Christian) European cities – emblematizing the Global North – searching for work. Original in its presentation of a character named Alí, the song allows him to directly address Ska-P's fan base to remind them that he has already been introduced as a character in track 3 of the album in the song titled "Chupones" (Leeches). It is in "Chupones" that Alí introduces himself to the audience as an already criminalized migrant worker that is apprehended and condemned for carrying ten grams of hashish while major drug dealers conduct their business in the Spanish territory with impunity. The creation of a character traversing songs underlines the importance Ska-P grants to lyrics, which are highlighted by their loud musical style – a common sound feature of participatory music defined by Thomas Turino as having "[d]ensely overlapping textures, wide tunings, consistently loud volume, and buzzy timbres" (Turino 2008, 46). Ska-P consistently used all of these in their albums and live concerts.

In "Alí, el magrebí" both melody and lyrics underscore Ska-P's belief in the social function of music to nourish communities and to inspire solidarity towards those less fortunate and suffering from injustices. The song is grounded in repetition both melodically and in the lyrics. On the one hand, Alí's name is repeated seventeen times – once by the lyric voice representing the band, and sixteen times by the chorus. On the other, Alí implores Allah five times in the song's last four lines. By having Alí address the public directly, Ska-P goes against the general tendency to discuss migration in statistical terms and the presence of migrant newcomers in abstract and general terms. The need to avoid abstractions and generalities was argued by Najat El Hachmi, the Moroccan-born Catalan writer who, in the prologue to her 2004 *Jo també sóc catalana* (I too am Catalan,) explained her mixed-genre text as a response to the abundance of statistical analyses assessing immigration since "people are not known through statistics" (2004, 12). As a text offering what the author calls "pensament de frontera" (border thinking), *Jo també sóc catalana* works with several genres at once – autobiography, analytical essay, and fiction. This bridging of genres aligns El Hachmi with the border thinking proposed by Chicana writer Gloria Anzaldúa in *Borderlands/La Frontera* (Martin-Márquez 2008, 346–7; Ricci 2010). Anzaldúa's discussion of the ability to traverse linguistic borders – Spanish and English in her case – as tools that allow for "border thinking" finds an echo in El Hatchmi's understanding of the similarities between the linguistic marginalization of her own native Amazigh, which is a minority language in Morocco spoken by Berbers, and that of her acquired Catalan. El Hatchmi makes this point when explaining to her son Rida, born in Catalonia, that "Amazigh has always been considered secondary, strictly an oral language, barbaric, they say [...] your other mother tongue, Catalan, was once persecuted and despised, it's not in vain that your mother feels that they are two sister languages" (2004, 27).

Border thinking is not articulated in "Alí, el magrebí" since the song follows the story of a migrant worker in constant motion. In this, the song adheres to a storyline similar to the one presented in "Africanos en Madrid." It begins by describing why Alí left his country – to run away from abject poverty – and ehow the journey implies much peril and personal loss. However, Ska-P expands the witnessing function present in "Africanos en Madrid" by producing a song with two sets of voices – that of Alí, and that of the chorus/band denouncing his situation – that moves beyond mere witnessing.

The lyrics also establish that migration processes are, at the core, narratives of the particular that need to be told by the actual agents, as Chab Samir does. Ska-P brings to the fore that the border crossing of subjects, money, material goods, cultural practices, ideologies, and symbols is tied to globalized capitalism, a point made by Joan Manuel Serrat in his 1989 "Salam Rashid" and his 1992 "Disculpe el señor." Indeed, transnational capitalism is central to Ali's plight since the naming in the song of all the European cities – London, Paris, Rome, Berlin, and Madrid – through which he has wandered looking for work, highlights how immigration, racism, and xenophobia need to be addressed within the global labour flows linked to transnational capital. It is not irrelevant that London, Paris, Rome, and Berlin are urban emblems of the wealth and power associated with the nations of the Global North.

Ska-P recognizes Alí's subjectivity by alluding to cultural and religious practices such as the holy month of Ramadan and the symbol of the *hilãl*, the "crescent moon" that is misidentified in the song as "media luna" (half-moon). The song realistically addresses clandestine migration for what it is: a brutal process by which the migrant worker wandering through Europe in search of a job suffers abject hunger but, more poignantly, lack of solidarity and general indifference from fellow human beings. This lack of social and ethical concern for immigrant workers in general, but North African migrant workers in particular, was horribly displayed in the early days of February 2000 when Spanish anti-Moorish xenophobia lead to, in the words of Juan Goytisolo, "escenas de saqueo de los pequeños negocios de los inmigrantes, incendios de chabolas y oratorios por encapuchados, caza despiada de magrebíes" (scenes of looting of small immigrant's businesses, the setting on fire of shacks and public phone establishments by hooded men, the merciless hunt of Maghrebi) (2000, 219).

Ultimately, and while the lyrics do not make a direct call for solidarity (as Ska-P does in the *Planeta Eskoria* song "Lucrecia" analysed in chapter 4), it is safe to assume that this was the song's ultimate objective based on the band's record of social commitment (see http://www.ska-p.com/) and their denunciation of Spanish racism and xenophobia, which extends to Spanish Immigration Laws in the 2000 song "Lucrecia." Tellingly, by the mid-1990s and within an increasingly diverse social landscape, actual migrant newcomers produced more compelling denunciations of Spanish racism, as is the case of Equatoguinean duo of Paloma Loribó and Piruchi Apo performing under the name Las Hijas del Sol.

Equatoguinean Responses to Racial Profiling: Las Hijas del Sol, Singing in Bubi and Spanish

Las Hijas del Sol first appeared on the musical scene in their native Equatorial Guinea where their talent was rewarded by the Hispano-Guinean Cultural Center in Malabo during the time Donato Ndongo-Bidyogo served as adjunct director (García-Alvite 2004, 156; Martin-Márquez 2008, 340). In 1992 they were selected to represent their nation at Seville's Expo' 92 and, sometime thereafter, Loribó and Apo fled their nation to engross the ranks of the Equatoguinean community living in the former metropolis. In so doing they joined the many thousands of Equatoguineans in exile escaping both the brutality of Teodoro Obiang Nguema's regime – in power since toppling his uncle Francisco Macías Nguema in 1979 – and the corruption of the Nguemist oligarchy.[4] In 1995, and already residing in Madrid, Las Hijas del Sol released *Sibèba*, their debut album, produced by the alternative label Nubenegra and sang almost entirely in Bubi. The only song in Spanish, "Tirso de Molina," is a rendition of "A ba'ele" (The foreigners), inviting an interconnected reading of the two pieces. Both songs offer a gendered understanding of the social process of migration and show the manners in which ethnicity, class, and gender intersect (see Pedraza 1991).

The duo released four more recordings during their run – two with Nubenegra, *Kottó* (1997) and *Kchaba* (1999) – and mostly sang in Bubi as *Sibèba*. At the beginning of the twenty-first century they were recruited by the multinational label Zomba records, releasing *Pasaporte mundial* (World Passport) (2001) and *Colores del amor* (Colours of love) (2003), mostly in Spanish, with El Retiro ediciones musicales, which works with Zomba records in Spain (García-Alvite 160). The five albums, all produced in Spain, are a testament to the social practices and systems of belief of the Bubi ethnic group to which the two artists belong. And, in producing these records, as García-Alvite indicates, "the Bubi singers were passing along the histories and indigenous knowledge of their place of origin as they struggle against material deprivation and cultural oppression" (García-Alvite 2004, 151). This is not an irrelevant task in the context of what continues to transpire in present-day Equatorial Guinea, where the Nguemist policies are bent on destroying Bubi culture – and all other perspectives that are not Fang, the group to which the majority of the Nguema clan belongs. In fact, the need to recover traditional Bubi songs and legends – as in "Boto I" (a song for the rite of fertility) and "O wato wa baye" (about the mother goddess of the Bubi people, Bisila) – is openly alluded by the artists in the CD liner.

Not surprisingly, and given their musical commitment to Bubi culture and traditions, Las Hijas del Sol were placed under the "world music" banner, resulting in the exoticization of the marketing and presentation of their albums.[5] And, while I agree with Philip V. Bohlman that when discussing world music "the old definitions and distinctions don't hold any more" (2002, xi), I also believe it is important to remember that, as the critic points out, world music is also "traditional music repackaged and marketed as popular music" that "owes its origins to the 1980s, *when the executives of record companies and advertising specialists determined that popular music from outside the Anglo-American and European mainstreams needed a distinctive name*" (Bohlman 2002, xiv-xv, emphasis mine). Indeed, as Stephen Feld persuasively argues in "A Sweet Lullaby for World Music" (2000), we must remember that while musical identities and styles are now more than ever manifestly transient and in continuous states of fusion due to globalization (Feld 2000, 145), "in the end, no matter how inspiring the musical creation, no matter how affirming its participatory dimension, the existence and success of world music returns to one of globalization's basic economic clichés: the drive for more and more markets and market niches" (Feld 2000, 168). The market's drive notwithstanding, we cannot overlook that in their work Las Hijas del Sol inscribed a central postcolonial tenet in the racial hierarchization processes taking place in late twentieth-century Spain. Indeed, Loribó and Apo had high degrees of control in the production of *Sibèba* since they were responsible for the musical arrangements of all songs – except for the three traditional ones – as well as the original authors of eight of the fifteen songs that constitute *Sibèba*. And, it bears repeating, Las Hijas del Sol offer a gendered understanding of the causes – escaping a brutally repressive military regime in their native Equatorial Guinea – processes, and consequences of, in this case, forced migration.

As postcolonial subjects, migrant women, and members of the African diaspora, Paloma Loribó and Piruchi Apo directly spoke – instead of being spoken about – to the constant fear, sorrow, and displacement experienced by migrant newcomers (Martin-Márquez 2008, 340). All of these experiences are at the core of both "A ba'ele" (The foreigners), track 3 of the album, and "Tirso de Molina," track 15. In fact, both begin with urban sounds – a motor roaring and the siren of a police car or an ambulance – mixed with those of African drums and the inconsolable wailing of a woman to which "A ba'ele" (The foreigners) responds:

No llores más.	Do not cry anymore
¡Ay, ay qué dura es esta vida!	Ah, Ah, how hard is this life!
¡Ay, ay, no, no, ya no puedo más	Ah, ah, no. no I cannot go
Antes canté sobre las burlas, ahora sobre el emigrante]	Before I sang about jokes now about the emigrant]
para el que el llanto se ha convertido en una rutina.]	For whom crying has become a routine.
En mi país, bín que mal, soy una persona como los demás]	In my country, mo' or less, I am a person like everyone else]
Cuando salimos de casa nos sentimos aliviadas]	When we left home we felt relieved
pero al llegar aquí encontramos problemas peores.]	But when we got here we encountered worse problems.]
¿Cómo llegaré a Atocha?	How will I get to Atocha?
¿Cómo llegaré a Gran Vía?	How will I get to Gran Vía?
¿Cómo llegaré a Bilbao?	How will I get to Bilbao?
¿Cómo llegaré a Tirso de Molina?	How will I get to Tirso de Molina?
Sin que la policía me ponga las manos encima]	Without the police getting their hands on me]
y sin que la policía me meta en el talego.	Without the police getting me in the pokey.
El problema de los extranjeros hay que vivirlo,]	Only those who experience being a foreigner]
sólo así podrás comprenderlo.	Can understand the problem.
lyöò aè weé	Lyöò aè weé
Lloro a los emigrantes diariamente detenidos y despreciados]	I cry for the emigrants that are daily detained and rejected.]
¿Qué puedo hacer? No puedo avanzar ni retroceder]	What can I do? I can't move forward nor back-up]
ese es mi vehículo y no tiene marcha atrás.	That is my vehicle and does not back up.[6]

The song addresses placelessness – the term belongs to Philip V. Bohlman when speaking of "placelessness in world music" (2002, 115) – by pointing first to a country of origin with the lyric "In my country." Then, by narrating a journey from that place of origin – "When we left home" – and, lastly, by exposing the condition of feeling displaced in the receiving country with "but when we got here we encountered worse problems." Placelessness is also at work in the series of questions seeking to determine how to get to the four well-known metro stations in the Madrid system – everyday destinations with which the migrant newcomer needs to become rapidly familiarized if s/he is to survive in the Spanish capital. Madrid, metonymically represented here by the references to the metro destinations of Atocha, Gran Vía, Bilbao, and Tirso de Molina, becomes the emblem for the place where displaced peoples and cultures inhabit.

And once again fear becomes the emotion connected to motion and mobility, as in Amistades Peligrosas's "Africanos en Madrid," since the distinctive attribute of placelessness is dreading capture and incarceration, in this case, by the Spanish police. Las Hijas del Sol, as postcolonial subjects seeking to navigate the metropolis, give testimony to their own experiences and to the anxieties and trepidations of black migrant subjects using Madrid's metro system. Indeed, the anaphoric repetitions presented in the questioning of how to arrive to each of the listed destinations serve to underscore the constant "without the police getting their hands on me / Without the police getting me in the pokey." In so doing, "A ba'ele" exposes the panic with which black immigrants experience the construction of transnational identities (see figure 5).

Fright, sorrow, and fear are at the centre of "Tirso de Molina," a rendition of "A ba'ele" in Spanish that stresses the suffering – as per the repetition of "grief" in the first four lines – of the singing voice. Here the postcolonial subject is a woman pleading with her Spanish audience to not make her feel "like a stranger." The CD liner lists Pablo Guerrero as the author of "Tirso de Molina"; however, as Susan Martin-Márquez has argued, given that Guerrero basically revisits the worries and trepidations originally articulated by Loribó and Apo in "A ba'ele" (The foreigners) this song needs to be read as a version of the original (Martin-Márquez 2008, 340). Here are the lyrics:

5. Madrid's Tirso de Molina Metro Station.
Copyright Javier Lafora, 2014.

Tirso de Molina

¡Ay, dolor, cómo siento el dolor!
¡Ay, dolor, más no puedo sufrir!
¡Ay, dolor, sólo puedo llorar!
¡Ay, dolor solo puedo cantar!
Camino por las calles
No hagas sentirme una extraña.
Me lo hace vivir
la policía de España.
Me lo hace sentir
la residencia en España

Ah, grief how I feel the pain!
Ah, grief I cannot suffer any longer!
Ah, grief, I can only cry!
Ah, grief, I can only sing!
I walk through the streers
Do not make me feel like a stranger.
It makes me experience it
the Spanish police.
It makes me feel it
residing in Spain.

Por trabajar	To work
en un país diferente	In a different country
dejé mi hogar,	I left my home,
mis paisajes y mi gente.	my landscapes and my people.
Duras son para mí	Hard are for me
las calles de Madrid.	Madrid's streets.
Como intrusas sin voz	Like intruders without a voice
de la Puerta del Sol nos echan.	They kick us out of the *Puerta del Sol.*
No sé llegar a Atocha.	I do not know how to get to Atocha.
No sé llegar a Gran Vía.	I do not know how to get to Gran Vía.
No sé llegar a Bilbao.	I do not know how to get to Bilbao.
No sé llegar a Tirso de Molina	I do not know how to get to Tirso de Molina.
Sin poder volver la vista	Without being able to turn my gaze
ni a delante ni atrás.	neither forward nor back
¿Cómo llegaré a Atocha?	How will I get to Atocha?
¿Cómo llegaré a Gran Vía?	How will I get to Gran Vía?
¿Cómo llegaré a Bilbao?	How will I get to Bilbao?
¿Cómo llegaré a Cuatro Caminos?	How will I get to Cuatro Caminos?

"Tirso deMolina" concludes with the same set of questions articulated by Las Hijas del Sol in "A ba'ele." Both stanzas – the third in the first song and the concluding one in the second – are governed by a desire to know how to find the way to four specific metro destinations in the nation's capital. By presenting us a Bubi and a Spanish version of their plight seeking to navigate the nodes and links shaping Madrid's metro system, Las Hijas del Sol participate in the articulation of a diasporic consciousness that operates in a global flow.

Exerting Violence on Black Men: Ella Baila Sola's "Que se te escapa el negro"

On 3 March 1996, by a narrow margin, the conservative *Partido Popular* ended the era of the Felipe González's Socialist governments by winning the general election. And, signalling a dramatic shift in the construction of Spanishness, José María Aznar, the new prime minister, began promoting an image relying on a "Castilianizing, monarchical, and homogenous historiographical paradigm" (Delgado 2002, 326; see also Delgado 2014). During Aznar's two mandates (1996–2000, 2000–4), the Spanish economy experienced an unprecedented growth – not seen since the years of *desarrollismo* – that had many in the media and financial sectors speaking of a "Spanish economic miracle." The (mis)perception that everything was golden in Spain at the cusp of the twenty-first century was summarized by Aznar with the infamous "España va bien" (Spain is doing great) phrase. However, the so-called "economic miracle" was accompanied by a strong precarization of the job market and unrestrained real estate speculation. As we now know now, the latter would bring the miracle crashing down in flames. In the musical arena – with less dire consequences – Spain also got to witness a similar scenario in the rise and fall of Ella Baila Sola.

The duo of Marta Botía and Marilia A. Casares performed under the name Ella Baila Sola from 1996 to 2001, releasing three albums with EMI-Odeon: *Ella Baila Sola* (1996), *E.B.S.* (1998), and *Marta y Marilia* (2000), which earned a nomination in the 2001 Latin Grammys. Highly successful during their run, Ella Baila Sola's first self-titled album sold over one million copies in Spain and close to seven hundred thousand throughout Latin America. In addition to their love songs that reached the top of the charts – "Amores de barra" (Bar's love affairs) and "No lo vuelvas a hacer" (Don't do it again), among others – their migration themed song "Que se te escapa el negro" enjoyed likewise commercial success.

The singing voices of Ella Baila Sola directly address a singular "you," the supposedly "good cop" of a couple of officers chasing a young black migrant man for illegally selling tobacco in the metro. The use of both *negro* and *negrito* make clear that the officer's justification for persecuting this particular migrant subject – he is selling "death" – is a laughable excuse, as attested by the ironic references to it being a sin to sell cigarettes in a country of, at that time, chain-smokers. In fact, by insisting on describing the migrant subject as *negro* and *negrito*, the song speaks to the racist workings of a cultural imaginary that has inscribed black persons as "negative difference" for over four hundred years "(Branche 2006, 2). This "negative difference" was much at work during the expulsion of 103 black African migrant workers in July 1996 by plane, and where some of them were administered tranquillizers to "keep them calm." The event stands out as a most troubling example of institutionalized racism. The legitimization of such an act – drugging people while being expelled – was sealed with the infamous phrase "there was a problem and it was solved" uttered by Major Oreja, the interior minister during José María Aznar's first presidency. Such articulation underscores how Spanish discursive parliamentary practices were used to legitimize the expulsion. Using a dominant strategy of racist discourse, that of the "negative other-presentation" – the categorization belongs to van Dijk (2005, 28) – the migrant workers to be deported were presented as a problem that needed to be solved by any means necessary. The episode exposes the brutal dimensions of patrolling Spain's borders at the national level, as in the deporting of drugged black African immigrants, or at the local level, as in the fictionalized persecution of the street vendor in "Que se te escapa el negro." In so doing, the song invited audiences to consider what policing the Spanish state actually entails, and how the securitization of migration persecutes individual subjects.

Moreover, and by presenting the migrant subject as a street vendor – a *vendedor ambulante*, known in Spain as "top manta," which literally means "top blanket" – the song reminded the audience that "the racial/colonial hierarchies that were put in place on a world scale during the European colonial expansion are now reproduced within the metropolitan global cities" (Grosfoguel, Cervantes-Rodríguez, and Mielants 2009, 7).[7] In depicting a black African migrant worker as a street vendor, Ella Baila Sola's song converses with Donato Ndongo's third novel *El metro* (The Subway) (2007), where we follow the hardships of Lambert Obama Ondo, a black migrant from Africa surviving in Madrid as a *vendedor ambulante*. Early in the novel we are informed that Obama Ondo is surprised by his predicament:

> Lambert Obama Ondo nunca había imaginado que los derroteros de su vida le condenarían a ser sólo un pobre vendedor ambulante. Cuando terminó de ordenar sobre la estera de coloures adquirida a un marroquí que andaba con ellas colgadas al hombro, inconmovible ante la Mirada indiferente de los muchos transeúntes que transitaban por la Puerta del Sol – de Madrid al Cielo, había oído a los más viejos del lugar – Obama Ondo fijó su mirada en esos escasos productos que constituían su negocio y todo su mundo, dispuesto a esperar lo que le proporcionara el nuevo día (Ndongo 2007, 19)

> Lambert Obama Ondo had never imagined that life's twists-and-turns would condemn him to be only a poor street vendor. When he finished organizing on top of the coloured blanket bought from a Moroccan that wandered around with them hanging from his shoulder, unmoved before

6. Street vendors in Madrid. Copyright Javier Lafora, 2014.

> the indifferent gaze of the many passers-by moving through the Puerta del Sol – "From Madrid to Heaven" he had heard from the older citizens of the city – Obama Ondo fixed his gaze on those few products that constituted his business and his whole world, ready to face what the new day was to bring (see figure 6).[8]

Ndongo's description brings to the fore the dim economic prospects of the undocumented migrants that have risked their lives to get to Spain. In narrating the life and death of Lambert Obama Ondo – he is murdered by a skinhead in Madrid's Metro – Donato Ndongo exposes how the realities of current discrimination, racism, exploitation, poverty, and forced migration need to be assessed against the "civilized" Western notions of human rights, democracy, egalitarianism, and freedom. I argue Ella Baila Sola's "Que se te escapa el negro" commits to the same project by calling attention to how all those mighty European notions and achievements are easily – and brutally – forgotten in the everyday life practices with which Spain, now a full-fledged European nation, entrusts its police to enforce immigration laws and to execute "border control." In so doing, Ella Baila Sola's "Que se te escapa el negro" works against exoticization while showing us the insidious nature of prejudice.

Conclusion

Amistades Peligrosas's "Africanos en Madrid," Barricada's "Oveja negra," Ska-P's "Alí, el magrebí," Las Hijas del Sol's "A ba'ele" (The foreigners) and "Tirso de Molina," as well as Ella baila sola's "Que se te escapa el negro" contribute to the imagination of race in 1990s Spain by exposing how migrant newcomers are (mis)represented as racialized non-white counterparts – mostly "black" and "moorish" – to a seemingly homogeneous (and white) Spanish identity. In this, the songs validate Jerome Branche's argument that Luso-Hispanic cultures operate within a five-hundred-year tradition that has "inscribed blackness as negative difference" (2006, 2). The topic of racism resonates loudly in the six songs studied in this chapter, though fittingly, more so, in Las Hijas del Sol's "A ba'ele" and "Tirso de Molina," since the actual migrant subjects musically denounce racism while also considering the social consequences of gender. Both Barricada's "Oveja negra" and Ella Baila Sola's "Que se te escapa el negro" denounce racism, policy brutality, and the criminalization of migration. And while all but Las Hijas del Sol's songs call attention to the complex social dynamics unleashed by transnationalism and the articulation of a global economy, "Alí, el magrebí" more clearly exposes transnational capitalism's contradictory pulls. On the one hand, those pulls need cheap labour from the Global South and East to enrich European nations, while, on the other, that same workforce was, and continues to be, detained, persecuted, and deported due to the European Union's Immigrations Laws at the national and transnational levels, maintaining Fortress Europe.

4
Twenty-First Century Musical Landscapes in Spain: From Ska and *Música mestiza* to Singing, Chilling, and Rapping against Racism

If Lucrecia Pérez's murder in November 1992 shocked Spain into facing its underlying racism and xenophobia, the events of February 2000 in El Ejido, the agricultural centre in the southern province of Almería, forced the country to recognize, in a most brutal manner, that racial prejudice had become unmanageable. In the 2000 episodes, migrant Moroccan workers endured three days of violent racist attacks that destroyed their houses, shops, mosques, and many buildings housing institutions providing services to them (Checa 2001). For writer and cultural critic Juan Goytisolo, exploitation and racial discrimination were at the heart of El Ejido's 2000 xenophobic aggressions, problems to which he had already called attention in an article published in *El País* in February 1998. Titled "El Ejido, quién te ha visto y quién te ve" (El Ejido, who has seen you and who sees you today), the author denounced the inhuman conditions in which Moroccan and black migrants worked and lived, criticizing Spaniards for forgetting their own past poverty and forced emigration. As a direct response to the 2000 racist attacks, Juan Goytisolo joined forces with the Algerian-French renowned political philosopher Sami Naïr (1946–), an expert on migrations, to produce *El peaje de la vida: Integración o rechazo de la emigración en España* (2000) (The toll of life: integration of the rejection of emigration in Spain).

The virulence that turned local protests on security issues into mob violence should be understood within Spanish discourses that have conjured up the image of the violent invading Moor throughout centuries. In the global arena, the identification of Muslims with terrorism is but one of the manifestations of the new racial discriminations so prevalent these days and where discourses, representations, and practices have shifted "from ethnic and color lines to religious and cultural affiliations or differentials (Gana 2008, 1573). This contemporary phase of racialization, emphasizing cultural and religious differences as sources of new prejudices and discriminations, has developed and thrives within the globalization of capital and the expansion of neoliberalism (Balibar 1991, 15-23, and Macedo and Gounari 2006, 3–35, among others). Indeed, the migrations propelled by neoliberal policies and transnational capitalism have been the source of modern racist and fascist activity, leading Étienne Balibar to described "migration as a substitute for the notion of race" (1991, 20).

In the case of Spain, the only country in Western Europe to have been Islamized for seven centuries (711–1492), some of the current racist manifestations take place within a particular historical situation in which Islam is not a "new reality."[1] Spain's Muslim past continues to be a conflictive one in the nation's cultural imaginary and is articulated as either alien to or substantive in the process of Spanish identity building (Zapata-Barrero 2004, 140). However, the emergence of different racist reconfigurations has not meant the end of the old racisms. As Jerome C. Branche argues when discussing the Luso-Hispanic worlds, the naturalization of negatively charged racial naming is one of the legacies of Spanish and Portuguese colonialism that black persons continue to endure (2006, 4). As I discussed in chapters 2 and 3, this reality was forcefully set out by Equatoguinean author Francisco Zamora Loboch in *Cómo ser negro y no morir en Aravaca*. And both Branche and Zamora Loboch, aware that racial hierarchies are interdependent of time and place, demonstrated that the devaluation of black persons has been supported by the weight of four hundred years of Spanish and Portuguese literary traditions.

To combat racisms old and new, and to address issues of citizenship in a globalized world, many states in Western Europe, including Spain, implemented multiculturalist policies with varying emphasis and degrees of success (see Soysal 1994; Velasco 2000). According to Harald Runblom the term "multiculturalism," in Europe, has no fixed definition; it can refer both to the description of a culturally, linguistically, and ethnically diverse society as well as, in its normative use, to the peaceful coexistence among groups of diverse origins (Runblom 1994, 624). It is in dialogue with this former understanding of multiculturalism – which foregrounds the need to work with and through difference to find democratically harmonious solutions – and against the new, and not so new, racial discriminations that Ska-P, Che Sudaka, and Chambao appeal to solidarity and denounce racism with songs released between

2000 and 2009. In their reflections on race in constitutional Spain, Concha Buika and El Chojin embark on different musical projects. Buika proposes a new multicultural, multiracial Spanish identity in her fusion of flamenco, jazz, and Caribbean rhythms while El Chojin, with raps published between 2009 and 2011, adheres to identity politics in the Spanish context and furthers the anti-racist stances first advanced in his 1999 "Mami, el negro está rabioso." All of the soundtexts analysed in this chapter attest to a "multicultural configuration of Spain" – a categorization that I borrow from Ana Corbalán and Ellen Mayock's *Towards a Multicultural Configuration of Spain: Local Cities, Global Spaces* (2015).

In assessing the works by Ska-P, Che Sudaka, Concha Buika, Chambao, and El Chojin, I also take into account the complex Spanish political landscape of the first decade and a half of the twenty-first century during which Spain dealt with both the international terrorism affiliated with Islamic fundamentalism – as per the 11 March 2004 Madrid terrorist attacks – and the devastating economic crisis of 2008, from which Spain has yet to recover as of late 2016. The precarious situation in which millions of Spaniards were left because of the implosion of the Spanish housing and banking markets, much political corruption at all levels of government, and the inadequacy of the responses by both the Spanish Socialist Workers' Party and the People's Party led to the vibrant grass-roots protests of 15 May 2011, creating what is known as the 15-M Movement that, in turn, gave rise to the party Podemos. Lead by Pablo Iglesias, Podemos jolted the Spanish political landscape by forcing a radical change to the two-party system in place since 1982. However the supposed historic breakthrough by the coalition Unidos Podemos (Together We Can) – with the joining of Izquierda Unida (United Left) – in the 26 June 2016 election did not materialize, as already discussed in the introduction. For its part, the Popular Party increased its number of seats in parliament, enabling Mariano Rajoy to be re-elected as prime minister of a minority government.

Ska-P's "Lucrecia" and the Case against Immigration Laws

In 2000 the band Ska-P, whose "Alí, el magrebí" I discussed in the previous chapter, also contributed to discussions on multiculturalism and *mestizaje* – hybrid social constructions within migratory transnational and global processes defining twenty-first century Spain – by releasing the fifteen-track album *Planeta Eskoria* (Planet Skum) (BMG). In songs such as "Lucrecia" (track 11) and "Mestizaje" (Cultural mixing) (track

14), which I am not discussing, Ska-P invited its public to embrace the cultural, ethnic, and religious diversity brought to the Spanish social landscape by migrant subjects while questioning globalization's impact on migratory processes. The album also focused on an array of other social and political issues such as the United States' invasion of Iraq in "Tío Sam" (Uncle Sam) (track 12), questioning Spain's bullfighting tradition in the song "Vergüenza" (Shame) (track 2), and addressing domestic violence in "Violencia machista" (Macho violence) (track 13) (see www.ska-p.com for the band's complete discography). The album's diverse social concerns corroborate Ska-P's anti-authoritarian ideological stance, as does the deliberate misspelling of *escoria* – meaning "dregs" or "scum" – with a "k" and its toying with Spanish phonetics (the letter "c" sounds like "k" when preceding "o").

Issues of migration and racial domination are central to Ska-P's "Lucrecia," the band's belated homage to Lucrecia Pérez, the black Dominican migrant woman to whom Carlos Cano's dedicated "Canción para Lucrecia" discussed in chapter 2. Racial domination, as a system, is produced by discriminatory practices "that result in the problematization, marginalization and exclusion of non-Europeans by Europeans" (van Dijk 2005, 2–3).[2] By speaking to this marginalization and exclusion in 2000, eight years after Lucrecia's 1992 murder, the band reminded their listeners that racism was still rampant – as evidenced in the El Ejido episodes – and needed to be forcefully denounced. To call attention to such matters in 2000 was a difficult task since other ghostly returns preoccupied Spaniards when the first mass grave of the Spanish Civil War was unearthed in Priaranzo de Léon under the initiative of the *Asociación para la recuperación de la memoria histórica* (The Association for the Recovery of Historical Memory) (see http://memoriahistorica.org.es.) The Civil War was very much present that year when José María Aznar secured, by absolute majority, a second term as prime minister and declared that "la Guerra Civil puede darse finalmente por concluída" (the Spanish Civil War can finally be considered to have concluded) (quoted by Charles Powell 2001, 625).

By honouring Lucrecia, the band asked the nation to face more recent "ghosts": those of the migrant workers killed in racist attacks since 1992. The band used the occasion to question racial phenotypes and the economic dislocations brought about by global capitalism. The lyrics, as listed in Ska-P's official website at http://www.ska-p.com/content/lucrecia, advance social solidarity; the repetition of words – and sounds and rhythms when listening to the song – serve several functions at once. First, it brings Lucrecia back from the dead forcing Spanish audiences to remember the shameful historical moment that ended the migrant worker's life. Second, repetition facilitates memorization of the lyrics since almost each one of the lines is repeated at least twice. Lastly, repetition – a strategy often employed in advertising – pounds anti-racist ideas into the minds of audiences and listeners. Throughout the musical and lyrical pounding, the band, by connecting migration to poverty, asks the public to understand that it is global capitalism that has prompted millions of destitute people from the Global South to migrate to the Global North. Moving from economic to legal concerns, the song also tackles the *Ley de Extranjería* (Immigration law) that for Ska-P is but institutionalized racism; this prompts the band to call all Spaniards to participate in civil disobedience by not following the law's mandates. In so doing, Ska-P renders visible their belief in music's ability to impact the public sphere and to inspire people to action through emotion.

By reminding the public that Lucrecia Pérez is the tragic emblem of Spain's racist violence against migrants, Ska-P validates the notion that "music is a particularly powerful resource for building and bonding communities" (Turino 2008, 210). For the band such bonding arises in solidarity, when individuals come together to collectively take a stance against racists, racism, and nationalistic ideologies that promote border controls. In so doing, Ska-P appears to denounce the discriminatory provisions driving the revisions proposed by the Partido Popular's *Ley de Extranjería, 8/2000* (Immigration Law 8/2000) where Spanish borders become permeable for certain groups of people, such as wealthy foreigners like the multimillionaire sheiks that have properties on the Andalusian coast and other privileged foreigners like Queen Sofia (born in Athens, Greece). By making Lucrecia Pérez's 1992 murder relevant in 2000, Ska-P impugned migratory policies reifying social and economic divides, demanding that both Queen Sofia and the multimillionaire sheik be subjected to *La Ley de Extranjería*.

Ska-P's concerns were well founded since it was in 2000 that the Partido Popular's *Ley de Extranjería, 8/2000* abolished "the many positive elements of the broadly supported previous law (4/2000), adopted just a few months earlier, but never implemented" (van Dijk 2005, 19). Secured in their new parliamentary majority, the PP disregarded the protests of all opposition parties as well as immigrant organizations to impose a law that meant migrants losing essential medical, legal, and educational benefits. Ultimately, Spain's *Tribunal*

Supremo annulled eleven provisions of the law, exposing the PP's willingness to curb the human rights of migrants. Ska-P's commitment to a multicultural, multiracial Spain at the dawn of the first decade of the twenty-first century will reverberate in Che Sudaka's semi-autobiographical 2003 song "Sin papeles" (Undocumented) and in Concha Buika's 2005 "New Afro Spanish Generation." According to Ska-P, the time has come for Spain to stop being "disoriented" – as suggestively proposed by Susan Martin-Márquez's *Disorientations: Spanish Colonialism in Africa and the Performance of Identity* (2008) – and finally embrace "the realities of a modern-day *convivencia*" (Martin-Márquez 2008, 355, emphasis mine). In fact, Ska-P more daringly stood against immigration control and was for full open borders (see Hayter 2000, for global open borders). This is the project to which Che Sudaka is fully committed.

Che Sudaka: Migrant Musicians, *Música mestiza*, and Being "Sin Papeles" (2003) in Barcelona

As already mentioned in the introduction, Che Sudaka was formed in 2002 and, with much irony, reappropiates the derogatory term "sudaca" to self-identify as a "grupo Argentino-Colombiano afincado en Barcelona" (Argentinean-Colombian group residing in Barcelona) (see http://www.chesudaka.com/index.php/en/) which shares with many of their followers and other migrant newcomers the experience of being undocumented. In the section entitled "La banda" (The band), which narrates the history of Che Sudaka, we are informed of their personal understanding of migration issues in Spain at the turn of the twenty-first century since: "los cuatro músicos sudamericanos [...] vivieron en su popria piel la dura vida del inmigrante sin papeles" (the four South American musicians lived in their own skin the hard life of the undocumented migrant) (see under "About" at https://www.facebook.com/chesudaka and www.chesudaka.com/index/php/es/la-banda). As mentioned in the introduction, the musicians, two brothers from Argentina, Leo and Kachfaz, and their Colombian peers Cheko and Jota (no last names to mark their anti-system stance), met while busking around Barcelona's historic Barrio Gòtic (Gothic Quarter). More specifically, they met around the area popularly known as Tripi Square – in allusion to drug induced "trips" that would take place in the area and to the surrealist sculpture placed at the centre of this location on September 1991, which can be experienced as a "trip." It is in honour of the particular location where they first met that Che Sudaka titled their first album *Trippi Town* (2003).

The Square was officially inaugurated on 23 September 1991 as part of the refiguration of the city of Barcelona, getting ready for its global close-up as the site of the 1992 Summer Olympic Games.[3] In praise of what journalist Lluis Permanyer considered a successful beautification process, he invited the reading public to visit the still unnamed location as follows: "Recientemente nació una plaza encantadora en plena calle Escudellers, que aún no ha sido bautizada, y de ahí que para localizarla tenga que precisar que está delimitada por las calles Arai y Carabassa" (Reccently a charming square was born in the middle of Escudellers Street, which has not yet been named, and hence to locate [the place], my need to specify that is delimited by Arai and Carabassa Streets) (Permanyer 1991, 9). The sculpture was a large-scale reproduction of the eighty-centimetre 1935 work titled "Monument" by leading Catalan surrealist artist Leandre Cristòfol (1908–98). In 1996 Barcelona's city hall honoured George Orwell's commitment to combat fascism during the Spanish Civil War by renaming the space *Plaça de George Orwell* (George Orwell Square).[4] For Che Sudaka, the Square – the popular designation of Tripi Square remains to this date – marks both the beginning of their journey as musicians and the one that will take them from undocumented migrants to citizens with legal status. Thus, their 2003 album pays homage to the place where, within the boundaries of Barcelona's urban centre, they first developed a sense of belonging to a global multiracial, multiethnic, multicultural community fully engaged in the musical hybridity that has come to define Barcelona's pulsating *música mestiza* scene.

To document this ebullient musical scene, journalist Miguel Amorós and photographer Xavier Torres-Bacchetta produced the book *Barcelona és bona si la música sona* (2012) (Barcelona is good if the music plays) where they explore how local and global musicians from diverse ethnic/racial identities, and an array of musical backgrounds, have contributed to the explosion of musical *mestizaje* in Catalonia's capital city. The volume's title is another play on the popular saying "Barcelona és bona si la bossa sona" (Barcelona is good if the purse is full).[5] Che Sudaka joins the list, along with the other seventy-nine Barcelona-housed bands/groups exploring *música* mestiza throughout the city. Among those, I call your attention to bands such as Microguagua (see https://www.facebook

.com/microguaguaband/) and RumbAmazigha (see www.rumba mazigha.com/es), both of which are examples of the emergence of new musical manifestations in Barcelona simultaneously underscoring both the heteregenous national/ethnic/racial origins of band's members as well as their varied musical styles. Microguagua define themselves as "el resultado natural de una ciudad mestiza en el alma como lo es Barcelona. Siete músicos de países, culturas y estilos musicales diferentes que se encuentran en los callejones del centro histórico dando vida a una banda fresca, vitalista, y llena de energía positiva, que productores y prensa todavía no pueden clasificar" (the natural result of a mixed city as Barcelona is in its soul. Seven musicians from countries, cultures, and different musical styles that met in the alleys of the historical centre, giving life to a fresh, lively, and full of positive energy band, that producers and the press cannot yet classify) (see "About"). For its part RumbAmazigha underscores their being a collective engaged with North African musical paradigms while concurring with Microguaga that their musical productions defy categorization: "Un proyecto del Taller de Musics que nace para impulsar y mezclar músicos de procedencias diversas, geográficas y estilísticas, Rumba catalana y música popular amazigha intercambiando sus lenguajes musicales, melodías y ritmos, para crear colectivamente un sonido popular, bailable, festivo, propio y sin etiquetas." (A Musicians Workshop's project created to promote and mix musicians from diverse geographical and stylistic origins, Catalan Rumba and Amazigh popular music exchanging their musical languages, melodies, and rhythms, to collectively create a popular, danceable, festive, particular sound without labels) (see "Inicio").

Microguagua and RumbAmazigha, as does Che Sudaka, embrace *mestizaje* as lived experience: as "a lived process, which encompasses, but is not limited to, ideology, involves the maintenance of enduring spaces for racial-cultural difference alongside spaces of sameness and homogeneity" (Wade 2005, 240). And while Wade's proposal to rethink *mestizaje* centres on Latin America, specifically on Colombian popular music, Venezuelan popular religion, and Brazilian popular Christianity, the migrant musicians of the above-mentioned bands, and in particular Che Sudaka, as undocumented migrants upon arrival attest to *mestizaje* being a "lived process" that takes place within the diverse diasporic communities living in twenty-first century Barcelona. In fact, the critic himself calls attention to the fact that the concept of *mestizaje* is receiving increasing attention in Europe when discussing "processes of racial and cultural mixture" (2005, 240). Indeed, discussions on *métissage*, hybridity, and *mélange* have taken place in French and Francophone postcolonials studies since the 1990s, as in the musical *métissage* assessment of the French *banlieue* musical scene (Cannon 1997; Oscherwitz 2004, among others).

Among the eighty bands/groups included in *Barcelona és bona si la música sona*, Che Sudaka is one of the most popular ones in terms of distribution and circulation, having already performed over 1,300 concerts throughout Europe and Latin America. The band believes in the social function of music. More importantly, they embrace that their transient musical identities and styles are in a constant state of fusion due to the borderless nature of their global cultural project, as summarized in the expression "Arriba la vaina hasta ke choke China Kon Afrika! (Hooray until China krashes with Africa! – I am using the letter "k" instead of the letter "c" to capture the use of the letter k in the original Spanish).

It is in this musical context that the dance-inviting cumbia "Sin papeles" resonates within Barcelona's contemporary multicultural and diasporic identity. By questioning social exclusion through a soundtrack that underscores the fluid and dynamic relation between popular music, identity, and place in twenty-first century Spain, the song speaks to the "diasporic cultural and political strategies in which migrants, refugees, and diaspora populations detached from nation-states situate themselves in global flows and build new homes for themselves" (Stokes 2004, 59). In true *música mestiza* fashion, Che Sudaka mixes cumbia rhythms with a melody that would be easily recognized by any of Sting's fans; namely, the single titled "Englishman in New York" from his second solo studio album *...Nothing Like the Sun* released in October 1987 by the label A&M Records. "Englishman in New York" was released in February 1988 as the third single from the album, becoming very popular in Europe throughout 1988.[6] Sting's song addresses migration, exposing, when compared to "Sin papeles," the class and economic hierarchies at the core of why individuals from certain nations can reside legally in the cities of the Gobal North, while others cannot. In this case, the individual from the United Kingdom is now residing legally in New York City, one of the emblematic global spaces/places of contemporary multicultural and diasporic identity.

Che Sudaka's "Sin Papeles" playfully samples the melody of "Englishman in New York," ironically rephrasing the famous line enunciated in the 1988 production where the English speaker establishes his legal status in the United States. In a parody of that coveted legal status, Che Sudaka presents the voice of a first-person migrant newcomer, identifying himself as a *sin papeles* (undocumented) in the European Union, and highlighting the criminalization of migration by alluding to the pistols carried by the Guardia Civiles (Spanish Police) and their show of force through *machista* attitudes. Moreover, the joke would not be lost on those familiar with Sting's "Englishman in New York" since the reference in the first line of the Che Sudaka song is not to drinking tea but rather *mate*. The Barcelona-based band refashions Sting's opening line where Britishness is established by the fact that the singing subject does not drink coffee, as New Yorkers do, but tea, a practice of everyday life that has come to be associated as a national identity marker for Britons. As it is well known, *yerba mate* is considered Argentina's national drink – as well as in other South American countries such as Paraguay, Uruguay, and Brazil. Thus, by bringing a cultural practice associated with a particular national identity – Argentina in this case, which speaks to the points of origin of two of the members of Che Sudaka – the band attests to the multicultural practices that take place in the global city of Barcelona. And while "Sin papeles" unequivocally shows the diverse vulnerabilities experienced by undocumented migrants – which are shared by the band members – the song, ultimately, is an invitation to a twenty-first century *convivencia* and to the recognition that *mestizaje* is a lived experience.

Concha Buika: Race and Multicultural Identities in Twenty-First Century Spain

Born María Concepción Balboa Buika in 1972, singer Buika praised the emergence of a multicultural Spain in "New Afro Spanish Generation," the opening track from her 2005 debut album *Buika* (Dro East West). The song does not directly address migration but, by focusing on racial and ethnic identity markers as they pertain to the definition of a "new generation," actively engages in the imagination of race in twenty-first century Spain. As evidenced by the song's title, the singer embarks on a bilingual effort where, as per the lyrics quoted below, English serves the artist to address racial categories such as Afro American (misspelled both "afro" and "american" in lower case letters) and "Afro Spanish" (also misspelled in lower cases). The consideration of racial and ethnic classifications also includes the Spanish gendered terms *paya* (used by Gypsies to define a non-Gypsy person) and *gitana* (Gypsy). All are relevant to the questioning of musical, national, and racial identities enacted by Buika, a second-generation Spanish black woman born in Palma de Mallorca to exiled Equatoguinean parents (see *Afro-Europe International Blog* 2009). Drawing upon the complex histories that intersect in her personal life, Buika, as an emblem of this "New Afro Spanish Generation," symbolizes the fusion of identities and subject positions, even interrogating the concept of gender by exploring its performative quality to expose the fluidities of said performances – an aspect to which Jerome Socolovksy calls attention in his November 2008 interview with the artist for National Public Radio (NPR).[7] She has also come to embody the hybridization of musical genres, the sheer personification of eclecticism.

In Spain, Buika was heralded for infusing the Spanish *copla* with new life, but in the US she has been placed within the "world music" niche, which I consider a ghettoization strategy. This approach was patently at work in the advertising booklet of the Los Angeles Philharmonic Orchestra for the 2010–11 Season. Under their "World Music Series" her 10 November 2010 concert was announced as follows: "Spanish-born Concha Buika is a mesmerizing presence, her voice reminiscent of Cesaria Evora and a flamenco singer" (Los Angeles Philharmonic Orchestra 2010, 16).[8] The reference to Cesaria Evora served to make Concha Buika identifiable and consumable precisely because of her "otherness" – both in terms of race and in terms of musical genres – which, according to the booklet's description, she supposedly shares with the Cape Verdean artist.

Tellingly, the presentation failed to mention that Buika's third album, *Niña de fuego* (Girl of Fire), had been nominated for the 2008 Latin Grammy Award for Album of the Year or that her second album, *Mi niña Lola*, had been awarded the "Premios Música 2007" (Music awards 2007) in the category Best Album in Spanish Song (Mejor Album Canción Española) in Spain. In fact, underscoring the 2008 Latin Grammy Award nomination would have proved to be a wiser marketing strategy since on 11 November 2010, and at the eleventh annual Latin Grammy Awards, Buika's fourth album, the 2009 *El ultimo trago* (The Last Drink) with Chucho Valdés, earned the 2010 Latin Grammy Award as "Mejor Álbum Tropical Tradicional" (Best Tropical Traditional Album). Rather, by having chosen to present Buika in comparison to Evora, the booklet portrayed the artists as equal in their difference, said difference being the commodity advertised to motivate concertgoers to buy tickets. However, to ensure Buika was not just (mis)represented as "another" Cesaria Evora, the booklet's description also identified her voice with that of a "flamenco singer" (Los Angeles Philharmonic Orchestra 2010, 16).

An illuminating observation since, as I argue, the performer's talents as a flamenco singer as well as her alliances to flamenco fusion are relevant to our appreciation of "Afro Spanish Generation." Written by Buika, the song, lasting just under six minutes, appears to have been primarily conceived for dancing. It pulsates with salsa rhythms that are enriched by Buika's engagement with the vocal ranges and tonalities particular to singers of flamenco. By de facto mixing the musicalities of salsa and flamenco, "Afro Spanish Generation" embraces hybridity and creolization thus becoming the ground where musical, national, and racial identities are questioned and reformulated. None of these aspects are foreign to flamenco since blending with other musical styles speaks to a tradition of experimentation that allow us to "trace a map of sub-genres within the general category of *flamenco fusión*, namely, the alloy of flamenco with other world sounds, comprising of rock, blues, and hip-hop, among others" (Pérez 2006, 76; see also Gamboa 2005, Paetzold 2009). Indeed, flamenco's ability to transcend boundaries was certified on November 2010 when the UNESCO inscribed this cultural form – "fusing song (*cante*), dance (*baile*) and musicianship (*toque*)" – on the Representative List of the Intangible Cultural Patrimony of Humanity (see Mitchell 1994 for a history of flamenco).

In going beyond the mere mixing of diverse musical patterns, the practice of flamenco fusión allows for "new modes of expression that help re-think the configurations of local identities and even address concerns about racial, sexual, and class issues at a local as well as at a global level," as Jorge Pérez argues when analysing the work of the female trio Las niñas in *Ojú* – an album integrating elements of hip hop, soul, funk, blues, and jungle into flamenco (Pérez 2006, 77). A similar desire for musical integration drives "Afro Spanish Generation," where the rethinking of identities takes centre stage, prompting Buika to challenge, without further elaboration, the "gitana" (Gypsy)-"*paya*" (non-Gypsy) dichotomy. I quote the lyrics from the CD liner, there are no page numbers:

We are living times of progress
We are the new afro spanish [*sic*] collective
From the spanish [*sic*] collective
We are the new afro spanish [*sic*] collective (three times)

Me da la gana de sentirme acompañada para el resto de mi vida Me da la gana de que me arañen un poquito el corazón] La soledad viene sin patria donde te pilla te mata, mi hermano	I feel like having company for the rest of my life I feel like having my heart a bit torn Solitude comes without fatherland Where he finds you he kills you, my brother]
Dame la mano, Tanta patria y tanta convicción Tú vas a acabar sin corazón yo no Porque yo libre soy,	Give me your hand So much fatherland and so much conviction You will end up without a heart not I Because free I am,
Chorus No soy americana, No llevo en la sangre, Ni raza gitana Ni paya llevo por dentro. I´m not afro american [*sic*] This is my country I am from the barrio Madrid siempre será el centro,	**Chorus** I am not American I do not carry in my blood Nor gypsy race Nor *paya* inside me. I am not Afro American This is my country I am from the *barrio* Madrid will always be the centre
New afro spanish [*sic*] generation. Nueva generación española New afro spanish [*sic*] generation Me da la gana de sentir la madre patria en el centro de mi tierra Ay porqué yo ya he tenido mucha guerra	New afro spanish [*sic*] generation. New Spanish generation New afro spanish [*sic*] generation I feel like feeling the motherland in the centre of my land Alas, I have had already had too much war]

Chorus

No soy americana,	I am not American
no llevo en la sangre,	I do not carry in my blood
ni raza gitana	Nor gypsy race
ni paya llevo por dentro.	Nor *paya* inside me.
I´m not afro american [*sic*]	I am not Afro American
this is my country	This is my country
I am from the barrio	I am from the *barrio*
Madrid siempre será el centro,	Madrid will always be the centre.
New afro spanish [*sic*] generation	
Y siento ansias de rendirme a tantas cosas	And I long to surrender myself to so many things]
que ya no siento tormento de na'	That I no longer feel torment for no'ting
Yo quiero el sur y el norte pa' mis venas	I want the South and North in my veins
Barrera pa' quien las quiera, ay dios	Barriers for those who want them, My God
Ay que ya libre soy	Alas, that finally free I am
No soy americana	I am not American
We are a new afro spanish [*sic*] collective	

The opening stanza, repeated three times, considers Spain's new multiethnic landscape a sign of progress prompting the singer's affirmation: "we are the new afro spanish [*sic*] collective." The same pronouncement is repeated as the song ends, both attesting to Buika's belief in multiculturalism and the advantages of diversity in constructing a unified nation. Tellingly, the articulation of this new collective identity is partially articulated in English – opening and closing stanzas, as well as the chorus. And as we shall see, Buika's use of the English language is a discursive strategy that goes to the heart of identity politics: while she is black and she is the daughter of African parents, she rejects the "Afro-American" label that appears to have been thrown at her. Thus, it is only in English and in response to this particular identifier that Buika can offer her "new Afro Spanish collective." Buika may have become familiar with said labels and the American racial stratification system during her 2000 stint in Las Vegas as a Tina Turner lookalike – she also played one of The Supremes.

Throughout the song the performer insists on repeating "No soy Americana" (I am not American) and "I'm not afro american [*sic*] / This is my country." These two assertions – "I'm not afro american [*sic*] / This is my country" – acquire their full relevance in English given that it is in the English language that the term "Afro-American" was born.[9] In so doing, Buika seems to be questioning the imposition of racial identities that belong to other countries and realities, and the references point to the United States as the originator of such impositions.[10] Both in Spanish and English Buika negates said markers and asserts, first in Spanish – "No soy Americana" – and then in English – "I'm not afro american [*sic*]. In both instances, and as songwriter and performer, Buika exerts her agency and her desire to reinforce a Spanish identity by rejecting labels from the country that has appropriated the term "American" for itself – the United States – and that has created the racial term "Afro-American" as an identity marker. By insisting on her Spanish nationality and that "Madrid siempre será el centro" (Madrid will always be the centre), the artist argues for the creation of a new "Spanish collective" – an Afro Spanish collective – that identifies Spain as her country of origin. Her literal and metaphorical underscoring of Madrid's centrality, the country's capital, further reinforces this positioning. It would be a mistake, however, to understand Buika's assertions about Spain and Madrid as patriotic.

To avoid such perceptions, the singer makes a point of questioning patriotic notions. She appeals to the shared experience of "solitude" while drawing attention to the element of violence involved in the defence of the fatherland, in the defence of boundaries. The experience of solitude is called upon to accentuate that this particular human experience transcends patriotic ideologies. Then the singing voice personalizes the argument by directly addressing a singular "you" to assert, in two enjambed lines, that patriotic convictions will end up leaving that person enslaved to such ideologies and, ultimately, without a heart – once more a metaphor for humanity. The power of the argument rests in its being personal; the enjambed sequence inscribes the singing voice's opposing position to accentuate the difference between her freedom and their enslavement: "Tanta patria y tanta convicción / Tú vas a acabar sin corazón yo no/ Porque yo libre soy" (So much fatherland and so much belief / You will end up without a heart not I / Because free, I am). Freedom from patriotic notions is also used by Buika to denounce "war" and "heroes" as two negative consequences associated with the defence of the motherland: "yo ya he tenido mucha guerra / A mí el héroe se me murió" (I have had enough war already / To me the heroe is dead). Ultimately, the specific references to the epistemic violence exerted in the defence of the motherland show that, while the song aims to engage our bodies by inviting us to dance to its salsa rhythms, through its lyrics, it also seeks to engage our minds. Thus, "New Afro Spanish Generation" stands as an anthem to the formation of new identities, the ones now defining present-day Spain and well represented in bands such as Che Sudaka, Microguagua, and RumbAmazigha.

Flamenco Chill and Chambao's "Papeles Mojados": *Pateras* and Migration As Death

Chambao's distinctive musical style first appeared in a double compilation CD titled *Flamenco Chill* (2002, Sony), assembled by the band and which included other followers of this particular fusion. The term "flamenco chill" identifies the flamenco-electronic modality that fuses flamenco sounds and *palos* with electronic music. The term "chambao" is a localism from the Spanish South that refers to any improvised beach tent seeking to shelter from the sun and wind. The resourceful but shifting and temporal nature of such refuge appears to symbolize well the band's several transformations, though Chambao's core continues to be María del Mar Rodriguez Carnero, known as Lamari. Originally a trio, formed by Lamari, Eduardo Casañ (El Edi) and Daniel Casañ (Dani), Chambao released their solo debut album *Endorfinas en la mente* (Endorphins in the mind) in 2003, which earned a Premios Ondas musical award. In 2005, they released *Pokito a poko* (Step by step) (Sony BMG). In 2006, with a new formation, Chambao produced a double CD compilation titled *Caminando* (Walking) (Sony BMG), which included a DVD; and in 2007 *Con otro aire* (With another air) (Sony BMG), which includes, as the first track, "Papeles Mojados" (Wet Papers). The song reached the top of Spain's *Cuarenta principales* by January 2008 and due to its success was rereleased in 2008 along with a new version – a duet with Greek performer Elena Paparizou – in the CD single titled *Papeles mojados* (Sony BMG) (see Paetzold 2009, 217; for Chambao's complete discography see http://chambao.es).

Written by Lamari, "Papeles mojados" incorporates North African music and vocals to reflect on the tragically failed journeys of migrant newcomers seeking to leave behind poverty and powerlessness and who have turned the Mediterranean into, "a *mare mortum* / *mare monstrum*, a rotten sea of dead bodies adrift, a liquid cemetery" (Sarnelli 2015, 150, emphasis in the original). It is in this liquid landscape of treacherous journeys that have shipwrecked *pateras* take centre stage in a song that brings into focus, "the sharp edges of fortress Europe[,] made most evident by the dreadful death toll of would-be migrants lost at sea during perilous crossings as they try to enter ... Spain, Italy, Malta, and Greece" (Geddes 2008, 29). The opening lines are in a Tuareg dialect from Algeria and are neither presented in the CD liner nor posted on any of the websites listings the lyrics, but can be heard in the YouTube video.[11] And thanks to Hakim Abderrezak's persistence, with the help of his colleagues from Algeria, we know that the lines in the Tuareg dialect repeat the words "papeles mojados." As the song begins, we are presented with stereotypical images that represent migrants as an invading dark mass with no agency. The images, all too familiar for the past three decades, continue to be constantly flashed on all media outlets, having become a staple of television daily news, and a contested issue in the political arena (Triandafyllidou, Modood, Zapata-Barrero 2006, 3).

"Papeles mojados" needs to be understood within the complex geographical notion of "Spanish-African borders" – the term is used by Jørgen Carling – that refer, on the one hand, to the combined length (eighteen kilometres) of the perimeters of the land borders between Morocco and the Spanish enclaves of Ceuta and Melilla (Carling 2007, 317). On the other hand, it refers to the maritime borders that "cover more than a thousand kilometers along the south coast of the mainland and around the Balearic and Canary Islands (Carling 2007, 317). It is in connection to the maritime borders that Chambao attests to the continuous symbolic and material relevance of *pateras* and *cayucos* in the socioeconomic, political, and cultural Spanish landscapes by narrating the story of those who leave a wake of wet documents after the drowning of one such boat. The popularity of the song cannot be overlooked since it shows how these tattered boats continue to represent migration as a naval invasion in the Spanish cultural imaginary well into the twenty-first century.

Despite the problematic stereotyping, Lamari's words, soulful voice, and heartbreaking rendition clearly appeal to compassion and empathy, thus linking emotion, music, and the materiality of migration for audiences and listeners. In at least one arena, that of massive popularity, the emotional plea appears to have succeeded since, as mentioned earlier, "Papeles Mojados" reached the top of Spain's *Cuarenta principale*s in early 2008. And while the melodic rhythms and musical blending of flamenco guitars and lutes may account for much of the song's success, it is my contention that its success also derives from the lyrics and their invitation to experience a wide range of emotions. Indeed, the lyrics invite audience and listeners, if they so wish, to empathize with the emotions felt by the migrants – the fear felt by those embarking on these treacherous journeys. They are also asked to consider sympathizing with the singer's heartbreak, or they may choose to share in the singer's rightful desperation, or respond to her appeal to "walk in their shoes." In all instances, the melodic ranges of flamenco, perfectly suited to sing about despair, heartbreak, and sorrow, serve Lamari well to expose how songs both "mean" and "do" something to their audience and listeners. In regards to "meaning," and as a performative speech act seeking to create understanding, Chambao's "Papeles mojados" is an important contribution to reimagining ways to combat racism and xenophobia. On the subject of "doing," Chambao brings forth empathy and compassion seeking to change the hearts and minds of their fellow citizens.

El Chojin: From "N.E.G.R.O." (2009) and Spanish Identity Politics to "Rap vs. Racism" (2011)

Ten years after "Mami, el negro está rabioso" (Mama the black man is mad), El Chojin's reiterated his compelling criticism of Spanish racism in "N.E.G.R.O.," a song from the 2009 album *Cosas que pasan, que no pasan y que deberían pasar* (Things that happen, that do not Happen, and that should happen) (Boa). This is the artist's tenth album and, according to *Rap: 25 años de rimas* – the history of Spanish rap co-authored by El Chojin and Paco Reyes – the record made him the Spanish MC with the most published references (318). This is a distinction that speaks to his relevance and popularity on the musical scene, of consequence when discussing a song such as "N.E.G.R.O." Indeed, it is here where El Chojin further theorizes race as lived experience, relying on the potentialities of identity politics to respond to his nation's overvaluation of whiteness (Bermúdez 89). The song marks an important development in El Chojin's socially conscious rhetoric, standing as a testimony of black consciousness in 2000s Spain. The effort to facilitate black agency through racial identification, is an untried endeavour in the Spain born after the constitution of 1978. And given that there have been no major shifts in regard to racism, or minor changes either according to the rapper, N.E.G.R.O. needs to be considered as one of the first manifestos arguing for the practice of identity politics and the defence of blackness in present-day Spain. When El Chojin released *Cosas que pasan, que no pasan y que deberían pasar* in 2009, Spain was marred by the bleak socio-economic outlook as a result of the implosion of the real state bubble in 2008 and the global financial crisis. In fact, the album's title could be understood as, at one level, referring to what was and was not transpiring with jobs, the economy, and, immigration.

In 2011, the prolific artist published the above-mentioned *Rap: 25 años de rimas, un recorrido por la historia del rap en España* with Paco Reyes, and the single-authored *Ríe cuando puedas, llora cuando lo necesites* (2011). And with Sony Music his album *El ataque de los que observan* (The attack of those who pay attention), which includes the identity politics manifesto "N.E.G.R.O," a song exposing Spain's social divisions along the colour line. For the rapper, racial divides have not lost their social significance and given his nation's continued refusal to admit its own racism, he raps to show us how race remains a central issue in twenty-first century Spain. The lyrics leave no doubt about the importance of racial hierarchies in the multiethnic landscape of constitutional Spain, since the very first line addresses the construction of blackness through the visual and discursive narratives perpetuating stereotypes. The rapper enumerates the list of hackneyed images populating Spanish television screens – these include *pateras*, African street vendors, and prostitutes on Spanish streets and highway exits – that end up reducing black persons to what Jerome C. Branche, when discussing slavery, describes as "the marginality and disempowerment of subpersonhood" (2006, 83).[12] The rapper then lists the many ways and forms in which blackness is devalued to finally present one of the song's central tenets: black persons are not to be taught, but respected. Respect, if we recall El Chojin's 1999 "Mami, el negro está rabioso," is what he has been demanding for the past decade through rap, a musical genre that arrived in late twenty-century Spain as the dominant modality for discussing race in the United States.

That the artist had to return to discussing racism in his 2009 "N.E.G.R.O." clearly indicates that respect continues to be hard to come by in Spain's current socio-racial dynamics, where concrete and everyday experiences of inequality render untrue egalitarian rhetoric. For El Chojin, a tenuous *convivencia* may arrive but, first, Spaniards need to become aware of the discursive practices reifying racism. To contribute to consciousness-raising he directly addresses questions of race and blackness at the end of the first decade of the twenty-first century.[13] And since rap, due to its own musical and social history, is the genre that can "sell" – literally and metaphorically – blackness to transcultural/

transnational audiences, El Chojin begins by inviting the audience to look up the pejorative and negative connotations assigned to the word "negro" in the dictionary of the Spanish language. And if one finds the term "negro, negra" (Black man, black woman) in the *Diccionario de la Lengua Española*, in its twenty-first edition from 1992, which is the one I have handy, the negative connotations are there for all to see, with the first one being: "[d]e color totalmente oscuro, como el carbon, y en realidad falto de color" (of totally dark colour, such as coal, and actually lacking in colour) (1992, 1015). El Chojin also calls attention to how the term means "sumamente triste y melancólico" (extremely sad and melancholic) (1992, 1015).

The central assumptions of the term are fully operative in racism, since, as in the definitions quoted, we see an attempt "to fix and naturalize the difference between belongingness and otherness" (Hall 1996, 445). By displaying how the term has been used as a weapon for marginalization, El Chojin appears to echo John Lipski's and Jerome Branche's scholarly endeavours – discussed in previous chapters – which centre on dismantling the vernacular expressions, the linguistic terminologies, and literary discourses that reify racial naming. And if, in regard to the power of the written word, Branche's motivation for writing *Colonialism and Race in Luso-Hispanic Literature* was to call attention to the "epistemic violence such writing has perpetrated and continues to perpetrate" (3), our rapper's impetus appears to be clear: promote black consciousness while bolstering the notion that "black does not equal inferior."

Indeed, using the power of strategic essentialism, El Chojin advances identity politics in Spain by boldly asking everyone to embrace the word *negro* without fear and with much pride (Bermúdez 2015). Agency, then, is derived from fully taking up the term and from rejecting the many euphemisms that are used in the Spanish language to avoid enunciating the term *negro*, among which we find the idiom, which I use in *Rocking the Boat*, "subsahariano" (sub-Saharian) or, among others, "morenito" (darkie). And while, as indicated by the title, the main focus of "N.E.G.R.O." is to address blackness as lived by the author and other fellow Spaniards, the experiences of Muslim women are made relevant by the discussion of the headscarf issue.[14] The cultural conflict of the hijab in the classroom focuses on the integration of migrant populations and has been a source of discord in many European nations. But soon after bringing up this issue, El Chojin returns to the central topic of the song, which is to utter and repeat the word "negro." By using participatory techniques to enact the enunciation of the word *negro*, El Chojin hints at the kind of effort that may be required to build a more equitable Spanish nation.

The artist returns to combat racism in the 2011 joint venture titled "Rap vs. Racismo" which was promoted by the Movimiento contra la Intolerancia (Movement against intolerance) and the Ministerio de Sanidad, Política Social e Igualdad (Ministry of Health, Social Politics and Equality). As per the YouTube video, El Chojin and thirteen other Spanish rappers – Lírico, Santo, El Langi, Kase O, Nach, Locus, Ose, Nervizzo, Sho Hai, Zatu, Gitano Antón, and Titó Xhelazz – take turns to discuss race and racism following the call-and-response structure of rap (for access to the video go to El Chojin-YouTube at https://www.youtube.com/watch?v=Zl8W6ddWfM8). This particular pattern of call-and-response facilitates community engagement since, instead of having a single musician, we have a group of rappers collectively creating and performing the song. In his El Chojin's Canal oficial de YouTube (Official YouTube channel), the famed rapper posted the video of "Rap vs. Racismo" by stating:

> Nuevo videoclip de El Chojin del tema "Rap vs. Racismo" donde cuenta con las colaboraciones de Lírico, Santo, El Langi, Kase O, Nach, Locus, Ose, Nervizzo, Sho Hai, Zatu, Gitano Antón, Titó y Xhelazz. El tema y el videoclip forman parte de una campaña de la ONG Movimiento contra la Intolerancia. El videoclip viene de manos de Bajocero Producciones.
>
> (New videoclip of El Chojin of the topic "Rap vs Racismo" where he counts with the collaboration of Lírico, Santo, El Langi, Kase O, Nach, Locus, Ose, Nervizzo, Sho Hai, Zatu, Gitano Antón, Titó, and Xhelazz. The rap and the videoclip are part of the campaign by the NGO Movement Against Intolerance. The videoclip comes from Bajocero Producciones.) (see https://www.youtube.com/watch?v=Zl8W6ddWfM8).

"Rap vs. Racimo" attests to how this musical modality is linked to larger social forces – in this particular case to actively combat racial discrimination. As per El Chojin's above description, the grounding element of this consciousness-raising activity is the participatory techniques used by all the rappers to engage the audience in a collective undertaking to eradicate racism and truly create a just and fair Spanish society for all. Aware that music allows people to interact within and across cultures, Movimiento Contra la Intolerancia not only was behind this particular 2011 campaign, but between 2011 and 2013 the ONG's website used the rap as its background music. And after the campaign activity the song, always readily available through El Chojin's YouTube channel, continues to serve as a constant reminder for the need to actively engage in questioning prejudiced conceptions of otherness and to fully embrace the ethnic/cultural/social/linguistic/religious mosaic that has defined constitutional Spain since the late twentieth century (see Dirlik 2008 for possible pathways to overcome political and cultural racialization).

Conclusion

As I pointed out in the introduction, the Spanish general elections of December 2015 and June 2016, as perplexing as they were and further complicating an already complex political environement, stood in stark contrast with what was transpiring, for example, in the 2016 presidential elections in the United States where the Republican candidate touted the creation of a "Fortress United States," which would separate itself from Mexico by a wall. And also in contrast with the anti-immigration sentiment behind why a narrow majority of British voters in Britain's Brexit referendum succeeded in having their nation leave the European Union. In Spain there were no anti-immigration calls from the mainstream parties to rally support. In fact, movements such as the *Indignados* and political parties such as Podemos place the blame of what ails Spain squarely on the shoulders of those who are "stealing" from the middle class and workers: bankers, tax dodgers, and low-paying jobs. But it would be misleading to assume that Spain had completely abandon its anti-migrant stances, which is what Juan Carlos Checa Olmos and Ángeles Arjona Garrido warn against in their "Anti-Immigrant Feeling in Spain" (2012) using data from the opinion survey firm, Análisis Sociológicos, Económicos y Políticos (Sociological, economic, and political analyses) for the period 1997–2007 (Checa Olmos and Arjona Garrido 2012, 42–4).

Moreover, the radical changes and upheaval brought by the severe economic crisis of 2008, and from which Spain continues to suffer as this book goes to press in 2017, have transformed the nation, once again, from a receiving to a sending society. Thus, while experiencing recession and high unemployment – at 20 per cent in April 2016 – *El País* bluntly stated that: "La crisis acelera la emigración de españoles a

Europa y América" (The crisis accelerates the emigration of Spaniards to Europe and America) (Nogueira 2012). The central point of the article is to underscore the astonishing change "de ser un país que batía récords de recepción de inmigrantes, desde el año pasado son más los que salen de España que los que llegan a ella" (from being a country that broke records for receiving immigrants, since last year there are more leaving Spain than those that come to nation) (Nogueira 2012). Among many factors, and as I have also explained in the introduction, the decrease can be explained by the fact that the impacted points of entry to Fortress Europe have moved further east, to the so-called Eastern Mediterranean route when Greece overtook Italy as the first European Union country of arrival.

In terms of the Spanish musical landscapes of the past thirty plus years, all the songs analysed in *Rocking the Boat* demonstrate that popular music is not – as Adorno argued – a mere commodity shaped by market forces. On the contrary, the various sites of production and reception of popular music encompass complex cultural and political realities that reveal artistic agency and ethical concerns. Only by studying music within the context of cultural studies and literary studies – through close textual reading – can we ascertain the role of artistic agency in the songs by Radio Futura, Mecano, Amistades Peligrosas, Barricada, Ska-P, Las Hijas del Sol, Che Sudaka, Ella Baila Sola, Chambao, Joan Manuel Serrat, Carlos Cano, Joaquín Sabina, Pedro Guerra, Chab Samir, Concha Buika, and El Chojin. Also close readings of their lyrics allow us to understand the songs' political and ethical concerns in regard to the racialization of immigration, the proposal of a new, twenty-first-century *convivencia*, and fresh musical landscapes for constitutional Spain. As I have argued in the previous four chapters these concerns are evident in each one of the songs, in manners that, on the one hand, share similar ethical and even political commitments, while, on the other, delineate new musical modalities that either embrace other rhythms and melodies or focus on topics that speak to current social issues.

In regard to new musical modalities we find 1980s Spain embracing African/Caribbean rhythms by Radio Futura – as per Santiago Auserón's poems "Un africano por la Gran Vía," "Semilla negra," "Paseo con la Negra Flor," and "Coplas añadidas a Semilla Negra" evaluated in chapter 1. Chapter 2 examines Joaquín Sabina's 1990s salsa song "La casa por la ventana," which, since it was recorded as a duet with Pablo Milanés, one of the titans from the *Nueva Trova Cubana*, also highlights other Cuban musical genres. And the same can be said in regard to the 1990s musical experimentation in "Africanos in Madrid" by Amistades Peligrosas with reggae-infused tonalities, as discussed in chapter 3. Other musical rhythms and genres are welcomed by Concha Buika's hybridization of flamenco, jazz, and Latin American sounds in her "Afro Spanish Generation" and by Chambao's lead singer Lamari with flamenco chill in her emotional appeal in "Papeles mojados" (both in chapter 4).

On the one hand, we find similar thematic concerns in the new musical topics addressed by Mecano's "No es serio este cementerio" and "El blues del esclavo," which, by bringing to the fore the ghosts of Spanish history and slavery, speak to relevant socio-economic issues in 1980s Spain, as discussed in chapter 1. On the other hand, Pedro Guerra's "Contamíname," examined in chapter 3, attests to the social issues of 1990s Madrid. The social function of music shines in Joan Manuel Serrat's incisive "Salam Rashid" discussed in chapter 1 as well as in his 1992 "Disculpe el señor" addressed in chapter 2. The social function of music is also central to Carlos Cano's ethical request for forgiveness in "Canción para Lucrecia," to El Chojin's blistering denunciation of racism in "Mami, el negro está rabioso," and the poignant plight by Chab Samir's "Patera," all evaluated in chapter 2. These original musical topics are also found in chapter 3 in the denunciation of police brutality and racist governmental practices in 1990s Spain in Barricada's "Oveja negra," Ska-P's "Alí, el magrebí," and Ella Baila Sola's "Que se te escapa el negro." But further denunciation of racism is also present in the 2000s in Ska-P's "Lucrecia," El Chojin's "N.E.G.R.O." and "Rap vs. racism," as well as in the condemnation the criminalization of migration in "Sin papeles" by the band Che Sudaka.

Since music is "quite uniquely both the most fluid of cultural forms (quite literally, as sound waves moving through air) and a vibrant expression of cultures and traditions, at times held onto vehemently in the face of change" (Connell and Gibson 2003, 9), it is not surprising that at the beginning of the twenty-first century, in part as an immediate response to the murder of Lucrecia Pérez (discussed in chapters 2 and 4) and the 2000 xenophobic attacks in El Ejido (discussed in chapter 4), explicit political actions against racism were promoted from within the realm of music. One such early example is the concert put on by the *Coordinadora Estatal de Inmigrantes con y sin papeles* (State coordinator of documented and undocumented immigrants), held in Madrid on 21 March 2001 under the sign "Música contra el Racismo" (Music against racism). Participants in said concert included singer-songwriters Pedro

Guerra, extensively discussed throughout *Rocking the Boat*, and Jorge Drexler (1964–, Uruguay), winner of the 2005 Music Academy Award for the song "Al Otro Lado del Río" (On the other side of the river) from the 2004 film *The Motorcycle Diaries* [directed by Walter Salles); as well as groups such as Alcohol Jazz (Spain, funk) and Habana Abierta (Cuba, self-described "timbaconrock" or "rumbaconfunk"), among others. The event, one among the hundreds of concerts that have taken place in Spain since Lucrecia Pérez's murder and the 2000 El Ejido anti-migrant/anti-Moroccan riots to denounce xenophobia and promote solidarity and *convivencia*, emblematizes how actively the realm of music participates in the social discourse fighting racism. And well into the twenty-first century, music's engagement with anti-racist stances continues as per, among other activities, Chab Samir's participation in the 2005 celebration of the "Semana Contra el Racismo" (Week against racism) at Zaragoza's "La Casa de las Culturas" (The house of cultures).

Other solutions were offered by musicians at the personal level such as Pedro Guerra's creation in 2000, in response to the anti-migrant riots of El Ejido, of the *Contamíname Fundación para el mestizaje cultural* (Contaminate me foundation for cultural hybridity) to promote intercultural dialogue, which was operative until 2009 (see www.pedroguerra.com). The foundation sponsored events such as Memorias en Transición: Encuentro Iberoamericano de Derechos Humanos y Ciudadanía" (Memories in transition: Iberoamerican encounter on human rights and citizenship) from 26 to 30 October 2009 in defence of human rights; it joined forces with the *Asociación para la Recuperación de la Memoria Histórica* (ARMH) to sponsor the event. The notion of promoting "iberoamerican encounters" is central to the musical endeavours of the band Che Sudaka, as developed in chapter 4. As also discussed in chapter 4, El Chojin has worked tirelessly to promote anti-racist subject positions.

The efforts are there and, as I have stated throughout *Rocking the Boat*, there is no doubt that musicians such as Joan Manuel Serrat, Carlos Cano, Joaquín Sabina, Pedro Guerra, El Chojin, as well as the duos Amistades Peligrosas, Las Hijas del Sol, and Ella Baila Sola, and the bands Barricada, Ska-P, Chad Samir, and Che Sudaka were and are committed, some of them from the early stages of the migratory processes reshaping the identity of constitutional Spain, to raising consciousness and solidarity for migrants and refugees. At the same time, in certain songs, these musicians also present compelling and forceful denunciations of contemporary racism and force Spaniards to look more closely and deeply at their reputed defences of democracy and human rights. In this sense, the songs more closely focused on migration and race have not only "rocked" notions of Spanishness to the core, they have also served and serve as cultural stimulation for the creation of musical communities that seek to transform notions of exclusion and inclusion and reshape power structures.

Ultimately, music is sustained by *convivencia* (living together) and *mestizaje* (comingling), and, as such, I conclude these lengthy reflections by calling attention to the Orquesta Àrab de Barcelona (OAB), included in the book *Barcelona és bona si la música sona* (2012) (Barcelona is good is the music plays), which I discussed in chapter 4 in relation to the city's effervescent musical landscape. The OAB was born in 2005 out of the desire of four Moroccan musicians led by Mohamed Soulimane, the musical director of the band and a migrant himself, to use their musical talents to "educar, difundir y ser portavoz de muchos compatriotas que no tienen voz" (to educate, disseminate [music of the Maghreb and the Middle East] and be a spokesperson for many compatriots who have no voice) (see "Biografía" [Biography] at www.orquestraarabdebarcelona.com). Soulimane is a classically trained violinist that understands the social function of music and along with his blended band of Catalan and Moroccan musicians considers the dissemination of Moroccan/Maghrebi music "as an important opportunity to explain our culture at a politically sensitive time where Islam is identified with terrorism, violence, and radicalism. For us it is just the opposite and that is what we try to convey with our rhythms, lyrics and music" (see "Biografía" [Biography] at www.orquestraarabdebarcelona.com).

If "Un africano por la Gran Vía" (1984), the first song analysed in *Rocking the Boat*, attests to the possible anxiety generated by the presence of a well-dressed black man in Madrid's Gran Via, the music produced by the OAB – I was not able to secure copyrights for any of the songs included in any of their three records: *Báraka* (2006), *Maktub* (It is written) (2008), and *Libertad* (Freedom) (2011) – speaks of peace, integration, love, and coexistence with lyrics in Arabic, Catalan, and Spanish, and melodies that blend Moroccan musical tradition with those of the Arab world in general, including influences from different Mediterranean nations. And if these kinds of popular music are not rock 'n' roll, new hybrid forms of urban music emerging in the twenty-first century are refashioning Spain's notions of homogeneity, boundaries, accommodation, and incorporation.

Notes

Introduction

1 Similar musical manifestations, beyond the scope of this study, can be found in France (see Lebrun 2012) and other Mediterranean nations (see Abderrezak 2016) since the early 1990s. The British electronica band Asian Dub Foundation (founded in 1993) is well known for their 2003 song "Fortress Europe" from their *Enemy of the Enemy* album (Ffrr Records) protesting the closed-border policies designed to prevent non-Europeans from entering the European Union.

2 The European Union was formed in 1993, whereas the European Economic Community (EEC) was born in 1957 to bring economic integration among its member states. Spain joined the EEC in 1986. In 2009 the EEC was incorporated and renamed as the European Community (EC). The community ceased to exist in 2009 when all EC institutions were absorbed into the European Union.

3 For migration in contemporary Spanish cinema see, among others, Santaolalla (2005) and Zecchi (2010); see Ballesteros (2015) for immigration cinema in/about the European Union. For literary productions, see, among others, Abrighach (2006) for Moroccan and Magrehbi migration in Spanish narrative; Ugarte (2010) for Equatoguinean literature and immigration/exile; Rueda and Martín (2010) for immigration in *Hispano-marroquí* literature; Ricci (2010) for "African Voices in Contemporary Spain"; and the volume edited by Faszer-McMahon and Ketz (2015) for African immigrants in contemporary Spanish writing. For the photographic coverage of the Moroccan population in Barcelona's Ciutat Vella by Catalan photographer Núria Andreu Castellví, see Nair (2000).

4 In her study of Concha Piquer's coplas Stephanie Sieburth convincingly argues that "through her voice and performance, [Piquer] played a role somewhere between therapist and ritual high priestess, a role that did much to enable the defeated to work through some of the intense traumatic feelings they carried within as they sang along with her" (2014, 7).

5 The small rafts (*pateras*) were mostly used by Moroccan and African nationals seeking to reach Spanish shores (Andalusia) across the Strait of Gibraltar in the 1990s. In the 2000s medium-sized *cayucos* were used mostly by migrants journeying from West Africa to the Canary Islands.

6 The migrant workers represented as invaders generally work in menial jobs with low wages. Migrant newcomers working in the middle or high levels of the occupational scale move without difficulty and experience few or no problems integrating.

7 See, among others, Tam Tam Go!'s "Espaldas Mojadas" (Wet backs), Celtas cortos's "El emigrante" (The emigrant), Miguel Ríos's "Libres (en medio de la noche) (Free, in the middle of the night), Manu Chao's "Clandestino" (Illegal immigrant), Bidinte's (Jorge da Silva Binidite) "La rumba del viajero" (The traveler's rumba), and "Samba da emigraçao" (Emigration's samba). Several rappers have also focused on these topics in songs such as "Alguien se acordará" (Someone will remember) by Krazé (Marcos Ela Edjang), "La nueva España (The new Spain) by Frank T. (Franklin Thsimini Nsombolay), and "Tierra prometida" (Promised land) by MC Nach (formerly known as Nach Scratch, born Ignacio Fornés Olmo), among others.

8 Though Chab Samir sings of clandestine migration across the Mediterranean in *patera*, he arrived in Barcelona in 1992 by plane with a tourist visa to attend the Olympic Games. He became an irregular migrant once his visa expired, later marrying a Catalan woman. Samir identifies as Spanish/Catalan/Moroccan.

9 For the musical practices of the Moroccan community in Barcelona in the late 1990s, including raï music, see Asensio (1999 and 2002), among others.

10 The so-called "Golpe de libertad" (Freedom coup), the military uprising of 3 August 1979 led by Teodoro Obiang, put an end to Macías's dictatorship. The hopes of a possible democratization of the country were short-lived, since Obiang's government turned out to be more brutal than that of his predecessor.

11 In the late 1990s and early 2000s, the great majority of migrant workers arriving from Latin America were from the Andean regions of Ecuador, Peru, and Bolivia.

12 Italy, Malta, and Greece also received support from the European Union to deter the further arrival of migrants from Africa.

13 Among the many successful bands of the 1980s are Siniestro Total, La Unión, Duncan Dhu, Golpes Bajos, Gabinete Caligari, Los Secretos, Glutamato Ye-Yé, Alaska y los Pegamoides, and Alaska y Dinarama (Ríos Longares 2001; del Val, Noya, and Martín Pérez-Colman 2014).

1. The Roaring 1980s

1 Elvis Costello is the stage name of Declan Patrick MacManus – see www.elviscostello.com.

2 The first decade of the twenty-first century brought a wave of nostalgia for the Spanish 1980s, as evidenced by the moniker "La Edad de Oro del pop español" (The golden era of Spanish pop), which was used to market from compilations DVDs and CDs to ring tones for mobile phones.

3 *Semilla del son* was produced and selected by Santiago Auserón in collaboration with the *Empresa de Grabaciones y Ediciones Musicales de Cuba* (EGREM), featuring performances by musical legends such as the Trio Matamoros, Francisco Repillado (aka Compay Segundo), Arsenio Rodríguez, and Beny Moré, among others.

4 Beny Moré is considered one of the greatest *soneros* of all time with several successful orchestras touring Mexico and Venezuela. Though he performed all kinds of Cuban popular music – *guajiras, boleros* – he is best known for his particular way with *sones* (see John Radanovich's 2009 book *Wildman of Rhythm: The Life and Music of Benny Moré*). Miguelito Cuní is also one of Cuba's most celebrated *soneros*, touring Venezuela with the Beny Moré's Orchestra in 1956 (see Helio Orovio's 1992 book *Diccionario de la música cubana*).

5 Known as "covermounts" – any cover gifts, promotions, and incentives used by the publishing industry to lure readers – they are used by Spanish and European newspapers to boost dwindling circulation, especially during the summer months. For its implicit devaluation of the cultural productions of popular music and film, it is considered a controversial practice.

6 For more on racialized visions in film in 1920s and 1930s Spain see Woods Peiro's chapters 1 to 3 (2012).

7 Epps precisely details this haunting:

> Africa, more closely than any other area of the world, haunts contemporary Spain, haunts it in all its component or contested parts, its unitary visions and peripheral dreams, its vertebrations and invertebrations, its border controls and linguistic policies, its charitable

gestures and enterprising investments, its "leyes de extranjería" and "derechos" and "deberes" of citizenship, its professions of singularity and its claims to universality, and, most acutely, its gestures of racial and ethnic tolerance (2005, 114).

8 According to Rosa Montero (1995) xenophobia was one of the negative consequences of Spain's rags-to-riches transformation. For an overview on xenophobia from the 1970s to 1996 see Barbadillo Griñán (1997); see also D'Ancona (2004).
9 For more on Spanish and European masculinities see, among others, the volumes by Powrie, Davies, and Babington (2004) and by Fouz-Hernández and Martínez-Expósito (2007).
10 On the demographics of the Atlantic slave trade, Lipski also relys on *The Trans-Atlantic Slave Trade: A Database on CD-ROM* (1999), which contains data on more than twenty-seven thousand slave voyages from 1595 and 1866 (46–7). For a scathing view of Europe's involvement in the slave trade see Luis de Sebastián's *África, pecado de Europa* (2006) where he argues for a politics of reparation.
11 The actual predicament of the slaves is made brutally evident in the dungeons at Elmina Castle (Ghana) that lead to the "Door of No Return," as I had the opportunity to experience on my visits to the castle in August 2008 and August 2013.
12 Mecano's use of the term "zulús" is questioned by Jorge Marí (2007) who contends that the trio's message of solidarity thus becomes nullified. I argue that the deployment of such a racially charged term does not negate the song's intention to call attention to slavery nor, in the context of 1980s Spain, to slave wages and the PSOE's economic policies that were harming Spanish unions and workers.
13 Among the many areas of contention between the two nations are the Rif War (1909–26), the participation of Moroccan soldiers on Franco's side during the Spanish Civil War (1936–9), the Ifni War (1957–8), and the conflicts regarding the Western Sahara, where the future of the Saharawi people remains unresolved as of 2017.
14 Edward Said's *Covering Islam: How the Media and the Experts Determine How We See the Rest of the World* (1981) exposed the role the US media played in stereotyping the Muslim world as problematical, worrisome, and threatening. The mechanisms identified by Said in 1981 have now become common practice worldwide.
15 The name *Els setze jutges* (The sixteen judges) derives from a famous tongue-twister in Catalonia, Valencia, and the Balear Islands (see Novell 2009).

2. The 1990s, Take One

1 The Federation of SOS *Racismo* Associations of Spain was established in 1995 by the joining of the various such agencies already existing in the Spanish territory (see www.sosracismo.org).
2 *AVE* is a play on the Spanish word "ave" – meaning "bird" – and the train's design, which resembles a bird.
3 The publication was clearly a PSOE enterprise since both Guerra and Tezanos were directly involved with Fundación Sistema – created in 1981.
4 In November 2012, the co-op Rosa Luxemburgo, constituted by several Aravaca's neighborhood associations, showed the self-produced video *Lucrecia Pérez, 20 años de un crimen racista* (Lucrecia Perez, 20 years of a racist crime).
5 He can be seen in such attire in a 1992 televised performance on TV1 on www.youtube.com/watch?v=w8BnbJNP_CI.
6 For more on Sabina's poetic collections see Javier Menéndez Flores and Joaquín Sabina's 2006 *Sabina en carne viva: yo también sé jugarmela boca*. In 2001, Sabina published *Ciento volando de catorce*, and in 2007 *Esta boca sigue siendo mía*, a collection of satirical verses from his days collaborating with the weekly *Interviú*.
7 In regard to personal ties among the four *cantautores*, Sabina's musical and poetic trajectory connects him first to Carlos Cano in the late 1960s working together in the *Manifiesto Canción Sur*. The untimely death of Carlos Cano in 2000 has Serrat posthumously "singing together" with the beloved Andalusian musician. Thanks to digitalization, both *cantautores* alternate stanzas interpreting Cano's "Antonio Vargas Heredia" in the 2001 album *Que naveguen los sueños* (Let the dreams' sail) (EMI Odeon 2001), a musical homage to Carlos Cano by other artists. Serrat sang Guerra's "Contamíname," along with Ana Belén, Víctor Manuel, and Miguel Ríos, on the 1996 album *El gusto es nuestro* (Our pleasure), the result of a successful tour, of the same title, that took them throughout Spain. In 2016 the four artists reunited to reprise the live concerts of 1996 under "El gusto es nuestro 20 años" (Our pleasure 20 years), once again singing "Contamíname."
8 The original Schegen accord eliminated border controls between France, Germany, and the Benelux countries (Belgium, the Netherlands, and Luxembourg). For more on the expansion of the original accord and the EU's configuration up until 2011 see Hix and Høyland's *The Political System of the European Union* (2011).

9 According to Thurmaier, chords are only placed in the first A, B, and C sections, because they are identical for the later sections in the song.

10 I thank Lorena Barrett for helping better my translation of the song:

Pardon, Sir
If I interrupt you, but in the entrance hall
There are a pair of poor people that
Insistently ask that you see them

They are not asking for donations, No.
They are not selling rugs made of sheep wool
Nor they are selling ebony made elephants.
They are poor people that have nothing of anything.
I did not understand

If they said that had nothing to sell or nothing to loose
But it seems
That you have something that belongs to them

Do you want me to tell them that the master is out?
Should I tell them to come tomorrow during visiting hours?
Or, should I better tell them, as you say
'Saint Rita, Rita, Rita,
What's been taken away, cannot be given back?'

Pardon me, Sir
The indigents have packed the vestibule
And they keep on arriving
From the rearguard, by land and by sea.

And since the master says that he is out.
And since they say that is an emergency
They have asked that I show them
The way to the pantry,
And that God will repay you

Would you give me the keys or should I oust them? Your call
Since while you and I talk
More indigents arrive and keep on arriving

Do you want me to call a policeman so he can check
if they have permit papers?
Or should I tell them, like the master says:
'I love you, you love me,
but let's not talk about money?'

Pardon, Sir
But this situation is going from bad to worse.
They are arriving by the millions
And, it appears that they are all coming here

I have tried to contain them, but as you can see
They have found you.
These are the indigent of which I was talking about.
I leave you with the gentlemen
And it is between all of you…

Unless you need anything else, I'll take my leave
If you need me, call me …
May God inspire you, May God protect you
Because these have yet to realize
That Karl Marx is long dead and buried.

11 Just before his passing in 2000, Cano released *De lo perdido y otras coplas* (Of what is lost and other stanzas) (EMI). Also in 2000, and as a joint venture with the NGO *Proyecto Mundo* (Project world) (Pontevedra, Galicia), he produced *Así cantan los niños de Cuba* (This is how Cuban children sing) to show his solidarity with the people of Cuba.

12 Created by Francisco "Pacho" Galán in the 1950s, the *merecumbé* is a musical production of Caribbean Colombia (Bermúdez 2007, 247).

13 Spain's northern region was not without geopolitical problems since, according to Prime Minister José María Aznar, the Basque Country was what was "wrong" with the nation at that time. The so-called Basque problem continued to challenge the Spanish state into the second decade of the twenty-first century. In an unanticipated turn of events, and as already stated in the introduction, the biggest challenge to Spain's constitutional unity has been driven since 2014 by Catalonia's quest for independence – as per the nonbinding 9 November 2014 citizen participation process on the political future of Catalonia and the 27 September, 2015 Catalan parliamentary elections that gave the majority to the *Junts pel Sí* (Together for yes) coalition. The referendum on independence from Spain was to take place on October 1, 2017 as *Rocking the Boat* was going to press.

14 I thank Eyda Merediz for helping me produce a more poetic translation of "La casa por la ventana."

15 See in particular: *Inequality, Growth, and Poverty in an Era of Liberalization and Globalization*, edited by economist Giovanni Andrea Cornia (2004), Branko Milanovic's *Worlds Apart: Measuring International and Global*

Inequality (2005), and *The Haves and the Have-Nots: A Brief and Idiosyncratic History of Global Inequality* (2012).

16 Developed during the 1970s to use music as a means to voice social and political concerns, the *nueva canción* revitalized Spanish popular music. Pedro Guerra admires Silvio Rodríguez and Pablo Milanés from the *nueva troba cubana* (New Cuban song), and Víctor Jara from the *nueva canción chilena* (New Chilean song).

17 A performance by Pedro Guerra of "Contamíname" on 8 July 2008 in the Auditorium Pilar Bardem in Madrid can be seen in at www.youtube.com/watch?v=63xrbVSXbXA (accessed 30 July 2016).

18 *Urotsukidōji* was originally created by Toshio Maeda in 1986, who was commisioned to do the series for *Wani* magazine.

19 The racist implications of the product can be still seen today on YouTube in a sequence titled "Evolución Conguitos" posted on 9 February 2014 and accessed 30 July 2016 at https://www.youtube.com/watch?v=_4AwGKzbMF4. See Diana Q. Palardy's detailed evaluation of the history of the advertising of Conguitos in Spain (2014).

20 Cola Cao is sold in what is by now a highly recognizable yellow container and promoted as an energy drink that can help the consumer become a better athlete. In one of the older television commercials, familiar to generations of Spaniards, the jinx insisted on underscoring its being the ideal meal for either breakfast or an afternoon snack – *merienda*. Racial stereotyping runs rampant throughout the commercial, beginning with the speaking subject selling the product that self-identifies itself as a "negrito" ("darkie" [*sic*]). See "Antiguo anuncio del cola cao de tv" (Older TV Cola Cao commercial) posted by Juan Raya on 11 May 2011 at www.youtube.com/watch?v=R5DzdXLjghU (accessed 30 July 2016).

21 Known simply as Khaled, the Algerian born artist is considered raï's most successful exponent, having revolutionized the form and achieving international recognition. See www.khaled-lesite.com.

22 Chab Samir's performance in a packed and boisterous disco – Discoteca Árabe de Terrasa – posted on 9 November 2011 on YouTube, does not indicate when the video was actually filmed. It can be seen at www.youtube.com/watch?v=tObPFQfoAVo (accessed 30 July 2016).

3. The 1990s, Take Two

1 The albums are: 1991's *Relatos de una intriga* (Tales of a scheme), 1993's *La última tentación* (The last temptation), 1995's *La Profecía* (The prophecy), 1997's *Nueva era* (New era), and the 1998 compilation *Grandes éxitos* (Bestsellers).

2 Susan Martin-Márquez offers a detailed and thorough evaluation of the fight for self-determination of the Saharawi people, the group most negatively affected by the Tripartite Agreement signed by Franco in November 1975, days before his death. In particular, she calls attention to how Spaniards have become "obsessed with the plight of the Saharawis" (2008, 325) paying little or no attention to the plight of Equatoguineans.
3 In his reading of Zurara's chronicle, Branche calls attention to how the narrator, in describing the findings of the voyages between 1434, when Gil Eannes rounded Cape Bojador, and 1444, when the first shipment of captives is taken to Lagos for sale, collapses "the different categories of items – vegetable, animal, and human – into the single class of 'booty'" (2006, 39).
4 A chilling account of Nguema's brutality and corruption can be found in Francisco Zamora Loboch's first novel, *Conspiración en el green (El informe Abayak)* (Conspiracy in the green [The Abayak dossier]) published in 2009.
5 For a detailed discussion of the implications of the two different jackets used in the presentation of the record to Spanish audiences and the rest of Europe and the United States see García Alvite (2004, 151).
6 I quote the Spanish version of the song from the CD liner, which is offered to the right of the Bubi version. The lyrics of the first fourteen songs are presented in Bubi and Spanish. The last song, "Tirso de Molina" is listed only in Spanish. Once more I thank Lorena Barrett for helping me render more poetically the English version of lyrics.
7 The vernacular expression "top manta" refers to the street vendors showing counterfeit products (from CDs and DVDs to purses, watches, belts, and other accessories) on a blanket. It is a racialized idiom since the term also indicates that these street vendors are black African migrants.
8 For alternative visions of gender, identity, and the nation in *El metro* see Montouri (2009); see Fra-Molinero (2009) for *El metro* as postcolonial novel and metaphor for slavery; and Ugarte as a "saga of the African Emigrant" (2010, 76–89).

4. Twenty-First Century Musical Landscapes

1 Sicily and the Balkans were also Islamized.
2 For more on racial domination see, among others, *Racism and Migration in Western Europe* by John Wrench and John Solomos (1993); Alfonso García Martínez's *La construcción social del racismo. Análisis y Perspectivas* (2004), and *Theories of Race and Racism: A Reader* by Les Back and John Solomos (2009).

3 As it is well known, the Socialist major of Barcelona from 1982 to 1997, Pasqual Maragall – grandson of Catalan leading poet Joan Maragall (1860–1911), who was also president of the Generalitat of Catalonia from 2003 to 2006 – supervised the large scale beautification campaign by which the city was inundated with banners commanding the city to "Barcelona, posa't guapa" (Barcelona, get dolled up).
4 The British writer (born Eric Arthur Blair, 1903–50), as indicated by a plaque, briefly lived in one of the buildings surrounding the square that now bears his name.
5 The actual saying goes beyond insisting that in order to enjoy Barcelona's many goodnesses, one needs money by stating: "Barcelona és bona si la bossa sona" però tant si sona com si no sona, Barcelona sempre és bona" (Barcelona is good if the purse is full, but even if it full or if it is not full, Barcelona is always good).
6 The song refers not to Sting (1951–), an Englishman himself, but to the English gay icon Quentin Crisp (born Denis Charles Pratt, 1908–99), admired by Sting, and who had moved to the East Village in Manhattan in 1981. The global star – in his own right and as the lead and bassist of the band The Police – interviewed Quentin Crisp in 1986.
7 In regard to subject positions and identities, Socolovksy made a point of highlighting Buika's bisexuality in his 12 November interview with the artist (Socolovksy 2011).
8 The booklet listed two female performers for the 10 November 2010 concert, Lila Downs and Buika. Downs is a Mexican-American singer, who, when convenient, is marketed either as a Mexican-American singer, within the tradition of Chicano music, or as "world music" performer.
9 For more on the conceptualization of African-American and other racial hierarchies in the United States see, among others, Michael C. Dawson's *Black Visions: The Roots of Contemporary African-American Political Ideologies* (2001) and Desmond King's *Separate and Unequal: African Americans and the U.S. Federal Government* (2007).
10 A discussion of the racial contracts in the articulation and development of the United States is beyond the scope of *Rocking the Boat* but, among others, the following are illuminating in this regard: Wahneema Lubiano (1997), Eduardo Bonilla-Silva (2014), and Douglas S. Massey (2007).
11 See the video at https://video.search.yahoo.com/search/video?fr=yfp-t&p=papeles+mojados#id=1&vid=5755ff6c438997279966d846df52c0c2&action=click.

12 As explained in chapter 3, this is a racialized expression that describes street vendors as black migrant subjects.

13 *Convivencia* is the historical term to describe the coexistence of Muslims, Jews, and Christians in Spain between 711 and 1492.

14 In the summer of 2016 the targeted clothing item is the burkini – a full-length swimsuit that covers the whole body except for the face, hands, and feet.

Bibliography

Abderrezak, Hakim. 2016. *Ex-Centric Migrations: Europe and the Maghreb in Mediterranean Cinema, Literature, and Music*. Bloomington: Indiana University Press.

Abrighach, Mohamed. 2006. *La inmigracion marroquí y subsahariana en la narrativa española actual*. Agadir, Marruecos: ORMES.

Adorno, Theodor. 1990. "On Popular Music." In *On the Record*, assisted by George Simpson, edited by Simon Frith and Andrew Goodwin, 301–14. New York: Pantheon.

Adrados, Javier, and Carlos del Amo. 2004. *Mecano: la fuerza del destino*. Madrid: La esfera de los libros.

Afro-Europe International Blog. 2009. "Concha Buika-New Afro Spanish Generation." *Afro-Europe International Blog*, 28 December. http://afroeurope.blogspot.ca/2009/12/concha-buika-new-afro-spanish.html.

Aguilar, Paloma. 2002. *Memory and Amnesi: The Role of the Spanih Civil War in the Transition to Democracy*. Translated by Mark Oakley. New York: Berghahn Books.

Allison, Mark. 2000. "The Construction of Youth in Spain in the 1980s and 1990s." In *Contemporary Spanish Cultural Studies*, edited by Barry Jordan and Rikki- Morgan-Tamosunas, 265–73. London and New York: Arnold.

Allison, Mark, Miguel Amorós, and Xavier Torres-Bacchetta. 2012. *Barcelona és bona si la música sona*. Barcelona: Satélite K.

Andersson, Ruben. 2014. *Illegality, Inc. Clandestine Migration and the Business of Bordering Europe*. Oakland, CA: University of California Press.

Andrés-Suárez, Irene, Marco Kunz, and Inés d'Ors. 2002. *La immigración en la literatura española contemporánea*. Madrid: Verbum.

Anzaldúa, Gloria. 1999. *Borderlands/La Frontera*. 2nd ed. San Francisco: Aunt Lute Books.

Aparicio, R. Frances. 2000. "Ethnifying Rhythms, Feminizing Cultures." In *Music and the Racial Imagination*, edited by Ronald Radano and Philip V. Bohlman, 95–112. Chicago and London: Chicago University Press.

Appadurai, Arjun. 1996. *Modernity at Large: Cultural Dimensions of Globalization*. Minneapolis: University of Minnesota Press.

Appiah, Anthony. 2005. *The Ethics of Identity*. Princeton, NJ: Princeton University Press.

Ares Queija, Berta, and Alessandro Stella, eds. 2000. *Negros, mulatos, zambaigos: Derroteros africanos en los mundos ibéricos*. Sevilla: Escuela de Estudios Hispano-Americanos. Consejo Superior de Investigaciones Científicas.

Asensio, Susana. 1999. "Etnomusicologia i emigració: marroquins a Barcelona." *Revista d'Etnologia de Catalunya* 14: 132–9.

– 2002. "The Politics of Hybridization in Rai Music." In *Songs of the Minotaur: Hybridity and Popular Music in the Era of Globalization. A Comparativ Analysis of Rebetika, Tango, Rai, Flamenco, Sardana, and English Urban Folk*, edited by Gerhard Steingress, 51–82. Hamburg: LIT Verlag.

Auserón, Santiago. 1998. *La imagen sonora: notas para una lectura filosófica de la nueva música popular*. Valencia: Episteme.

– 1999. *Canciones de Radio Futura*. Valencia: Pre-Textos.

– 2012. *El ritmo perdido. Sobre el influjo negro en la canción española*. Barcelona: Ediciones Península.

Back, Les, and John Solomos. 2009. *Theories of Race and Racism: A Reader*. 2nd ed. London and New York: Routledge.

Baker, Houston A., Jr. 1984. *Blues, Ideology, and Afro-American Literature: A Vernacular Theory*. Chicago: University of Chicago Press.

Balfour, Sebastian. 2005. "The Reinvention of Spanish Conservatism: The Popular Party since 1989." In *The Politics of Contemporary Spain*, edited by Sebastian Balfour, 146–68. London and New York: Routledge.

Balibar, Étienne. 1991. "Is There a 'Neo-Racism." In *Race, Nation, Class: Ambiguous Identitities*, edited by Étienne Balibar and Immanuel Wallerstein 17–27. London: Verso.

Ballesteros, Isolina. 2015. *Immigration Cinema in the New Europe*. Bristol and Chicago: Intellect.

Barbadillo Griñán, Patricia. 1997. *Extranjería, racismo y xenofobia en la España contemporánea: la evolución de los setenta a los noventa*. Madrid: Centro de Investigaciones Sociológicas: Siglo XXI.

Baroja, Pío. 1937. *El árbol de la ciencia*. Madrid: Espasa Calpe.

Bauman, Zygmunt. 1997. "The Making and Unmaking of Strangers." In *Debating Cultural Hybridity: Multicultural Identities and the Politics of Anti-Racism*, edited by Pnina Werbner and Tariq Modood, 46–57. London, New Jersey: Zed Books.

Bensaad, Ali. 2007. "The Mediterranean Divide and its Echo in the Sahara: New Migratory Routes and New Barriers on the Path to the Mediterranean." In *Between Europe and the Mediterranean: The Challenges and Fears*. Translated by Penny Allen, edited by Thierry Fabre and Paul

Sant-Cassia, 51–69. Houndmills, Basingstokem Hampshire and New York: Palgrave Macmillan. http://dx.doi.org/10.1057/9780230287334_5.
Bermúdez, Silvia. 2001. "Rocking the Boat: The Black Atlantic in Spanish Pop Music from the 1980s and the '90s." *Arizona Journal of Hispanic Cultural Studies* 5 (1): 177–93. http://dx.doi.org/10.1353/hcs.2011.0034.
– 2007. "Lucrecia Pérez en el imaginario cultural de España: del racismo a la ética del perdón." In *Memoria colonial e inmigración: La negritud en la España posfranquista*, edited by Rosalía Cornejo Parriego, 239–50. Barcelona: Bellatera.
– 2010. "La España Constitucional: Democracia y Cultura, 1978-2008." *Revista de Estudios Hispánicos* 44 (3): 533–43.
– 2015. "Encrucijadas raciales y políticas identitarias: El Chojin y la función social del rap en español." In *Encrucijadas globales: Redefinir España en el siglo XXI*, edited by José Colmeiro, 107–123. Madrid: Iberoamericana/Vervuert.
Bermúdez, Silvia, and Jorge Pérez. 2009. "Introduction: Spanish Popular Music Studies." *Journal of Spanish Cultural Studies* 10 (2): 127–33. http://dx.doi.org/10.1080/14636200902990661.
Bermúdez, Silvia, and Roberto Strongman. 2015. "Introduction: Mediterranean Manifesto: From *Mashrabiya* and the Doha Tower to Fortress Europe." *Journal of Mediterranean Studies* 24 (2): 137–46.
Béroud, Sophie. 2006. "Manipulations et mobilisations: L'Espagne du 11 au 14 mars 2004." *Critique Internationale* 31 (2): 53–66. http://dx.doi.org/10.3917/crii.031.0053.
Beverley, John. 2004. *Testimonio: On the Politics of Truth*. Minneapolis: University of Minnesota Press.
Bohlman, Philip V. 2002. *World Music: A Very Short Introduction*. Oxford and New York: Oxford University Press. http://dx.doi.org/10.1093/actrade/9780192854292.001.0001.
Bonilla-Silva, Eduardo. 2014. *Racism without Racists: Color-Blind Racism and the Persistence of Racial Inequality in America*. 4th edition. Lanham, Maryland: Rowman & Littlefield Publishers.
Bowman, Paul. 2008. *Deconstructing Popular Culture*. Basingstoke (England) and New York: Palgrave MacMillan.
Branche, Jerome C. 2006. *Colonialism and Race in Luso-Hispanic Literature*. Columbia and London: University of Missouri Press.
– ed. 2008. *Race, Colonialism, and Social Transformation in Latin America and the Caribbean*. Gainesville: University Press of Florida.
Calvo Buezas, Tomás. 1993. *El crimen racista de Aravaca. Crónica de una muerte anunciada*. Madrid: Jóvenes contra la Intolerancia (JCL).
Cannon, Steve. 1997. "Paname City Rapping: B-Boys in the Banlieues and Beyond." In *Postcolonial Cultures in France*, edited by Ale G. Hargreaves and Mark McKinney, 150–66. London: Routledge.

Carling, Jørgen. 2007. "Migration Control and Migrant Fatalities at the Spanish-African Borders." *International Migration Review* 41 (2): 316–43. http://dx.doi.org/10.1111/j.1747-7379.2007.00070.x.

Cervera, Rafa. 2002. *Alaska y otras historias de la Movida*. Barcelona: Random House- Mondadori.

Checa, Francisco, ed. 2001. *El Ejido: la ciudad-cortijo. Claves socioeconómicas del conflicto étnico*. Barcelona: Icaria.

Checa Olmos, Juan Carlos, and Ángeles Arjona Garrido. 2012. "Anti-Immigrant Feeling in Spain." *Polish Sociological Review* 177: 39–53.

Cisneros, J. David. 2008. "Contaminated Communities: The Metaphor of 'Inmigrant as Pollutant' in Media Representations of Immigration." *Rhetoric and Public Affairs* 11 (4): 569-601.

Clemente, Josep Carles. 1994. *Historias de la transición 1973/1981. El fin del apagón*. Madrid: Fundamentos.

Colectivo, Ioé. 1996. "La inmigración marroquí en Cataluña." In *Atlas de la inmigración magrebí en España. Atlas 1996*, edited by Bernabé López García, 146–51. Madrid: Universidad Autónoma.

Coleman, Mathew. 2005. "Permeable Borders and Boundaries in a Globalizing World: Feeling at Home amidst Global Poverty." In *Holding the Line: Borders in a Global World*, edited by Heather Nicol and Ian Townsend-Gault, 293–307. Vancouver: University of British Columbia Press.

Colmeiro, José. 2003. "*Canciones con historia*: Cultural Identity, Historical Memory, and Popular Songs." *Journal of Spanish Cultural Studies* 4 (1): 31–46. http://dx.doi.org/10.1080/1463620032000058668.

Connell, John and Chris Gibson. 2003. *Sound Tracks: Popular Music, Identity and Place (Critical Geographies)*. London: Routledge.

Corbalán, Ana and Ellen Mayock, eds. 2015. *Towards a Multicultural Configuration of Spain: Local Cities, Global Spaces*. Madison: Fairleigh Dickinson University Press.

Cornia, Giovanni Andrea, ed. 2004. *Inequality, Growth and Poverty in an Era of Liberalization and Globalization*. Oxford and New York: Oxford University Press. http://dx.doi.org/10.1093/0199271410.001.0001.

Cox, Arnie. 2012. "Tripartite Subjectivity in Music Listening." *Indiana Theory Review* 30.1 (Spring): 1–43.

D'Ancona, Cea. 2004. *La activación de la xenophobia en España:¿Qué miden las encuestas?* Madrid: Centro de Investigaciones Sociológicas.

Dawson, Michael C. 2001. *Black Visions: The Roots of Contemporary African-American Political Ideologies*. Chicago: University of Chicago Press.

de Miguel, Maurilio. 1986. *Joaquín Sabina*. Madrid: Ediciones Júcar.

– 2005. *Eso será poesía (Sabina antes de Sabina)*. Madrid: Ediciones Martínez Roca.

de Sebastián, Luis. 2006. *África, pecado de Europa*. Madrid: Editorial Trotta.

de Vicente, Juan. 1993. "Los inmigrantes negroafricanos en la CAM." In *Inmigrantes extranjeros en Madrid*, coordinated by Carlos Giménez Romero, 251–336. Madrid: Comunidad de Madrid.

de Wenden, Catherine Wihtol. 2007. "Does Europe Need New Immigration?" In *Between Europe and the Mediterranean*, edited by Thierry Fabre and Pau Sant-Cassia, 28–40. Translated by Penny Allen. Houndmills, Basingstoke, Hampshire, and New York: Palgrave Macmillan.

del Val, Fernán, Javier Noya, and C. Martín Pérez-Colman. 2014. "¿Autonomía, sumisión o hibridación sonora? La construcción del canon estético del pop-rock español." *Revista Espanola de Investigaciones Sociologicas* 145: 147–80.

Delgado, Elena. 2002. "La nación deseada: Europeización, diferencia y la utopía de (las) España(s)'. In *From Stateless Nations to Postnational Spain*, edited by Silvia Bermúdez, Antonio Cortijo, and Timothy McGovern, 207–21. Boulder: Society of Spanish and Spanish-American Studies.

– 2014. *La nación singular. Fantasías de la normalidad democrática española (1996-2011)*. Madrid: Siglo XXI.

Dirlik, Arif. 2008. "Race Talk, Race, and Contemporary Racism." *Publications of the Modern Language Association of America* 123 (5): 1363–79. http://dx.doi.org/10.1632/pmla.2008.123.5.1363.

Du Bois, W.E.B. 1900 (1996). "The Present Outlook for the Darker Races of Mankind." In *The Oxford W.E.B. Du Bois Reader*, edited by Eric Sundquist, 47–54. Oxford: Oxford University Press.

– 1903. *The Souls of Black Folk*. Chicago: A.C. McClurg.

El Chojin and Paco Reyes. 2010. *Rap: 25 años de rimas, un recorrido por la historia del rap en España. 2nda Edición*. Barcelona: Viceversa Editorial.

El Chojin. 2011. *Ríe cuando puedas, llora cuando lo necesites*. Madrid: Espasa Calpe.

El Hachim, Najat. 2004. *Jo també sóc catalana*. Barcelona: Columna.

– 2008. *L'Ultim Patriarca*. Barcelona: Planeta.

Epps, Bradley. 2005. "Between Europe and Africa: Modernity, Race, and Nationality in the Correspondence of Miguel de Unamuno and Joan Maragall." *Anales de la Literatura Española Contemporánea* 30 (1–2): 97–132.

– 2010. "To Be (a Part) of a Whole: Constitutional Patriotism and the Paradox of Democracy in the Wake of the Spanish Constitution of 1978." *Revista De Estudios Hispánicos* 44 (3): 545–68.

Fanon, Frantz. 1961. *Les Damnés de la Terre*. Paris: François Maspero.

Faszer-McMahon, Debra, and Victoria Ketz. 2015. *Across the Straits: New Visions of Africa in Contemporary Spain*. Burlington: Ashgate Press.

Feld, Stephen. 2000. "A Sweet Lullaby for World Music." *Public Culture* 12 (1): 145–71. http://dx.doi.org/10.1215/08992363-12-1-145.

Flesler, Daniela. 2008. *The Return of the Moor: Spanish Responses to Contemporary Moroccan Immigration*. West Lafayette, Indiana: Purdue University Press.

Fouce, Héctor. 2006. *El futuro ya está aquí*. Madrid: Velecío Editores.

Fouce, Héctor, and Fernand del Val. 2013. "La movida. Popular Music as the Discourse of Modernity in democratic Spain." In *Made in Spain. Studies in Popular Music*, edited by Silvia Martínez and Héctor Fouce, 125–134. New York. Routledge.

Fouz-Hernández, Santiago, and Alfredo Martínez Expósito. 2007. *Live Flesh: The Male Body in Contemporary Spanish Cinema*. London: I.B. Tauris.

Fouz-Hernández, Santiago. 2009. "Me cuesta tanto olvidarte: Mecano and the *Movida* Remixed, Revisited and Repackaged." *Journal of Spanish Cultural Studies* 10 (2): 167–87. http://dx.doi.org/10.1080/14636200902990695.

Fra-Molinero, Baltasar. 1995. *La imagen de los negros en el teatro de Siglo de Oro*. México, D.F. and Madrid: Siglo Veintiuno Editores.

– 2000. "Ser mulato en España y América: Discursos legales y otros discursos literarios." In *Negros, mulatos, zambaigos. Derroteros africanos en los mundos ibéricos*, edited by Berta Ares Queija and Alessandro Stella, 123–47. Sevilla: Escuela de Estudios Hispano-Americanos, Consejo Superior de Investigaciones Científicas.

– 2009. "Novela postcolonial, emmigración y metáfora de la esclavitud." *Afro-Hispanic Review* 28 (2): 81–96.

Frith, Simon. 1981. *Sound Effects: Youth, Leisure, and the Politics of Rock 'n' roll*. New York: Pantheon Books.

– 1996. *Performing Rites: On the Value of Popular Music*. Cambridge, MA: Harvard University Press.

Frontex. No date. "About." Accesed 30 March 2017. frontex.europa.eu/about-frontex/origin/

– No date. "Eurosur." Accessed 1 July 2016. http://frontex.europa.eu/intelligence/eurosur/.

Gabilondo, Joseba. 2003. "Historical Memory, Neoliberal Spain, and the Latin American Postcolonial Ghost: On the Politics of Recognition, Apology, and Reparation in Contemporary Spanish Historiography." *Arizona Journal of Hispanic Cultural Studies* 7 (1): 247–66. http://dx.doi.org/10.1353/hcs.2011.0169.

Gallero, José Luis. 1991. *Sólo se vive una vez: Esplendor y ruina de la movida madrileña*. Madrid: Ardora.

Gamboa, José Manuel. 2005. *Una historia del flamenco*. Madrid: Espasa Calpe.

Gana, Nouri. 2008. "Introduction: Race, Islam, and the Task of Muslim and Arab American Writing." *Publications of the Modern Language Association* 123 (5): 1573–80. http://dx.doi.org/10.1632/pmla.2008.123.5.1573.

Garber, Steve. 2007. "The European Union and the Racialization of Immigration, 1985–2006." *Race/Ethnicity: Multidisciplinary Global Contexts* 1 (1): 61–87.

García-Alvite, Dosinda. 2004. "Strategic Positions of Las Hijas del Sol: Equatorial Guinea in World Music." *Arizona Journal of Hispanic Cultural Studies* 8 (1): 149–62. http://dx.doi.org/10.1353/hcs.2011.0291.

García-Soler, Jordi. 1976. *La Nova Cançó*. Barcelona: Edicions 62.

García Martínez, Alfonso. 2004. *La construcción social del racismo: Análisis y Perspectivas*. Madrid: Dykinson.

Gates Jr., Henry Louis. 2008. "Reading 'Race,' Writing, and Difference." *Publications of the Modern Language Association* 123 (5): 1534–9. http://dx.doi.org/10.1632/pmla.2008.123.5.1534.

Gebrewold, Belachew. 2007. "Conclusion–Securitization of Migration and the Civilizing Process." In *Africa and Fortress Europe. Threats and Opportunities*, edited by Belachew Gebrewold, 171–9. Hampshire, England and Burlington, VT: Ashgate.

Geddes, Andrew. 2008. *Immigration and European Integration: Beyond Fortress Europe?* 2nd ed. Manchester and New York: Manchester University Press.

Gilroy, Paul. 1993. *The Black Atlantic: Modernity and Double Consciousness*. Cambridge, MA: Harvard University Press.

González Lucini, Fernando. 2006. *...y la palabra se hizo música: La canción de autor en España*. 2 vols. Madrid: Fundación autor.

Goytisolo, Juan, and Samir Naïr. 2000. *El peaje de la vida: integración o rechazo de la emigración en España*. Madrid: Aguilar.

– 2003. *España y sus Ejidos*. Madrid: Edición HMR, Hijos de Muley-Rubio.

Graham, Helen, and Antonio Sánchez. 1995. "The Politics of 1992." In *Spanish Cultural Studies: An Introduction: The Struggle for Modernity*, edited by Helen Graham and Jo Labanyi, 406–18. New Oxford: Oxford University Press.

Graham, Helen. 1995. "Popular Culture in the 'Years of Hunger.'" In *Spanish Cultural Studies: An Introduction: The Struggle for Modernity*, edited by Helen Graham and Jo Labanyi, 237–45. New Oxford: Oxford University Press.

Grosfoguel, Ramón, and Margarita Cervantes-Rodríguez, eds. 2002. *The Modern/Colonial/Capitalist World-System in the Twentieth-Century: Global Processes, Antisystemic Movements, and the Geopolitics of Knowledge*. Westport, CT: Greenwood Press.

Grosfoguel, Ramón, Margarita Cervantes-Rodríguez, and Eric Mielants. 2009. "Introduction: Caribbean Migrations to Western Europe and the United States." In *Caribbean Migration to Western Europe and the United States. Essays on Incorporation, Identity, and Citizenship*, edited by Margarita Cervantes-Rodríguez, Ramón Grosfoguel, and Eric Mielants, 1–17. Philadelphia: Temple University Press.

Gross, Joan, David McMurray, and Ted Swedenburg. 1992. "Rai, Rap, and Ramadan Nights: Franco-Maghribi Cultural Identities." *Middle East Report (New York, N.Y.)* 178: 11–16. http://dx.doi.org/10.2307/3012981.

Guerra, Alfonso, and José Félix Tezanos, eds. 1992. *La década del cambio. Diez años de gobierno socialista 1982–1992*. Madrid: Editorial Sistema.

Gugelberger, Georg M., ed. 1996. *The Real Thing: Testimonial Discourse and Latin America*. Durham: Duke University Press.

Guillot, Eduardo. 1992. *Radio Futura*. Valencia: La Máscara.

Guillén, Nicolás. 1979. "Sensemayá: Canto para matar una culebra." In *Nueva antología mayor*, edited by Ángel Augier, 256. La Habana: Editorial Letras Cubanas.

Hall, Stuart. 1996. "What is This 'Black' in Black Popular Culture?" In *Stuart Hall: Critical Dialogues in Cultural Studies*, edited by David Morley and Kuan-Hsing Chen, 468–78. London and New York: Routledge.

Haley, Alex. 2007. *Roots: The Saga of an American Family*. New York: Vanguard Books.

Hayter, Teresa. 2000. *Open Borders: The Case against Immigration Controls*. London and Sterling, VA: Pluto Press.

Hix, Simon, and Bjørn Høyland. 2011. *The Political System of the European Union*. 3rd edition. New York: Palgrave Macmillan.

Izquierdo Escribano, Antonio. 1992. *La inmigración en España 1980–1990*. Madrid: Centro de Publicaciones, Ministerio de Trabajo y Seguridad Social.

Játiva, Juan Manuel. 2004. "Chab Samir pone música a una jornada de amistad hispano- Marroquí." Last modified 26 March. http://elpais.com/diario/2004/03/26/cvalenciana/1080332302_850215.html.

Jover, Eduardo. 2002. *Toda una vida*. Madrid: La Esfera de los Libros.

Juliá, Santos. 2000. "The Socialist era, 1982-1996." In *Spanish History since 1808*, edited by José Alvarez Junco and Adrian Shubert, 331–44. London: Arnold; New York: Oxford University Press.

Kern, Soeren. 2009. "Immigration Policy a Casualty of Unemployment." *World Politics Review*, 13 May. http://www.worldpoliticsreview.com/articles/3750/immigration-policy-a-casualty-of-unemployment-in-spain.

King, Desmond. 2007. *Separate and Unequal: African Americans and the U.S. Federal Government*. Rev. Ed. New York: Oxford University Press.

Kleiner-Liebau, Désirée. *Migration and the Construction of National Identity in Spain*. Madrid and Frankfurt: Iberoamericana/Vervuert, 2009.

Kutzinski, Vera. 1993. *Sugar's Secrets: Race and the Erotics of Cuban Nationalism*. Charlottesville, VA: University of Virginia Press.

Labanyi, Jo. 2002. "Introduction: Engaging with Ghosts; or Theorizing Culture in Modern Spain." In *Constructing Identity in Contemporary Spain: Theoretical Debates and Cultural Practice*, edited by Jo. Labanyi, 1–14. Oxford and New York: Oxford University Press.

La lengua de las mariposas, dir. José Luis Cuerda, prod. Sogetel, 1999.

Lebrun, Barbara. 2012. "Carte de Séjour: Revisiting Arabness and Anti-Racism in 1980s France. *Popular Music* 31(3): 331–46.

Lesende, Tito, and Fernando Neira. 2006. *201 discos para engancharse al pop/rock español*. Madrid: Fundación Autor.

Lewis, Marvin A. 2007. *An Introduction to the Literature of Equatorial Guinea: Between Colonialism and Dictatorship*. Columbia, MO: Missouri University Press.

Lipsitz, George. 1994. *Dangerous Crossroads: Popular Music, Postmodernism and The Politics of Place*. London: Verso.

Lipski, John M. 2005. *A History of Afro-Hispanic Language: Five Centuries, Five Continents*. Cambridge and New York: Cambridge University Press. http://dx.doi.org/10.1017/CBO9780511627811.

Los Angeles Philharmonic Orchestra. 2010. "Lila Downs. Buika." Concert booklet for the 2010–11 Season, 16. Los Angeles.

Lowe, Lisa. 2006. "The Intimacies of Four Continents." In *Haunted by Empire: Geographies of Intimacy in North America*, edited by Ann Laura Stoler, 191–212. Durham: Duke University Press. http://dx.doi.org/10.1215/9780822387992-008.

Lozano, María Carmen. 2002. "The Sounds of Immigration: Cultural and Legal Discourse in Spanish Pop Music and Las Leyes de Extranjería (Spanish Immigration Laws)." MA thesis, University of California, Santa Barbara.

Lubiano, Wahneema. 1997. *The House That Race Built: Black Americans, U.S. Terrain*. New York: Pantheon Books.

Macedo, Donaldo, and Panayota Gounari. 2006. "Globalization and the Unleashing of New Racism: An Introduction." In *The Globalization of Racism*, 3–35. Boulder: Paradigm.

Marí, Jorge. 2007. "'No somos unos zulús': música de masas, inmigración negra y cultura española contemporánea." In *Memoria colonial e inmigración: La negritud en la España posfranquista*, edited by Rosalía Cornejo Parriego, 81–102. Barcelona: Bellaterra.

Martín Corrales, Eloy. 2002. *La imagen del magrebí en España: Una perspectiva histórica siglos XVI–XX*. Barcelona: Ediciones Bellaterra.

Martin-Márquez, Susan. 2008. *Disorientations: Spanish Colonialism in Africa and the Performance of Identity*. New Haven, CT: Yale University Press. http://dx.doi.org/10.12987/yale/9780300125207.001.0001.

Martín Muñoz, Gema. 2000. "Lo real y lo irreal en la representación occidental del Mundo musulmán." *Revista de Occidente (Madrid, Spain)* 224: 106–22.

Martínez, Sílvia, and Amparo Sales Casanovas. 2013. "Afterword: Mediterranean Love Songs: A Conversation with Joan Manuel Serrat." In *Made in Spain: Studies in Popular Music*, edited by Sílvia Martínez and Héctor Fouce, 196–204. New York and Oxford: Routledge.

Massey, Douglas S. 2007. *Categorically Unequal: The American Stratification System*. New York: Russell Sage Foundation.

Mazouzi, Bezza. 2002. "Raï." In *The Garland Encyclopedia of World Music*. Vol. 6, *The Middle East*, edited by Virginia Danielson, Scott Lloyd Marcus, and Dwight Reynolds, 269–75. New York: Garland Publications.

Menéndez Flores, Javier. 2000. *Joaquín Sabina: perdonen la tristeza*. Barcelona: Plaza & Janés.

Menéndez Flores, Javier, and Joaquín Sabina. 2006. *Sabina en carne viva: yo también sé jugarme la boca*. Barcelona: Ediciones B.

Méndez Lago, Mónica. 2000. *La estrategia organizativa del Partido Socialista Obrero Español (1975–1996)*. Madrid: Centro de Investigaciones Sociológicas.

Middleton, Richard. 2006. *Voicing the Popular: On the Subjects of Popular Music*. New York and London: Routledge.

Milanovic, Branko. 2005. *Worlds Apart: Measuring International and Global Inequality*. Princeton, NJ: Princeton University Press.

– 2012. *The Haves and the Have-Nots: A Brief and Idiosyncratic History of Global Inequality*. New York: Basic Books.

Mitchell, Timothy. 1994. *Flamenco Deep Song*. New Haven, CT: Yale University Press.

Moliner, María. 1977. *Diccionario del uso del español. 2 volúmenes. Reimpresión*. Madrid: Gredos.

Montero, Rosa. 1995. "Political Transition and Cultural Democracy: Coping with the Speed of Change." In *Spanish Cultural Studies: An Introduction*, edited by Helen Graham and Jo Labanyi, 315–20. Oxford and New York: Oxford University Press.

Montuori, Chad. 2011. "Representing Gender on the Move from Africa to Spain: Donato Ndongo's *El metro*." *Black Women, Gender, and Families* 5(2): 44–65.

Moore, Robin. 1997. *Naturalizing Blackness: Afrocubanismo and Artistic Revolution in Havana 1920–1940*. Pittsburgh: University of Pittsburgh Press.

Mullings, Beverly. 2004. *Caribbean Tourism: Trouble in Paradise?*, edited by Tracey Skelton, 97–117. London and New York: Arnold.

Nail, Thomas. 2015. *The Figure of the Migrant*. Stanford: Stanford University Press.

Nair, Parvati. 2000. "Albums of no return: Ethnicity, Displacement and Recognition in Photographs of North African Immigrants in Contemporary Spain." *Journal of Spanish Cultural Studies* 1 (1): 59–73. http://dx.doi.org/10.1080/713683434.

– 2006. "Practices of Migration Voicing Risk." *Interventions* 8 (1): 67–82. http://dx.doi.org/10.1080/13698010600622707.

Nash, Mary. 2005. "La doble alteridad en la comunidad imaginada de las mujeres inmigrantes." In *Inmigración, géneros y espacios urbanos. Los retos de la diversidad*, edited by Mary Nash, Rosa Tello, and Núria Benach, 17–31. Barcelona: Edicións Bellaterra.

Navarro, Josep María, ed. 1997. *El Islam en las aulas: contenidos, silencios, enseñanza*. Barcelona: Icaria.

Navarro, Manuel. 1992. "Cambios sociales en los años ochenta." In *La década del cambio. Diez años de gobierno socialista 1982–1992*, edited by Alfonso Guerra and José Félix Tezanos, 642–83. Madrid Editorial Sistema.

Ndongo Bidyogo, Donato. 1984. *Antología de la literatura guineana*. Madrid: Editora Nacional.

– 2007. *El metro*. Barcelona: El Cobre.

Ngom, Mbaré. 1993. "La literatura africana de expresión castellana: La creación literaria en Guinea Ecuatorial." *Hispania* 76 (3): 410–18. http://dx.doi.org/10.2307/343796.

– 2004. *La recuperación de la memoria: creación cultural e identidad nacional en la literatura hispano-negroafricana*. Madrid: Universidad de Alcalá.

Nichols, William J., and H. Rosi Song. 2014. *Toward a Cultural Archive of La Movida: Back to the Future*. Madison: Fairleigh Dickinson University Press.

Nogueira, Charo. 2012. "La crisis acelera la emigración de españoles a Europa y América." Accessed 25 January 2016. http://sociedad.elpais.com/sociedad/2012/04/16/actualidad/1334595551_993723.html.

Nordland, Rod. 2015. "A Mass Migration Crisis, and It May Yet Get Worse" *New York Times*, 31 October. Accessed 18 March 2016. http://www.nytimes.com/glogin?URI=http%3A%2F%2Fwww.nytimes.com%2F2015%2F11%2F01%2Fworld%2Feurope%2Fa-mass-migration-crisis-and-it-may-yet-get-worse.html%3F_r%3D1.

Novell, Pepa. 2009. "Cantautoras catalanas: De la *Nova Cançó* a la *Nova Cançó D'ara*. El paso y el peso del pasado." *Journal of Spanish Cultural Studies* 10 (2): 135–47. http://dx.doi.org/10.1080/14636200902990679.

Núñez Seixas, Xosé Manoel. 2005. "From National-Catholic Nostalgia to Constitutional Patriotism: Conservative Spanish Nationalism since the Early 1990s." In *The Politics of Contemporary Spain*, edited by Sebastian Balfour, 121–45. London and NewYork: Routledge.

Omi, Michael, and Howard Winant. 1994. *Racial Formation in the United States*. 2nd edition. New York: Routledge.

Ordovás, Jesús. 1984. *Historia de la música pop española*. Madrid: Alianza.

– 1989. *Radio Futura*. Madrid: Ediciones Cúbicas.

Orovio, Helio. 1992. *Diccionario de la música cubana: biográfico y técnico*. 2nd edition. La Habana: Editorial Letras Cubanas.

Oso Casas, Laura. 2009. "Dominican Women, Head of Households in Spain." In *Caribbean Migration to Western Europe and the United States: Essays on Incorporation, Identity, and Citizenship*, edited by, Ramón Grosfoguel, Ana Margarita Cervantes- Rodríguez and Eric Mielants, 206–29. Philadelphia, Temple University Press.

Oscherwitz, Dayna L. 2004. "Pop Goes the *Banlieue*: Musical *Metissage* and the Articulation of a Multicuralist Vision." *Contemporary French and Francophone Studies* 8 (1): 43–50. http://dx.doi.org/10.1080/10260210310001635496.

Paetzold, Christopher. 2009. "Singing Beneath the Alhambra: The North African and Arabic Past and Present on Contemporary Andalusian Music." *Journal of Spanish Cultural Studies* 10 (2): 207–23. http://dx.doi.org/10.1080/14636200902990711.

Palardy, Diana Q. 2014. "The Evolution of Conguitos: Changing the Face of Race in Spanish Advertising." *TransModernity Journal of Peripheral Cultural Production of the Luso-Hispanic World* 4(2): 38–56.

Palés Matos, Luis. 1988. "Intermedios del hombre blanco." In *Poesía completa y prosa Selecta* edited by Margot Arce de Vazquez, 169–70. Caracas: Biblioteca Ayacucho. Reimpresión.

Pancani, Dino, and Reiner Canales. 1999. *Los necios: Conversaciones con cantautores hispanoamericanos*. Santiago de Chile: LOM Ediciones.

Pedraza, Silvia. 1991. "Women and Migration: The Social Consequences of Gender." *Annual Review of Sociology* 17 (1): 303–25. http://dx.doi.org/10.1146/annurev.so.17.080191.001511.

Pérez, Jorge. 2006. "The Soundscapes of Resistance: Notes on the Postmodern Condition of Spanish Pop Music." *Journal of Spanish Cultural Studies* 7 (1): 75–91. http://dx.doi.org/10.1080/14636200600558711.

Pérez-Sánchez, Gema. 2007. *Queer Transitions in Contemporary Spanish Culture: From Franco to La Movida*. Albany: State University of New York Press.

Permanyer, Lluís. 1991. "Cristòfol, en una plaza pública." *La Vanguardia*, 23 September, 1991: 9.

Porras Nodales, Antonio. 2004. "Las elecciones generales de marzo de 2004: aspectos Problemáticos y consecuencias." *Revista de Estudios Políticos* 126 (octubre–diciembre): 29–58.

Powell, Charles. 2001. *España en democracia, 1975–2000*. Barcelona: Plaza & Janés.

Powrie, Phil, Ann Davies, and Bruce Babington. 2004. *The Trouble with Men: Masculinities in European and Hollywood Cinema*. London and New York: Wallflower.

Pratt, Ray. 1990. *Rhythm and Resistance: Explorations in the Political Uses of Popular Music*. New York, Westport CT, and London: Praeger.

Quintero-Rivera, Angel G., and Roberto Márquez. 2003. "Migration and Worldiew in Salsa Music." *Latin American Music Review/Revista de Música Latinoamericana* 24.2: 210-32.

Radano, Ronald, and Philip V. Bohlman. 2000. "Introduction: Music and Race, Their Past, Their Presence." In *Music and the Racial Imagination*, edited by Ronald Radano and Philip V. Bohlman, 1–53. Chicago: Chicago University Press.

Radanovich, John. 2009. *Wildman of Rhythm: The Life and Music of Benny Moré*. Gainesville: University Press of Florida.

Ramos Espejo, Antonio, and Juan José Téllez. 2004. *Carlos Cano. Una vida de coplas*. Sevilla: Andalucia Abierta.

RedAragon.com. 2005. "Concierto de Chad Samir en Huesca."Accessed 1 July 2016. http://www.redaragon.com/agenda/fichaevento.asp?id=29484.

Ricci, Cristián H. 2010. "African Voices in Contemporary Spain." In *New Spain, New Literatures*, edited by Luis Martín-Estudillo and Nicholas Spadaccini, 203–31. Nashville: Vanderbilt University Press.

Ríos Longares, Carlos José. 2001. *Y Yo Caí … enamorado de la moda juvenil. La movida en las letras de sus canciones*. Alicante: Agua Clara.

Romanos, Eduardo. 2013. "Collective Learning Processes within Social Movements: Some Insights into the Spanish 15-M/Indignados Movement." In *Understanding European Movements: New Social Movements, Global Justice Struggles, Anti-Austerity Protest*, edited by Cristina Flesher Fominaya and Laurence Cox, 203–19. London: Routledge.

Roy, Joaquín, and Aimee Kanner. 2001. "Spain and Portugal: Partners in Development and Democracy." In *The European Union and the Member States: Cooperation, Coordination and Compromise*, edited by Eleanor E. Zeff and Ellen B. Pirro, 235–63. Boulder, CO: Lynne Rienner.

Rueda, Ana, and Sandra Martín. 2010. *El retorno/el reencuentro: La inmigración en la literatura hispano-marroquí*. Madrid: Iberoamericana: Editorial Verveurt.

Runblom, Harald. 1994. "Swedish Multiculturalism in a Comparative European Perspective." *Sociological Forum* 9 (4): 623–40. http://dx.doi.org/10.1007/BF01466305.

Sabina, Joaquín. 2001. *Ciento volando de catorce*. Madrid: Visor.

Safdar, Anealla. 2016. "Crisis looms as a new wave of refugees reaches Europe." *Al Jazeera*, 1 March. Accessed 12 March 2016. http://www.aljazeera.com/news/2016/03/crisis-looms-wave-refugees-reaches-europe-160301185424809.html.

Saïd, dir. Llorenç Soler, prod. Ferran Llagostera, 1998.

Said, Edward. 1981. *Covering Islam: How the Media and the Experts Determine How We See the Rest of the World*. New York: Pantheon Books.

Sampedro, Víctor and Josep Lobera. 2014. "The Spanish 15-M Movement: A Consensual Dissent?" *Journal of Spanish Cultural Studies* 1–2. Accessed 8 January 2016. http://www.tandfonline.com/doi/abs/10.1080/14636204.2014.938466?journalCode=cjsc20.

Sánchez, Antonio. 2002. "Barcelona's Magic Mirror: Narcissism or the Rediscovery of Public Space and Collective Identity?" In *Constructing Identity in Contemporary Spain. Theoretical Debates and Cultural Practice*, edited by Jo Labanyi, 294–310. Oxford: Oxford University Press.

Sánchez Fuarros, Íñigo. 2013. "Music and Migration in Multicultural Spain." In *Made in Spain. Studies in Popular Music*, edited by Sílvia Martínez and Hector Fouce, 144–53. New York and London: Routledge.

Sánchez Jiménez, María Ángeles. 2005. "La articulación del derecho de extranjería." In *Derecho de extranjería: un análisis legal y jurisprudencial del régimen jurídico del extranjero en España (jurisprudencia y formularios)*, coordinated by María Ángeles Sánchez Jiménez, 95–104. Murcia: Diego Marín.

Santaolalla, Isabel. 2002. "Ethnic and Racial Configurations in Contemporary Spanish Culture." In *Constructing Identity in Contemporary Spain. Theoretical Debates and Cultural Practice*, edited by Jo Labanyi, 55–71. Oxford: Oxford University Press.

– 2005. *Los "otros": "etnicidad" y "raza" en el cine español contemporáneo*. Zaragoza: Prensas Universitarias de Zaragoza and Ocho y Medio.

Santos, Juliá. 2000. "The Socialist era, 1982–1996." In *Spanish History since 1808*, edited by José Alvarez Junco and Adrian Shubert, 331–44. London: Arnold; New York: Oxford University Press.

Sarnelli, Laura. 2015. "The Gothic Mediterranean: Haunting Migrations and Critical Melancholia." *Journal of Mediterranean Studies* 24 (2): 147–65.

Seaton, Albert. 1981. *The Fall of Fortress Europe, 1943–1945*. New York: Holmes & Meier Publishers.

Shuker, Roy. 2001. *Understanding Popular Music*. 2nd ed. London, New York: Routledge.

– 2005. *Popular Music: The Key Concepts*. 2nd ed. London, New York: Routledge.

Sieburth, Stephanie. 2014. *Survival Songs: Conchita Piquer's Coplas and Franco's Regime of Terror*. Toronto: University of Toronto Press.

Snyder, Jonathan. 2015. *Poetics of Opposition in Contemporary Spain: Politics and the Work of Urban Culture*. New York: Palgrave Macmillan.

Socolovksy, Jerome. 2011. "Concha Buika's African-Inspired Flamenco." *National Public Radio*, 7 February. Accessed 7 March 2012. http://www.npr.org/templates/story/story.php?storyId=96864556.

Soysal, Yasemin. 1994. *Limits of Citizenship: Migrants and Postnational Membership in Europe*. Chicago: Chicago Univerity Press.

Spartacus, dir. Stanley Kubrick, prod. Edward Lewis, 1960.

Stokes, Martin. 2004. "Music and the Global Order." *Annual Review of Anthropology* 33 (1): 47–72. http://dx.doi.org/10.1146/annurev.anthro.33.070203.143916.

Swedenburg, Ted. 2003. "Rai's Travels." *Middle East Studies Association Bulletin* 36 (2): 190–3. http://dx.doi.org/10.1017/S0026318400044837.

Tango, Cristina. 2006. *La transición y su doble. El rock y Radio Futura*. Madrid: Biblioteca Nueva.

Téllez, Juan José. 1999. *Carlos Cano. Una historia musical andaluza*. Madrid: Fundación de Autor.

Tilmatine, Mohand. 2011. "Moroccan Undocumented Immigrants in Spain since the End of the 20th Century." In *The Encyclopedia of Migration and Minorities in Europe: From the 17th Century to the Present*, edited by Klaus J. Bade, Pieter C. Emmer, Leo Lucassen, and Jochen Oltmer, 579–80. New York: Cambridge University Press.

Todorov, Tzvetan. 2006. "Race and Racism." In *The Postcolonial Studies Reader*, 2nd ed., edited by Bill Ashcroft, Gareth Griffiths, and Helen Tiffin, 213–15. London and New York: Routledge.

Tofiño-Quesada, Ignacio. 2003. "Spanish Orientalism: Uses of the Past in Spain's Colonization in Africa." *Comparative Studies of South Asia, Africa and the Middle East* 23 (1-2): 141–8. http://dx.doi.org/10.1215/1089201X-23-1-2-141.

Triandafyllidou, Anna, Tariq Modood, and Ricard Zapata-Barrero. 2006. "European Challenges to Multicultural Citizenship: Muslims, Secularism and Beyond." In *Multiculturalism, Muslims and Citizenship: A European Approach*, edited by Tariq Modood, Anna Triandafyllidou, and Ricard Zapata-Barrero, 1–22. London and New York: Routledge.

Turino, Thomas. 2008. *Music as Social Life: The Politics of Participation*. Chicago and London: The University of Chicago Press.

Ugarte, Michael. 2010. *Africans in Europe: The Culture of Exile and Emigration from Equatorial Guinea to Spain*. Urbana: University of Illinois Press.

van Dijk, Teun A. 2005. *Racism and Discourse in Spain and Latin America*. Amsterdam and Philadelphia: John Benjamins. http://dx.doi.org/10.1075/dapsac.14.

Vázquez Aguado, Octavio. 1999. "Negro sobre blanco: inmigrantes, estereotipos y medios de comunicación." *Comunicar Revista científica iberoamericana de comunicación y educación* 12: 55–60.

Vázquez Montalbán, Manuel. 1969. *Antología de la 'nova cançó' catalana*. Barcelona: Ediciones de cultura popular.

– 1971. *Crónica sentimental de España*. Barcelona: Lumen.

– 1972. *Joan Manuel Serrat*. Madrid: Júcar.

Velasco, Juan Carlos. 2000. "El multiculturalismo, ¿Una nueva ideología? Alcance y límite de la lucha por las identidades culturales." In *Hacia una ideología para el siglo XXI: ante la crisis civilizatoria de nuestro tiempo*, edited by José Alcina and María Calés, 146–63. Madrid: Akal.

Villamandos, Alberto. 2007. "Paseo con la negra flor: sujetos subalternos en la canción popular de la 'movida'." In *Memoria colonial e inmigración: La negritud en la España posfranquista*, edited by Rosalía Cornejo Parriego 102–23. Barcelona: Bellaterra.

Viñuela, Eduardo. 2009. *El videoclip en España (1980–1995). Gesto audiovisual, discurso y mercado*. Madrid: Instituto Complutense de Ciencias Musicales.

Wade, Peter. 2005. "Rethinking *Mestizaje*: Ideology amd Lived Experience." *Journal of Latin American Studies* 37 (2): 239–57. http://dx.doi.org/10.1017/S0022216X05008990.

Wrench, John, and John Solomos. 1993. *Racism and Migration in Western Europe*. Oxford and Providence, RI: Berg.

Woods Peiró, Eva. 2012. *White Gypsies: Race and Stardom in Spanish Musicals*. Minneapolis: Minnesota University Press.

Zamora Loboch, Francisco. 1994. *Cómo ser negro y no morir en Aravaca*. Barcelona: Ediciones B.

– 2008. *Desde El Viyil y otras crónicas*. Madrid: SIAL Ediciones.

Zapata-Barrero, Ricard. 2004. *Inmigración, innovación política y cultura de Acomodación en España*. Barcelona: Fundació CIDOB.

Zarata, Iñaki. 1992. *Barricada*. Navarra: Editorial La Máscara.
Zecchi, Barbara. 2010. "Veinte años de inmigración en el imaginario fílmico español." In *Imágenes del Otro: Identidad e inmigración en la literatura y el cine*, edited by Montserrat Iglesias Santos, 157–84. Madrid: Biblioteca Nueva.
Žižek, Slajov. 1991. *Looking Awry: An Introduction to Jacques Lacan through Popular Culture*. Cambridge, MA: Massachusetts Institute of Technology Press.

Discography

Amistades Peligrosas. 1991. "Africanos en Madrid." *Relatos de una intriga*. EMI.
Barricada. 1992. "Oveja negra," *Balas blancas*. Polygram.
Belén, Ana, and Víctor Manuel. 1994. "Contamíname." *Mucho más que dos*. BMG.
Buika, Concha. 2005. "Afro-spanish generation." *Buika*. Dro West.
Cano, Carlos. 1994. "Canción para Lucrecia." *Forma de ser*. Dahur.
– 2001. "Antonio Vargas Heredia." *Que naveguen los sueños*. EMI-Odeon.
Che Sudaka. 2003. *Trippi Town*. K Industria.
Ella Baila Sola. 1996. "Que se te escapa el negro." *Ella Baila Sola*. EMI-Odeon.
– 2000. *Marta y Marilia*. EMI-=Odeon.
El Chojin. 1999. "Mami, el negro está rabioso." *Mi turno*. Re velde.
– 2009. "N.E.G.R.O." *Cosas que pasan, que no pasan y que deberían pasar*. Boa.
Guerra, Pedro. 1994. "Contamíname." *Golosinas*. BMG Ariola.
Las Hijas del Sol. 1997. *Kottó*. Nubenegra.
– 1999. *Kchaba*. Nubenegra.
Mecano. 1986. "No es serio este cementerio." *Entre el cielo y el suelo*. BMG.
– 1988. "El blues del esclavo." *Descanso dominical*. BMG.
Orquesta Àrab de Barcelona. 2006. *Báraka*. Temps Record.
– 2008. *Maktub*. World Village.
– 2011. *Libertad*. World Village.
Pitbull. 2008. "The Anthem." *Boatlift*. TVT.
Radio Futura. 1984. "Un africano por la Gran Vía." *La ley del desierto/ La ley del mar*. Ariola.
– 1987. "La negra Flor." *La canción de Juan Perro*. Ariola, 1987.
– 1987. "Paseo con la negra Flor." *Maxisingle*. Ariola, 1987.
– 1992. "Paseo con la negra Flor." *Tierra para bailar*. BMG Ariola.
Sabina, Joaquín. 1980. *Malas companies*. CBS.
– 1990. *Mentiras piadosas*. Ariola.
– 1992. *Física y Química*. Ariola.
– 1994. "La casa por la ventana." *Esta boca es mía*. BMG/Ariola.
– 1996. "Mi primo, el nano." *Mi, me, contigo*. BMG.
Serrat, Joan Manuel. 1989. "Salam Rashid." *Material Sensible*. BMG Ariola.
– 1992. "Disculpe el señor." *Utopía*. BMG.
Ska-P. 1994. "Alí, el magrebí." *Ska-P*. AZ Records.
– 2000. "Lucrecia." *Planeta Eskoria*. BMG.

Index

TORONTO IBERIC

1 Anthony J. Cascardi, *Cervantes, Literature, and the Discourse of Politics*
2 Jessica A. Boon, *The Mystical Science of the Soul: Medieval Cognition in Bernardino de Laredo's Recollection Method*
3 Susan Byrne, *Law and History in Cervantes' Don Quixote*
4 Mary E. Barnard and Frederick A. de Armas (eds), *Objects of Culture in the Literature of Imperial Spain*
5 Nil Santiáñez, *Topographies of Fascism: Habitus, Space, and Writing in Twentieth-Century Spain*
6 Nelson Orringer, *Lorca in Tune with Falla: Literary and Musical Interludes*
7 Ana M. Gómez-Bravo, *Textual Agency: Writing Culture and Social Networks in Fifteenth-Century Spain*
8 Javier Irigoyen-García, *The Spanish Arcadia: Sheep Herding, Pastoral Discourse, and Ethnicity in Early Modern Spain*
9 Stephanie Sieburth, *Survival Songs: Conchita Piquer's* Coplas *and Franco's Regime of Terror*
10 Christine Arkinstall, *Spanish Female Writers and the Freethinking Press, 1879–1926*
11 Margaret Boyle, *Unruly Women: Performance, Penitence, and Punishment in Early Modern Spain*

12 Evelina Gužauskytė, *Christopher Columbus's Naming in the* diarios *of the Four Voyages (1492–1504): A Discourse of Negotiation*
13 Mary E. Barnard, *Garcilaso de la Vega and the Material Culture of Renaissance Europe*
14 William Viestenz, *By the Grace of God: Francoist Spain and the Sacred Roots of Political Imagination*
15 Michael Scham, Lector Ludens*: The Representation of Games and Play in Cervantes*
16 Stephen Rupp, *Heroic Forms: Cervantes and the Literature of War*
17 Enrique Fernandez, *Anxieties of Interiority and Dissection in Early Modern Spain*
18 Susan Byrne, *Ficino in Spain*
19 Patricia M. Keller, *Ghostly Landscapes: Film, Photography, and the Aesthetics of Haunting in Contemporary Spanish Culture*
20 Carolyn A. Nadeau, *Food Matters: Alonso Quijano's Diet and the Discourse of Food in Early Modern Spain*
21 Cristian Berco, *From Body to Community: Venereal Disease and Society in Baroque Spain*
22 Elizabeth R. Wright, *The Epic of Juan Latino: Dilemmas of Race and Religion in Renaissance Spain*
23 Ryan D. Giles, *Inscribed Power: Amulets and Magic in Early Spanish Literature*
24 Jorge Pérez, *Confessional Cinema: Religion, Film, and Modernity in Spain's Development Years (1960–1975)*
25 Joan Ramon Resina, *Josep Pla: Seeing the World in the Form of Articles*
26 Javier Irigoyen-García, *"Moors Dressed as Moors": Clothing, Social Distinction, and Ethnicity in Early Modern Iberia*
27 Jean Dangler, *Edging Toward Iberia*
28 Ryan D. Giles and Steven Wagschal (eds): *Beyond Sight: Engaging the Senses in Iberian Literatures and Cultures, 1200–1750*
29 Silvia Bermúdez, *Rocking the Boat: Migration and Race in Contemporary Spanish Music*

www.ingramcontent.com/pod-product-compliance
Lightning Source LLC
LaVergne TN
LVHW041113090826
844660LV00061B/878/J
9781442648524